Where Jesus L

Jim Gettel writes from the perspective of someone who has accompanied many churches on the journey into deeper and more faithful discipleship. He believes that the fundamental method for learning to join in God's mission is apprenticeship. We learn to follow Christ more faithfully by our companionship with others on the journey. It has been so from the beginning and in this book Jim offers us a way to practice walking that journey in the midst of the changing realities of our own time.

The Rt. Rev'd Jeffrey D. Lee,
Bishop, Episcopal Diocese of Chicago

Clergy, lay leaders, and anyone engaged in congregational development or passionate to enliven the Jesus Movement within their church community will find this book thoughtful and thought provoking. Jim Gettel asks the right questions and carefully guides us to the fundamental reality that relationships matter—especially relationship with Jesus. In a time when "brand loyalty" seems to have no relevance, this book provides a clear and convincing argument that relationship with Jesus is the paramount statement of loyalty that will breathe spiritual life, transformation, and growth into our own lives and into the lives of others. If you want to be a better disciple and/or foster discipleship in others, you must read this book!

The Rt. Rev'd Wendell N. Gibbs, Jr.,
10th Bishop, Episcopal Diocese of Michigan

For Edie,
With appreciation for
your ministry and companionship
along the Way.
Jim

Where Jesus Leads

HELPING CHRISTIAN COMMUNITIES TO FOLLOW

Jim Gettel

Where Jesus Leads
Copyright © 2017 Jim Gettel

Published by
Deep River Books
Sisters, Oregon
www.deepriverbooks.com

Unless otherwise noted, all Scripture quotations are from New Revised Standard Version Bible, copyright 1989, Division of Christian Education of the National Council of the Churches of Christ in the United States of America. Used by permission. All rights reserved.

Scriptures marked NASB are taken from the New American Standard Bible, copyright 1960, 1962, 1963, 1968, 1971, 1972, 1973, 1975, 1977, 1995 by The Lockman Foundation. Used by permission. All rights reserved.

Scriptures marked NIV are taken from the New International Version, copyright 1973, 1978, 1984, 2011 by Biblica, Inc. Used by permission of Zondervan. All rights reserved.

Scriptures marked NLT are taken from the Holy Bible, New Living Translation, copyright 1996, 2004, 2007, 2013 by Tyndale House Foundation. Used by permission of Tyndale House Publishers, Inc., Carol Stream, Illinois 60188. All rights reserved.

Scriptures marked KJV are taken from the King James Version, public domain.

Scriptures marked TM are taken from The Message: The Bible in Contemporary English, copyright 1993, 1994, 1995, 1996, 2000, 2001, 2002. Used by permission of NavPress Publishing Group. All rights reserved.

ISBN: 9781632694331
Library of Congress: 2017930094

Cover design by Jason Enterline
Printed in the USA

Thanksgivings

For so much love, I give thanks to God.

For clergy and lay leaders who invite me to work with Christian communities and make it possible for me to experience each time what Jesus means when he says his joy will be in us and our joy will be complete.

For mentors and friends who've encouraged and helped me to take more steps along the way, including The Reverend David Boyd and Bishops Arthur Vogel, Jeffrey Lee, Roger White, Ed Leidel and Wendell Gibbs.

For saints who have offered us wonderful examples in thought, word and deed; some are identified here, and others, including my parents, have helped me to know God's love.

For my daughter Sarah's work in helping to make this writing presentable; and the editing work by Alexis Miller, Kit Tosello and Tamara Barnet and publication by Andy Carmichael of Deep River Books.

And, especially, for my life journey with Jenny and for the faith, hope and love we share.

> *"Remember, I am with you always."*
> Matthew 28:20

Where Jesus Leads:

Pathways for Leading Christian Communities Today

TABLE OF CONTENTS

Part 4: Leading with Jesus

Tools for Christian Leadership

INTRODUCTION

O n our journeys together in life and community, leadership makes all the difference. As Christians, we strive to *follow* Jesus along the pathways of our lives *and*, as we also become Christian leaders, we *help Jesus lead* others along his Way. This book is designed to help you engage your path with Jesus and identify where Jesus is leading you and preparing you to lead others.

On a path together with Jesus

In our own lives and in our church communities, we can identify when we're walking with Jesus and when we're not. We might lose sight of the path at times, but over time we can see the directions our paths have taken us—where we have journeyed with Jesus and where we have gone astray. Our paths may feel like we are leaving home or returning. As we reflect back on our journeys, however, we discover that our destination is always less important than whether we are following where Jesus leads.

I have been privileged to journey with leaders of one faithful church community for more than a decade. In the few years before I came to know them, this community courageously left its one-hundred-year-old building, moved to a storefront while building a new church, and then moved into its new building in a growing area. During this journey, with a youthful and charismatic pastor, the church's average Sunday worship attendance grew from about 65 to 150.

Then the church's growth stalled. Even with a new building and new people and terrific enthusiasm and hospitality, the church was having trouble following its new path. The community carried along characteristics of the older, smaller congregation. Although the church was beginning to develop some ministry teams, the governing board still oversaw much of the day-to-day life of the congregation. The pastor was still careful to operate within the tacit approval of a few long-time, family-style leaders—patriarchs and matriarchs. And overall, the community was primarily a group of personal networks unified around the person and role of the popular pastor. The pastor largely focused on maintaining a direct pastoral relationship with each member, coordinating the work of a small leadership circle, personally conducting worship, and personally leading programs, such as evangelism training. The church needed transformation in leadership styles and structures, communications, and programs to grow into a larger congregation. As the congregation felt a continuing call to grow, it needed both to make these organizational changes and to fully engage its expanded mission (evangelism, outreach, and so on) with adequate resources, planning, and leadership.

Then this church community not only stalled—it began to fall apart. The popular pastor left to take a position with a slightly larger neighboring parish, and the new associate pastor became the primary pastor. This transition began in turmoil as several members followed the former pastor to the neighboring parish, and several others left the local church in anger over new policy decisions made at the national church level. Perhaps a third of the members left, and you can imagine that fewer new people found this community inviting and hospitable.

At that time, I was asked to meet with the church's leaders and begin to help them address their conflicts. At the first leadership retreat, I asked the board to begin by engaging in prayer and Scripture study, and several members angrily argued, "We don't have time for this." I insisted, and each of the leaders identifies this confrontation as the turning point for the community. Pretty soon, this kind of listening and discernment became the heart of the leaders' personal relationships, approach, and success.

Of course, that was only the beginning for this community to once again follow where Jesus leads. The new pastor began to focus on training mature leaders who would be an effective and non-anxious presence and remain accountable for parish unity, growth, and development. The church added significant training and small groups, for leaders and parishioners, in healthy congregations, boundaries, family systems, and church growth. New leaders adopted a covenant and developed effective leadership habits, including supporting common plans in a unified, reflective, calm, and nonreactive way; focusing on their own behaviors; speaking for themselves and directly to others; and remaining imaginative about strengths, resources, and options.

At the same time that this church community was beginning to deal with its conflicts, another nearby church closed after years of struggling to survive. Rather than seeing the challenge of integrating another failing community as an additional threat, church leaders welcomed these new members and invited them into leadership roles and training with them side-by-side. Instead of developing a split personality, the church community created a shared identity formed from the unusually successful marriage of the two families.

The vision for the church community soon grew from simply adding new members to enthusiastically encouraging lay leaders to prepare themselves and the community to grow and be of greater service to the world. Through blessing and mentoring leaders, more than fifty lay-led ministries were established based on the passions, gifts, and abilities of individuals and teams. In outreach, this included supporting a successful international refugee program. The church's pastoral care program has trained more than 160 lay chaplains from more than sixty-six churches (in eleven denominations) for service in hospitals and the broader community. Contemporary worship is led by a joyful and talented praise band comprised of church members. The youth group has grown through activities, mission trips, and pilgrimages. In each area, the pastor and the board helped leaders establish effective and accountable ministry teams that work together in an overall culture of mature leadership, shared values, and agreed purposes. The church culture does not rely heavily or exclusively on the authority of the pastor or the board.

The church has become one of the larger and healthier churches in the area. Unfortunately, after a few years, the pastor and the regional church authority came into significant personal conflict, and the authority removed the pastor. Nevertheless, with the groundwork of following Jesus and sharing leadership that had been established, it was relatively easy to remind congregational leaders of their roles as disciples and the need for maturity (Ephesians 4) in yet another painful and difficult transition. While the regional judicatory and new interim pastor certainly expected to find a belligerent community fragmented by anger and conflict, what they instead discovered was a community with leaders grieving but striving to support one another, maintain peace in unity, and continue along the Way.

This story is just one example of faithful Christian leadership today. By calling this journey "faithful," I do not mean "perfect" or "without struggle." Nor do I mean that we should try to replicate where this church went or what this church did. But the story illustrates how we can begin to face challenges and step out in faith once again. Our first step as Christian leaders is always recognizing that we are on a journey with Jesus and with one another, and that we can follow where Jesus leads and lead with Jesus. This book is designed to help you take this journey together with God, your community, and others you lead with.

Following Jesus together

Because the kingdom of God is all about loving relationships—God with us, and us loving God and loving others as Jesus loves us—the Christian Way is a shared journey. Along the Way, we grow in our relationships with God, with each other, and within ourselves. Like the first disciples, we each need to learn the Way in relationship with Jesus and in relationships with other people.

Of course, this is a personal journey for you. Jesus says, "Follow me" (e.g., Matthew 4:19, Mark 10:21, John 21:19), and he promises that he will be with you now and always (Matthew 28:20). Christians are people who follow Jesus. Christians go where Jesus leads. We know Jesus personally and keep Jesus in sight. By following Jesus, we take a new, different, narrow, and life-giving path. Christians have a Way of life that follows Jesus into God's kingdom. In effect, Jesus said to Nathanael, one of his first followers, "Are you amazed because I know who you are? You will see greater things than this, even heaven being revealed to earth!"[1]

At the same time, Jesus asks Christians to participate with him in his transformation of this world. Speaking to the apostles, he said "Very truly, I tell you, the one who believes in me will also do the works that I do and, in fact, will do greater works than these, because I am going to the Father" (John 14:12). Jesus calls his followers the salt of the earth, the light of the world, a city on a hill (Matthew 5). In these images, he identifies his followers as leaders. We are to help give the world flavor, vision, hope, and refuge through our presence and activities. Jesus proclaims, "Out of the believer's heart shall flow rivers of living water!" (John 7:38). Christians become streams of life for others. Jesus asks each of us both to follow him and to help guide others along his Way.

So, while this is a personal journey, we are not going alone. Our Christian journey always involves a three-way conversation in community with God and with people with whom we are traveling along the Way. Consider how this is different from leadership in other contexts. In those situations, we might begin by asking ourselves personal questions: Where am I going? Why am I going there? Who is going with me? How will I get there? The third question implies extending these personal questions to the teams, groups, organizations, or communities we are leading: Where are we going? Why are we going there? Who is going with us? How will we get there? As Christians, however, even before we ask these individual and collective questions, we ask questions about Jesus: Where is Jesus leading us? Why is he leading us there? Who is Jesus taking us to? How will we get there? Christian leadership has a different source, different purposes and objectives, and different applications.

This is why this book focuses on where Jesus leads, where we are going together, and how we are also leading others along the path we are traveling together. We need to see what Jesus is trying to do with us, see the realities we face, and see the challenges of the people we are journeying with—all at the same time. We ask the same questions— where, why, who, how?—to engage Christian life and leadership from all three important perspectives, not just from one or two of them. Who are you journeying with? Who needs to be part of your conversation about Christian leadership? Before you begin, think about who you can take with you on this journey. Ask them to share this journey with you.

Learning together

The chapters in this book introduce the importance and purposes of discipleship, certain steps in discipleship, and ways to grow Christian communities, lead transformation, and share love. Each chapter introduces an important topic about following Jesus or leading others to follow, identifies related scriptures, and contains questions for personal reflection and for group discussion. Engaging with God and one another about your journey together is more important than learning the chapter material. The chapters cover Christian discipleship and leadership topics briefly and with enough foundational material for you to have important conversations together about leading with Jesus.[2]

The primary purpose of each chapter is to encourage discernment and growth—together—for your Christian journey in your unique context. I hope you'll hear the living, prophetic voice of Jesus in your own life and in the life of your community. Please focus on inviting God and one another into these conversations for the purpose of hearing and following Jesus. Prayer, reflection, and conversation will lead to mutual discernment, transformation, and action by enabling you to hear and articulate your unique mission to respond to God's calling in the world, to identify people you are called to serve, and to recognize the ways in which you will serve.

Finding new paths

For many people today, talking about journeying together in Christian community is problematic. Much has been written about how traditional Christian churches have declined since 1965. Our times are described as "post-Christian." Many people are inclined to reject both the active movement and the inheritance and traditions of Christianity and instead look for new experiences of mission (significance, purpose, contribution) and community (belonging, trust, relationship). Even people who describe themselves as Christians are more likely to see their faith as an individual choice or concern, rather than a Way of life that is nurtured in community. Today's church members may also begin to feel disconnected as church communities lose spirit and energy, decline in members and financial resources, and become unsustainable.

For more and more people, "Christianity" no longer offers a central context, attitude, and culture for living. In many places, the institutional church neither provides answers contemporary Christians and non-Christians need for daily life nor offers an effective foundation for vibrant and growing Christian communities. Traditional churches seem to become even less effective when they react to the changing world by trying to preserve and restore Christian belief systems, ideologies, philosophies or theologies (orthodoxies), charismatic leaders or institutional organizational structures (authorities), or church practices, customs, or habits (cultures or traditions). In our post-Modern, post-Christian time, people are too wary of how earlier beliefs, habits, authorities, and institutions failed us to simply accept this approach.

The decline of the church has led contemporary Christian leaders to grapple with the relevance of the church and their roles in it, and to begin to discover new paths. In our time, there are strong feelings both of trepidation and of hope that we may create "new" communities that truly respond to God's desires and human needs in a changed and changing world. In this valuable conversation, the new, vital church has been described as the emergent church (Doug Pagitt, Tony Jones, Dan Kimball, and Karen Ward), the externally-focused church (Rick Rusaw and Eric Swanson), the metamorphosed church (Carl George), the missional church (Alan Roxburgh, Reggie McNeal, and others), the new apostolic church (George Hunter), the new reformation (Phyllis Tickle), the once and future church (Loren Mead), the permission-giving church (Bill Easum), the purpose-driven church (Rick Warren), the rediscovered, seeker-driven church (Bill Hybels), the reinvented church or the church on the other side (Brian McLaren), the resurrected church (Mike Regele), the twenty-first century church (Leith Anderson), the untamed church (Alan Hirsch), and more. These faithful contemporary church leaders recognize that institutional churches need to immediately change in very significant ways and need to keep changing. As might be expected, many people are wrestling with what these "new" communities will look like. The answer to that question would seem to give Christian leaders a sense of direction and "means to success" in the ongoing Christian movement.

A radical discovery throughout this movement is that people are rejecting churches because the churches do not look or act much like Jesus.[3] More and more people have trouble imagining a church that shows God's love to the world.[4] Both Christians and non-Christians intuitively recognize that traditional churches often have "lost their way" and are not successfully following where Jesus leads. The reexamination of Christian community is producing new excitement that Christianity may begin to find its way again and respond to people and the world in new ways, and more in the way Jesus intends. The radical discovery is that people are looking for churches and leaders that act like Jesus and follow where Jesus leads.

The challenge of Christian leadership is not just a challenge of organizational development or creating "better" churches. The real challenge is gaining a clear vision of what a church community needs to look like today to meet the needs of God's kingdom. Much that is written about Christianity is a reaction to what is wrong with the church. We can be more proactive and more effective by focusing first on following Jesus rather than on changing the church. There's greater value in learning what to do than in learning what to undo. Then, when we do change our churches, we can make our communities more effective in acting like Jesus, following where Jesus leads, and leading with Jesus.

A path focused on Jesus

Jesus is the Leader and the Way. Jesus invariably reminds people to "follow" him rather than try to grasp truth, life, or love through other instruments, principalities, or powers. He says, "I am the way, and the truth, and the life. No one comes to the Father except through me" (John 14:6). Our mission as Christian leaders is not in trying to reform our orthodoxies, authorities, organizations, practices, or traditions to make them work for us once more. Our mission is following where Jesus leads.

Wherever the Christian movement authentically goes, Jesus will lead. The foundational question we need to constantly engage is where Jesus leads—how we can become his followers and in turn become new leaders in this time and place. Like the earliest disciples, Christian leaders need to continually experience and learn how to live in close relationship with Jesus,[5] how to follow Jesus along the Way, how to create loving Christian communities that share God's love, how to help make new and stronger disciples, and especially how to serve and lead in making the world more reflective of God's kingdom of love. The joy of our work as Christian leaders includes walking with Jesus and one another, discovering new life, and striving to show forth God's presence and love to the world.

Engaging Jesus

Jesus wants to engage us as leaders for his kingdom mission in the world. Engagement is far more than simply participating. Engagement is a betrothal moving toward passionate and loving commitment. It is a lifelong process of attracting, preparing, involving, connecting, confronting, employing, empowering, and meshing us together so we can lead with Jesus (Ephesians 4).

To begin engaging Jesus, read and reflect on 1 Corinthians 3:9–17.

Questions for Personal Reflection:

1. How do you follow Jesus?

2. How is Christianity important in your life?

3. Why do you come to church? What type of actions, reactions, or invitations are you seeking from others in your church community?

4. When have you found your faith supported or strengthened in the church community?

5. When have you found yourself drifting away from a church community? What was happening in the church or in you?

6. What draws and excites you about your calling into Christ and the church?

7. As you study this book, what is one thing you hope God will do in your life?

Questions for Group Discussion:

1. What is the foundation St. Paul says we build upon?

2. How has Jesus changed the world?

3. Who are Christians?

4. How does a church community follow Jesus?

5. What is the role of the Christian church in the world today? How are Christians meant to change the world through our presence and activities?

6. Why do we need to follow Jesus together?

7. Why is our time described as "post-Christian"? Is it?

8. Why do Christians and non-Christians have trouble seeing the importance of Christianity?

9. What are some ways your church could change to follow Jesus more closely? What "stumbling blocks" would need to be removed?

10. What does the author mean when he says, "The challenge of Christian leadership is not just a challenge of organizational development or creating 'better' churches"? What do we need to do as leaders?

PART 1:

Following Jesus on the Way

1.1

Good News of God's Kingdom

J esus of Nazareth leads a movement that has profoundly impacted humankind. Even for those who do not accept Christianity as a religion or way of life, the influence of Christianity on human history during the last two millennia is undeniable. What Jesus taught and demonstrated during a three year period in Palestine changed world thinking about individual human worth and the significance of brotherhood, freedom, and the pursuit of justice in human relations. A new attitude and culture provided the context and creativity for centuries of human development that initiated admirable achievements in art, architecture, literature, music, philosophy, politics, religion, science, and other areas of human endeavor.

For Christians, the coming of Jesus into the world is the most significant event in human history. People who believe in Jesus recognize him as the incarnation of a Person of God who came into the world at a particular moment in history and, having conquered death, continues to lead a movement that is still growing. In this context, Jesus' life, death, resurrection, and continuing real presence provide the true relationship and purpose of our lives: helping us to reconcile and experience deeply loving relationships among God and people. To the extent we allow Jesus to have a continuing impact on our lives, we see him as our leader and ourselves as his followers.

The Good News of the Christian gospels is that a new movement with a powerful leader has come into a world waiting expectantly for change. And yet, the nature of the leader and the nature of his kingdom are different from what people expected.

The Person Jesus

In the New Testament, Jesus is named the "King of kings and Lord of lords" (Revelation 19:16), the "Son of God and King of Israel" (John 1:49), and the "ruler of kings on earth" (Revelation 1:5). The word "christ" or "messiah" literally means "the liberating king promised by God." And Jesus describes himself as a king who frees people from captivity. Eighty-one times, the New Testament calls Jesus the "Son of Man"—using the term from the liberation dream in the book of Daniel (7:13–14, 26):

> *In my vision at night I looked, and there before me was*
> *one like a son of man, coming with the clouds of heaven.*
> *He approached [God] and was led into his presence.*
> *He was given authority, glory and sovereign power; all*
> *nations and peoples of every language worshiped him. His*
> *dominion is an everlasting dominion that will not pass*
> *away . . . and all rulers will worship and obey him.*

Mark describes how at the moment of Jesus' baptism, "just as he was coming up out of the water, he saw the heavens torn apart and the Spirit descending like a dove on him. And a voice came from heaven, 'You are my Son, the Beloved; with you I am well pleased.'" (1:10–11). Jesus is not only the Son of Man but the Son of God:

> Then the miracle of all miracles takes place. The Son of
> God becomes a human being. The Word became flesh.
> The One who had dwelled from all eternity in the Father's
> glory, the One who was in the form of God, who in the
> beginning had been the mediator of creation so that the
> created world can only be known through him and in him,
> the One who was very God (1 Cor. 8:6; 2 Cor. 8:9; Phil.
> 2:6ff.; Eph. 1:4; Col. 1:16; John 1:1ff.; Heb. 1:1ff.)—this
> One takes on humanity and comes to earth. He takes on
> humanity by taking on human qualities, human 'nature',
> "sinful flesh," human form (Rom. 8:3; Gal. 4:4; Phil. 2:6ff.)
> . . . God's mercy sends the Son in the flesh, so that in
> his flesh he may shoulder and carry all of humanity.[1]

God's kingdom has come

Matthew summarizes the beginning of Jesus' public ministry, saying: "From that time Jesus began to proclaim, 'Repent for the kingdom of heaven has come near'" (Matthew 4:17). When each of the gospels refers to Jesus proclaiming the Good News, it is, "Repent, for the kingdom of heaven is near." (See also Mark 1:14, Luke 8:1.) Another proper translation of the Greek words used in these passages is "The kingdom of heaven is already here."

The message is the greatest pronouncement: God has come near; God is at hand. It's now possible for ordinary people to live in the presence and under the authority of God. Jewish hearers had a basic understanding of what this kingdom of God would be like from prophecies in the Hebrew Scriptures. The king would descend through the house of David as the "shoot of Jesse" and bring justice, righteousness, and especially peace. Christians believe these prophecies are about Jesus and reveal the nature of this kingdom (see, e.g., Micah 5:2–4, Zephaniah 3:14–18, Isaiah 40:1–11). The prophets proclaim that God is coming to save us: "Then the eyes of the blind shall be opened, and the ears of the deaf unstopped; then the lame shall leap like a deer, and the tongue of the speechless sing for joy" and as people who are saved, we "shall obtain joy and gladness, and sorrow and sighing shall flee away" (Isaiah 35:4–10).

The Good News is that the kingdom of God has come near. But it has not come in the way many people expected it to come. Some hearers were surprised and disappointed to find that Jesus did not create a human kingdom like the house of Israel; he created an entirely new relationship between God and human beings. He came as the suffering servant described in Isaiah 52:13–53:12. Jesus tells the Pharisees: "The kingdom of God is not coming with things that can be observed; nor will they say, 'Look, here it is!' or 'There it is!' For, in fact, the kingdom of God is among [or within] you" (Luke 17:20–21). Jesus proclaims that the kingdom of God may be present now, saying in three gospels, "But truly I tell you, there are some standing here who will not taste death before they see the kingdom of God" (Luke 9:27, Matthew 16:28, Mark 9:1).

The mission of Jesus

Jesus' ministry made manifest the healing and saving power of God already operating in the world. In prison, John the Baptist heard what Jesus was doing and sent some of his followers to ask Jesus who he was: "'Are you the one who is to come, or are we to wait for another?' Jesus answered them, 'Go and tell John what you hear and see: the blind receive their sight, the lame walk, the lepers are cleansed, the deaf hear, the dead are raised, and the poor have good news brought to them. And blessed is anyone who takes no offence at me.'" (Matthew 11:2–6). Jesus' response alludes to Isaiah 35:1–10 and Isaiah 61:1–2:

> *The spirit of the Lord God is upon me,*
> *because the Lord has anointed[2] me;*
> *he has sent me to bring good news to the oppressed,*
> *to bind up the broken-hearted,*
> *to proclaim liberty to the captives,*
> *and release to the prisoners;*
> *to proclaim the year of the Lord's favour,*
> *and the day of vengeance of our God;*
> *to comfort all who mourn.*

Jesus also used these words to describe himself in the synagogue at Nazareth, saying, "Today this scripture has been fulfilled in your hearing" (Luke 4:21). His Galilean hearers became infuriated because Jesus proclaimed the fulfillment of this prophetic dream not in some remote future, but then and there in the person who was speaking to them. Jesus was the one anointed as king to proclaim and realize God's kingdom. And Jesus preached that in his power and presence the kingdom of God is a living reality, although not yet in a full and final way. "But if it is by the finger of God that I cast out the demons, then the kingdom of God has come to you" (Luke 11:20).

Jesus proclaims a kingdom in which he wants us to participate.[3] In the Lord's Prayer, Jesus tells us to pray, "God's kingdom come, God's will be done, on earth as it is in heaven" (Matthew 6:10). The whole prayer is a kingdom prayer. We are praying that we will more and more fully experience and respond to the presence of God in our lives.[4] While this kingdom was not exactly what Jewish tradition expected of a Messiah, this is not just a heavenly kingdom but an earthly kingdom in which a divinely appointed king will in some way carry out God's judgment upon sin and reestablish God's people as a nation wholly acceptable to

God. God's kingdom arrives in the incarnate, divinely ordained king, Jesus, and the life of the kingdom can therefore be lived here and now.

Jesus' message of the kingdom of God is that God's will may be done on earth, during this life. We do not have to wait for death and heaven or a second coming to participate more fully in God's kingdom right now. Only Jesus' saving grace and love opens the kingdom of God. But if we are already part of God's family and kingdom, we can more fully and more immediately participate in that reality right now. Jesus does not say that the kingdom is already fulfilled. But his Good News is that it is possible to live right now in the presence and under the reign of God. Jesus will lead his followers in the Way of living in God's kingdom.

If we are Christians, we are a kingdom people (Matthew 5:48). And Jesus says we may participate in his kingdom through repentance. In asking us to repent, Jesus asks each of us to change our ways of life to experience life as God designed it and wants it to be.

Repentance

In Christianity, we're asked to fully commit our lives to living in relationship with God and other people. This is a commitment so complete that Jesus says we are born again. We are new creations (2 Corinthians 5:17, Ephesians 4:24, Colossians 3:10). Our entire lives change, not because we decide to follow a new philosophy or creed, but because we decide to see God in every aspect of life. We begin to "abide" in Jesus. For Jesus, the important thing is to live in God's presence and accept God's love. We do that, he says, through repentance: "Repent, for the kingdom of heaven has come near" (Matthew 4:17).

Nicodemus was a "ruler of the Jews" and an important Pharisee who came to Jesus at night, clearly not wanting to be seen but curious about a teacher who could do miracles and seemed to have come from God and to have God with him (John 3). Jesus told him that a person must be reborn to see the kingdom of God. When Nicodemus asked how this can possibly happen, Jesus answered that we are reborn by being baptized, washed clean, and then born again spiritually. Jesus proclaims that the way to enter the kingdom of God is to be reborn.[5]

Jesus tells people to "repent" to prepare to participate in the kingdom of God. The word repent is *metanoia*, from the Greek word for "mind."

The word is about thinking, about changing one's mind, about second thoughts. Even more, it is about a change of heart. Repentance is reorienting, reprioritizing, or restructuring our lives to focus on the reality of God and God's love for us and presence in our lives. Repentance is preparing the way of the Lord. Repentance is seeking first the kingdom of God and God's righteousness. Repentance is preparing one's self to live in God's presence.

In Mark 10:17–27, a man eagerly comes to Jesus and asks what he should do to inherit eternal life. Jesus says to the man, "You know the commandments," and lists those from the Ten Commandments dealing with human relationships. The man tells Jesus he has kept these commandments from his youth. He responds in such a way as to show his understanding that this is not enough; he knows he must do more. Jesus' response is unusually special: "Jesus, looking at him, loved him" (v. 21). Jesus invites the man to a life with him: "You lack one thing; go, sell what you own, and give the money to the poor, and you will have treasure in heaven; then come, follow me" (v. 21).The man goes away shocked and grieving, for he cannot do this. The kingdom of God was at hand, but this man could not make the changes necessary to enter it.

Jesus told the man he lacked only one thing, but it was the most important thing—repentance. Jesus asked the man to restructure his life and become a disciple. For the man, the cost of discipleship was too high. Elsewhere Jesus describes the means of entering the kingdom of God in similar terms of high cost: "Again, the kingdom of heaven is like a merchant in search of fine pearls; on finding one pearl of great value, he went and sold all that he had and bought it" (Matthew 13:45–46). To repent and follow Jesus, we may be called to give up more than riches: "'Whoever comes to me and does not hate father and mother, wife and children, brothers and sisters, yes, and even life itself, cannot be my disciple. Whoever does not carry the cross and follow me cannot be my disciple'" (Luke 14:26–27). Discipleship calls us to fully devote ourselves to the one great task of entering the kingdom of God.

Jesus exclaims at the conclusion of the story in Mark, "'How hard it is [for those who trust in wealth] to enter the kingdom of God'" (Mark 10:24).[6] This man's weakness in answering the call was devotion to material wealth, but we each have our treasures stored up, things we are not willing to give up in restructuring our lives to orient them to God. Repentance is about changing our orientation. We may need to take a new path in life. How hard it will be to enter the kingdom of God: So hard, Jesus says, that "For mortals it is impossible, but not for God; for God all things are possible" (Mark 10:27).

Jesus says, "Unless you change and become like children, you will never enter the kingdom of heaven" (Matthew 18:3). If we wish to prepare ourselves to live in the kingdom of God, we must repent. We must restructure our lives to orient them to God. We must become disciples of Christ. We must recognize that our present path in life is misdirected and that we need an entirely new set of beliefs, perceptions, and behaviors. This is being born again, born into the kingdom of God so that we may live in God's presence and under God's reign. Repentance is not just perpetual change, or abandoning our current dissatisfaction; it's moving meaningfully into our future with reverence to God.

We begin by experiencing repentance as a completely positive step of moving toward God, not a negative one of beating ourselves up. Repentance may be difficult because it requires shedding our developed ways and habits, becoming like children, but it is not a punishment. Repentance is misunderstood if it is seen just as a way to free ourselves from sin—whatever we are doing wrong in our relationships with God and other people—through contrition. Repentance is not, as many people believe, the emotional experience of feeling bad about or confessing what one has done wrong. John the Baptist and Jesus did not say, "Feel really bad, for the kingdom of heaven is near." They said, "Repent!" Misunderstanding Jesus' call to repentance keeps many sincere Christians from experiencing the adventure of closer relationship with God and from the transformed living in God's kingdom that Jesus offered.

The focus of repentance is a change of heart. Our behaviors change from the inside out, by our personal choice and by God's grace, as we enter into a renewed relationship with God. Jesus helps his disciples make this character transformation both through a mystical event of being reborn in the Spirit and through a series of understandings and experiences. But it is not a one-time thing. Jesus taught his disciples to restructure their lives not once and for all but continually.

Repentance happens by asking God to be part of our lives—the most important part. Jesus said, "Ask, and it will be given you; search, and you will find; knock, and the door will be opened for you. For everyone who asks receives, and everyone who searches finds, and for everyone who knocks, the door will be opened" (Luke 11:9–10). A Christian life is a life of choosing to be aware of God's presence and, from that awareness, of beginning to manifest God's presence in the world. We embark on this spiritual path by acknowledging the need we have for God in our lives and acting from that awareness toward a stronger relationship with God. With a longing to know God better and to see God's grace more fully established in our lives, we can ask God to be with us (Matthew 7:7–8).

Jesus essentially says, "If you change your way of life, you can participate in God's kingdom right now."

A kingdom of love for today

To the world's surprise, the new way of life commanded in God's kingdom is ... *love.* Jesus says the rule of law in his kingdom is "Love the Lord your God with all your heart, and with all your soul, and with all your strength, and with all your mind; and your neighbor as yourself" (Luke 10:27). The repentance Jesus asks is this: transform your whole heart, soul, mind, and actions to be part of this kingdom of love. Jesus calls this the "greatest commandment" not because it is possible to command love or make it a moral rule; Jesus simply shares the greatest spiritual truth: that you are a living member of God's kingdom if you do this. In the kingdom of God, we respond to God's love by loving God—and by loving each other because we are all children of God. In the process, we are also transformed by love; God's love at the heart of all creation is made manifest. God's kingdom offers people the gift of salvation through a new way of life, not just a system of ideas, laws, or morality. That way of life opens the extravagance of God's unlimited love flooding creation both in time and in eternity.

Of course, Christians also expect to follow Jesus into everlasting life. Jesus said, "Very truly, I tell you, anyone who hears my word and believes him who sent me has eternal life, and does not come under judgment, but has passed from death to life. Very truly, I tell you, the hour is coming, and is now here, when the dead will hear the voice of the Son of God, and those who hear will live" (John 5:24–25). And "Do not let your hearts be troubled. Believe in God, believe also in me. In my Father's house there are many dwelling places. If it were not so, would I have told you that I go to prepare a place for you? And if I go and prepare a place for you, I will come again and will take you to myself, so that where I am, there you may be also" (John 14:1–3).

But followers of Jesus are not really participating in God's kingdom if they are only waiting for a perfection or realization of that kingdom in the next life through some sort of belief in Jesus. By his resurrection, Jesus has destroyed death and made all things new. We need to participate in this new creation. As we shall see, Jesus calls his followers to follow him today, in this life, and he commissions his disciples to live with him and continue his mission in this world. This is why he calls each of his followers to take up our crosses and follow him, not just wait for him to come again. The revelation of heaven coming near is more about our relationship with God and others through Jesus (how) than about a time (when) and place (where).

The kingdom of God is an entirely new way of life. In the Beatitudes, Jesus shares images of a paradoxical, new reality where the poor, not the rich, are blessed, and the meek, not the strong, inherit the earth. The merciful obtain mercy. The pure in heart see God. Heaven belongs to those who are persecuted for righteousness' sake (Matthew 5:3–12). Blessed are the peacemakers who not only refrain from murder but from all conflict (5:21–26). Blessed are the pure in heart who avoid even adultery of the mind (5:27–30). Blessed are the meek who do not resist an evildoer (5:38–41). Blessed are the merciful who give to everyone who begs from them (5:42). Blessed are those who are persecuted for righteousness' sake and who love their enemies and pray for those who persecute them (5:44). Each righteous response to life goes further than any rule and is based in love.

Participating in the kingdom of God doesn't just happen to us. We need to approach God purposefully and change our lives to act as if the kingdom of God is available right now and we belong to it. We need to answer a call to be disciples of Jesus. We need to take on the character of Christ. And we need to participate in kingdom-fulfilling actions (Isaiah 61, Matthew 25:31–45). Jesus' Way is not just about Christians being saved so that we can go to heaven, but about turning to a new path, being transformed, and participating in the transformation of the world as a greater realization of God's kingdom. Christians have a critical mission in this world that goes far beyond changing other people's belief systems.

In fact, the only way we will change other people's thinking to help them live the Way of Jesus is by showing forth God's love.

Christians have a radically unique perspective of both the world and their life purposes and responsibilities. As people who dare to take Christ's name, Christians must be Christ's presence in the world for the world (2 Corinthians 4:5). We must have the same concern for the world and its people that Jesus did, and his love was so strong that he died for it. The purpose of our lives is to love what God loves by living in his love (John 15:9). Accordingly, Christians need to change the world by making it more loving and more revealing of God. Christianity is not peaceful, comfortable, static, or passive; it is active and loving. Christians are both servants and change agents. They are both followers of Jesus' Way and leaders to a new world God wants to spring forth. This is the movement where Jesus leads.

Engaging Jesus

To continue engaging Jesus, read and reflect on Matthew 16:13–28.

Questions for Personal Reflection:

1. How would you answer Jesus' question, "Who do you say that I am?" (Matthew 16:15, Mark 8:29, Luke 6:27)

2. Who is Jesus to you?

3. How is God's kingdom coming?

4. How do you help reveal God's kingdom?

5. What are opportunities you have to live more fully in God's kingdom of love?

6. How could you be a new creation (2 Corinthians 5:17, Ephesians 4:24, Colossians 3:10)? What positive new paths do you need to take?

7. Do you repent continually? How?

8. What would repentance require in your life? What are opportunities you have for repentance?

Questions for Group Discussion:

1. What is the Good News?

2. What does Matthew 16:13-28 say about who Jesus is? What other Scriptures particularly speak to you about who Jesus is?

3. How has Jesus come to change the world? What is the mission of Jesus (and his disciples)?

4. How is Jesus asking his followers to change their lives?

5. How may a church community help support a journey of repentance?

6. If "God's kingdom has come near," what is the kingdom of God like?

7. What is God's dream or desire for the world?

8. Jesus' message of the kingdom of God is that God's will may be done on earth, during this life. We do not have to wait for death and heaven or a second coming to participate more fully in God's kingdom right now. Does that sound strange to you, or does it make sense that we're not just waiting to be saved sometime in the future?

9. How do we participate more fully in God's kingdom right now?

10. Is the theology described in this chapter engaging and empowering? How is it different from what you have been taught? How does it fit with your personal experiences?

11. Reflect on Luke 4:16–21, Matthew 11:2–6, and Isaiah 61:1–2. What are some ways we can participate in the kingdom of God?

12. Where are we called to share God's love? To whom are we sent?

13. How do we help others live into God's kingdom?

14. How does your church community help reveal God's kingdom?

15. What are opportunities your church has to live more fully into God's kingdom of love?

16. Who is helping to reveal God's kingdom today?

1.2

The Way of Jesus

Jesus gathers and forms people into a new kingdom people. In the second half of the first chapter of the gospel of John, Jesus begins to call disciples to a new way of life. John the Baptist first identifies Jesus to his disciples as the Lamb of God,[1] the one who baptizes with the Holy Spirit, the Son of God. Then Jesus invites two of John's followers, Andrew and another, to "Come and see," and Andrew goes to find his brother, Peter, and proclaims that he has found the Messiah. Jesus also calls Philip to "Follow me" and Philip in turn finds Nathanael and proclaims Jesus to be the one described in the Mosaic Law and the prophets. Then Nathanael identifies Jesus as the Son of God. As soon as these young men identify Jesus, they leave everything and follow him.

Living with Jesus

When Jesus invites people to "come and see" and calls them to "follow me," he asks them to come to know him deeply by living with him and sharing his way of life. The call to discipleship—to follow Jesus along his Way—was a big commitment and a serious business in the rabbinical tradition of the time. When a teacher or rabbi asked a person to become his disciple, saying "Follow me," he was asking the person to "leave your family and your home and your business and all of your possessions and join my way of life." A person who accepted this invitation left all of his former life behind and lived wherever his rabbi lived. He served almost as a personal slave, making certain all of the rabbi's personal needs were met. He learned from the rabbi by memorizing everything the rabbi taught, the rabbi's "yoke" or way of life.[2] Most importantly, by living with the rabbi, disciples learned by his example. A disciple remained with a rabbi until he had learned everything the rabbi could teach him. Then the disciple also became a rabbi.

Discipleship happens by people being introduced to Jesus, living with him, and coming to know him, and then being sent out to serve with and for him. From living with Jesus, the first followers became believers and then went out and proclaimed the Good News of Jesus themselves. A disciple is not a person who simply studies the teachings of Jesus; a disciple is a person who actually lives with the teacher and shares his life, who truly comes to know Jesus, and who obeys and serves Jesus. Discipleship is not something you "believe" or "know" or "have." Rather, it is a path you are on, where you are continually learning from and growing closer to Jesus Christ. In this manner we come to know Jesus. In Jesus' way of life, we also experience and come to know his Father (John 14:7).

Becoming a disciple means actually living with Jesus. We can only come to live with Jesus if we recognize him not only as an historical figure, but as a living person present with us. For Christians, Jesus' story does not end with his crucifixion. He is resurrected and appears to his disciples on the road to Emmaus, in the upper room and at the Sea of Galilee. His resurrection means that Jesus lives now! Jesus is with us day by day (Matthew 28:20) and "is able for all time to save those who approach God through him, since he always lives to make intercession for them" (Hebrews 7:25). To become Christians, it is not enough for us to believe that Jesus once was or will be again; we must experience his immediate presence in our lives now. We must overcome the idea of a separation from Jesus in time and place. Jesus is not just a sacrifice for us. Jesus is alive, and his ongoing life makes him accessible to us today. If we accept Jesus into our lives, Jesus comes to be present with us today and helps us to have closer relationships with God and one another in our daily lives. We can become disciples who actually live in relationship with Jesus now and experience the reality of Jesus' life in our own. And we will begin to live in loving relationships with God and one another right now.

Jesus invites us to live with him. Jesus then models life for us and makes available to us a life lived in relationship with God, a life reconciled to God. When Jesus said, "The kingdom of God has come near," he did not just mean that God eventually will come to redeem or judge the world. He meant that through him, by living his faith, with him as mediator or mentor, we are able to participate in God's kingdom now. We are able to be aware of God's presence, to live under God's sovereignty in accordance with God's will, and to be reconciled with God. If we live with Jesus, we too are reconciled with God, because God accepts us and loves us. If we accept him, Jesus helps us develop a personal relationship with God and a right relationship to others in God's kingdom.

Jesus is the Messiah, the leader who is savior or deliverer. He is the bread of life, not as manna that sustains physical lives, but in terms of offering a relationship with God that sustains spiritual lives (John 6:35). What Jesus offers is more than himself: "You search the scriptures because you think that in them you have eternal life; and it is they that testify on my behalf. Yet you refuse to come to me to have life" (John 5:39–40). The life that Jesus offers is the continuous, expansive, encompassing, and personal love of God.[3]

Christ in us

Living with Jesus means participating in his ongoing life in the world and letting his presence in our lives transform us and make our lives new. Although Christians follow the example of Jesus, we are not just trying to be like Jesus, to be imitators of Jesus. We believe that Jesus still lives, and lives on earth through the lives of his followers. Jesus is present and lives in my life:

> *Remember, I am with you always, to the*
> *end of the age. (Matthew 28:20)*

> *It is no longer I who live, but it is Christ*
> *who lives in me. (Galatians 2:20)*

As we live with and follow Jesus, we become more Christ-like. We begin more and more to reflect God's love in Jesus. As we grow closer to Jesus, his love and life show forth more brightly from our own. Because Jesus lives his life in us, we can follow his example (1 Peter 2:21), have the same thoughts and purpose (Philippians 2:5), walk as he walked (1 John 2:6), act as he acted (John 13:15), love as he loved (Ephesians 5:2; John 13:34, 15:12), forgive as he forgave (Colossians 3:13), and "lose our lives for the sake of our brothers and sisters just as he lost his life for our sake" (1 John 3:16).[4] If we truly have Jesus in our lives, his presence works to shape us more into his own image (Galatians 4:19), more into God's image as we were created to be (1 John 3:2): "All of us, with unveiled faces, seeing the glory of the Lord as though reflected in a mirror, are being transformed into the same image from one degree of glory to another; for this comes from the Lord, the Spirit" (2 Corinthians 3:18).

Christian belief

Jesus asks us to "believe" in him to have everlasting life (John 6:29, 6:40, 8:24, 11:25–26; Mark 16:16).[5] This belief is more than just intellectual assent to a proposition. This belief is recognizing Jesus as the Son of God and putting our trust in Jesus—to walk with him into the kingdom of God. Following Jesus is actually living in relationship with our living Lord; it is not simply having some form of knowledge or faith or holiness, which many Christians strive for.[6] Belief is obedience: hearing his voice, leaving everything and following. It is coming to know Jesus by spending time with him.[7] Following Jesus, walking behind him, is a journey in personal relationship with him, not a set of principles or a life program.

When Jesus tells his disciples at the Last Supper that he is going ahead to prepare a place for them, Thomas asks how they can possibly follow Jesus if they do not know where he is going. Jesus tells them, "I am the way and the truth and the life" (John 14:5–6). For his followers, to know Jesus is to know where they are going, why they are going there, and that they will have the strength to follow where Jesus leads. There are many roads, but Jesus is the Way. There are many possible perspectives and meanings, but Jesus is the one sure Truth. There are many ways of living, but Jesus gives new and abundant Life.

The way of life Jesus brings with him into the world is kingdom love. This way of life accepts and celebrates the amazing extravagance of God's love and, through that love, the possibilities of sharing and participating in a heavenly kingdom right now. That kingdom is realized as love flows beyond the limits of time, place, law or morality, or human desire. God's kingdom is not complete or utopian, but alive and growing like love itself.

Instead of Roman power or Pharisaic interpretation of the Law or priestly religion, Jesus offers himself as the Way for people to love God and love one another. Jesus is himself the Lord and Lawgiver—the most perfect expression of the Law. Saint Paul explains that the Law guided and protected people until Jesus came, but now Jesus is our guide and protector (Galatians 3:23–26). Jesus will bring about the reality of holiness, righteousness, justice, and peace that the Law sought, but in a way which goes far beyond the Law itself. Following a set of rules is not an adequate expression of the overflowing love to be found in God's kingdom. People will understand and live according to the Law not by following the precepts of the scribes and Pharisees but by following and living in community with Jesus himself. Jesus does not just say "Follow the Law." He says "Follow me." Following Jesus, of course, will never be in conflict with the Great Commandment, the rule of law in the kingdom of God (Galatians 5:14). The person who carefully and attentively follows Jesus along the Way will be living in the kingdom according to God's sovereign rules—whether or not he or she pays any attention to the Law itself. The Law is fulfilled when the kingdom of God is realized through love.

Jesus said, "For the gate is narrow and the road is hard that leads to life; and there are few who find it" (Matthew 7:14; see also Luke 13:24). The "narrow gate" Jesus speaks about is not a limitation or rule, but an approach, an openness to and faith in God. Truth derives from spiritual relationship with God, not from rules God made and imposed once and for all for everyone. The Law of love is less of a moral imperative and more of a statement of spiritual reality that we are able to participate in God's kingdom through love: "God is love, and those who abide in love abide in God, and God abides in them. ... We love because he first loved us" (1 John 4:16, 19). Our life choices are made in response to God's love for us. If we choose a Christian spiritual path, we discover that the "basis" for our choices in life is not a criterion but a personal relationship with God,[8] not a method or rule but a journey of love.[9]

Jesus asks for a change of heart to a kind of love or purity that goes beyond rules. Christianity is a personal transformation, the creation of a new character by God's grace in our personal relationships with God and other people. This only happens by living in relationship with Jesus. The walk of faith is more than "doing one's duty," belonging to a particular group, performing a certain ceremony, or following a particular rule, doctrine, or moral code. Jesus does not provide a new rulebook for repentance or living in God's kingdom. Repentance is a change in the way we approach our lives, not a new set of rules or beliefs.

The repentance that leads to kingdom living does not come from following a prescribed ethic or morality. The Way of Jesus is something we can only experience and participate in, not a body of ideas or principles. A way of living replaces an ethic. Right and wrong have to do not with the Law but with a person's faith: his or her relationship with God. As disciples, we need to be careful not to grasp hold of rules too tightly. The hardest challenge is that the Christian journey is an evolution and a process, not a creed or a formula. Although it is much easier to live by rules than to live in loving relationships, that is not how Christians are called to live. Christians are personally responsible for their relationships with God and other people. This is a profoundly different and more challenging spiritual path. The law Jesus brings with him into the world is kingdom love.

The Way means having the empowering presence of Christ in our lives so that we can live a new life of loving God and loving others. And following Jesus and living in the Way is the only way we can believe in Jesus. It is not surprising that people are looking to connect more with Christianity as a captivating way of life (rather than an ethical system or something that is fulfilled only in a future life or another realm), and are beginning to ask how it is possible to actually be a "follower" of Jesus today.[10] The continuing challenge for Christians is to follow closely, to keep Jesus in sight, to spend time with Jesus, to become more like him and closer to the image of God in whom we are created.

Engaging Jesus

To continue engaging Jesus, read and reflect on John 1:35–51.

Questions for Personal Reflection:

1. When has Jesus been present in your life? What experiences have you had in your life of meeting, living with, and serving Jesus?

2. How were you introduced to Jesus?

3. Think about a timeline of your life history. When did you

grow closer to God? When did you fall away?

4. How do you live with Jesus day by day? In the words of Saint Richard of Chichester (1197-1253), what are ways that you "know Jesus more clearly, love Jesus more dearly, and follow Jesus more nearly day by day?"[11]

5. Do you believe in Jesus?

6. Is Christianity a way of life for you? How?

7. How might you participate more fully in life with Jesus?

Questions for Group Discussion:

1. What (or whom) is the way to a loving relationship with God?

2. How is repentance different from the types of things many of us do during the season of Lent?

3. How is repentance different from following moral principles?

4. How do we continuously choose to live in God's presence now?

5. What does it mean for Jesus to be present in our lives? How do we begin to experience that presence?

6. How do we acquire faith in Jesus?

7. Does your church community share Christianity as a way of life? Or something else?

8. How is Christianity as a way of life different from other ways of living?

9. How do people come to know Jesus today? How do we introduce people to Jesus?

10. How do people come to our church community? How are adults formed in the faith when they come?

11. Does our community share its expectations for a spiritual journey? What is the spiritual path that a person can expect?

12. Do people in the congregation or coming to the congregation understand and participate in the discipleship process?

13. Where are most people in the congregation on the Way?

14. How might your church participate more fully in life with Jesus?

Following Jesus

The call of Jesus is both a difficult challenge and the greatest opportunity. The choice to follow Jesus creates a serious predicament for those who might accept discipleship. Jesus says both that his "yoke" or Way is easy (Matthew 11:30) and that his disciples must die by taking up a cross to follow him (Matthew 10:28, 16:34; Mark 8:34; Luke 9:23, 14:27). A paradox of true Christianity, of following Jesus in this life and into the next, is that his followers must lose their lives to find them.

Answering the call

Disciples hear the call of Jesus. In Mark 1:16–18, "As Jesus passed along the Sea of Galilee, he saw Simon and his brother Andrew casting a net into the lake—for they were fishermen. And Jesus said to them, 'Follow me and I will make you fish for people.' And immediately they left their nets and followed him." In Mark 1:19–20, "As he went a little farther, he saw James son of Zebedee and his brother John, who were in their boat mending the nets. Immediately he called them; and they left their father Zebedee in the boat with the hired men, and followed him." In Matthew 9:9, "As Jesus was walking along, he saw a man called Matthew sitting at the tax booth; and he said to him, 'Follow me.' And he got up and followed him." Similarly, in John 1:43, "he found Philip and said to him, 'Follow me.'"[1] Jesus' followers know they are called. Jesus directly tells them to get up and follow him and even what they are following him for: to live within the kingdom of God and to bring others into that kingdom.

So a first question for each disciple is "Have I been called?" Does Jesus exclude anyone from living with him and participating in God's kingdom? Some people believe that sinful people are excluded. But in Matthew 12:31 and Mark 3:29, Jesus says that every sin will be forgiven except blasphemy against the Spirit. And even for those who crucified him, Jesus asked, "Father, forgive them; for they do not know what they are doing" (Luke 23:34). Only people who themselves choose to have nothing to do with God are excluded from the king's banquet (Matthew 22:1–9).[2] Otherwise, everyone is invited (Matthew 22:10). If we wonder whether we are called, all we need to do is ask. Jesus said, "Ask, and it will be given you; search, and you will find; knock, and the door will be opened for you. For everyone who asks receives, and everyone who searches finds, and for everyone who knocks, the door will be opened" (Luke 11:9–10).

Trusting in Jesus

People who hesitate to follow Jesus may not doubt that they are called to this new life, but they may not feel they are ready to accept the invitation Jesus makes (Matthew 22:12–13). Like the rich young man in Mark 10, we may not feel ready to make the changes we need to make to follow Jesus and "enter the kingdom of God" (v. 24). No disciple is ready. Jesus reminds us, "For mortals it is impossible, but not for God; for God all things are possible" (v. 27). No one has the power to follow Jesus in their own strength.

Disciples fail when they do not have Jesus supporting them. In Matthew 14:28–31, when Peter saw Jesus walking on the sea, he knew he could not step out of the boat on his own and asked, "Lord, if it is you, command me to come to you on the water." Jesus said, "Come." So Peter got out of the boat, started walking on the water, and came toward Jesus. But when he noticed the strong wind, he became frightened, and beginning to sink, he cried out, "Lord, save me!" Jesus immediately reached out his hand and caught him, saying to him, "You of little faith, why did you doubt?" Like Peter walking on the water, each of us will need to rely on Jesus to support us each step of the Way.

Even being on the path with Jesus doesn't guarantee spiritual growth and success, but Jesus will hold on to us if we let him. We must continually be aware of who Jesus is and believe he is holding us, leading us, protecting us, and guiding us as our shepherd along the Way (1 Peter 2:25). This is true even after we begin to follow Jesus. Disciples stumble

(John 16:1). Jesus took Peter, James, and John with him to pray in the Garden of Gethsemane and they immediately fell fast asleep (Matthew 26:40–41). When the authorities came to arrest Jesus, all the disciples scattered like sheep (Matthew 26:31, 56). When Peter and John found enough courage to follow after Jesus and witness his trial before the Sanhedrin, Peter denied Jesus (John 18). Fortunately, Peter continued to trust Jesus, and Jesus restored him to the Way (John 21). Another disciple who had walked with Jesus along the same Way completely lost his trust in Jesus: Judas Iscariot became a traitor (Luke 6:17) and a thief (John 12:6), betrayed our Lord (Matthew 26:24) and, full of remorse, committed suicide.

Obeying Jesus

Because the Way of Jesus has nothing to do with our own strength or power, we must understand it as *his* Way, not *ours*. Our way is disobedience (not listening and following) and sin, and takes us out of the kingdom along the path of all individuals since Adam and Eve. Only those who truly hear the shepherd's voice (John 10:4) and know him are able to follow along the Way. We do not choose our own way; we follow his Way.

When Jesus recommissioned Peter for ministry as his disciple, he warned that Peter would no longer be able to go "wherever he wished" (John 21:18–20). Christians may be led to painful places, places they do not choose and would rather not go. Along with Jesus, the first apostles and the next generations of disciples—including Stephen (the first martyr, Acts 6) and Paul—all faced persecution and death. Christian discipleship comes from following Jesus wherever Jesus leads, and that takes away all power and control and makes the follower wholly vulnerable.

Those who do not understand the necessity of this fundamental and complete obedience cannot follow Jesus. As they were going along the road, someone said to Jesus, "I will follow you wherever you go." And Jesus said to him, "Foxes have holes, and birds of the air have nests; but the Son of Man has nowhere to lay his head" (Luke 9:57–58; Matthew 8:19–20). This person offers himself to discipleship, but he does not understand the hardship, and thus the obedience, needed to follow Jesus. A Christian has only Jesus to trust in.

When Jesus calls people to "Follow me" and become his disciples, the disciples hear and immediately obey. Those who hesitate miss the call. The followers of Christ accept the urgency of following Jesus. Andrew, Peter, John, James, Matthew, Phillip, Nathanael, Bartimaeus and other disciples immediately follow Jesus. They get up and go with Jesus at the very moment he calls them. Nothing is said about their motivations— what they were looking for or whether they were dissatisfied with their lives or professions—and there is no lengthy process of discernment.

Leaving everything

Trusting in Jesus means leaving everything else behind. In Mark 10, we see the stark contrast between blind Bartimaeus, who follows Jesus, and the rich young man, who does not. Bartimaeus leaves his cloak—his only shelter and all that he has—and risks going to Jesus. The rich young man cannot bring himself to sell everything and give to the poor so that he can come and follow Jesus. The followers of Jesus must be willing to leave everything.

Another person says, "I will follow you, Lord; but let me first say farewell to those at my home." Jesus replies, "No one who puts a hand to the plow and looks back is fit for the kingdom of God" (Luke 9:61–62). This person also puts something before Jesus and before moving into the kingdom: tying up loose ends in his former life. He places his own conditions on answering Jesus' call. Jesus says that looking back, even while preparing to move forward, will prevent entering the kingdom.

Jesus says to someone else, "Follow me." But that person says, "Lord, first let me go and bury my father." He simply asks to fulfill the fourth commandment, "Honor your father and your mother," by first burying his father. But not even the Law can come before following Jesus and fulfilling the kingdom of God, and he responds, "Let the dead bury their own dead; but as for you, go and proclaim the kingdom of God" (Luke 9:59–60, Matthew 8:21–22). Jesus says, "Whoever loves father or mother more than me is not worthy of me; and whoever loves son or daughter more than me is not worthy of me; and whoever does not take up the cross and follow me is not worthy of me" (Matthew 10:37–38). The first disciples who answered the call did not turn back with concerns about what they had left behind. Their focus was on Jesus, not what they owned or who they knew or even their close ties to family relations.

Disciples must enter a new way of life and leave the old behind. Jesus says, "For those who want to save their life will lose it, and those who lose their life for my sake, and for the sake of the gospel, will save it" (Mark 8:35). Life with Jesus requires disciples to die to their old lives—symbolized and accomplished in the sacrament of baptism—and accept a new life that may include rejection, persecution, suffering, and even death at the hands of others who deny God's presence, love, and sovereignty. Dietrich Bonhoeffer wrote:

> Following Christ means taking certain steps. The first step, which responds to the call, separates the followers from their previous existence. A call to discipleship thus immediately creates a new situation. Staying in the old situation and following Christ mutually exclude each other. . . . At first, that was quite visibly the case. The tax collector had to leave his booth and Peter his nets to follow Jesus.

> The point was to really walk with Jesus. It was made clear to those he called that they only had one possibility of believing in Jesus, that of leaving everything and going with the incarnate Son of God. . . . Those called must get out of their situations, in which they cannot believe, into a situation in which faith can begin. . . . If they want to learn to believe in God, they have to follow the Son of God incarnate and walk with him.[3]

The difficulty of discipleship, or following Jesus, is that nothing else can come before it. Life with Jesus comes first in time and energy. This urgency comes entirely out of who Jesus is and the kingdom he wants to share. Life in the kingdom of God comes first; otherwise, it is not that kind of life. This is why "many are called, but few are chosen" (Matthew 22:14). Nothing can come before Jesus. We either follow or not.

Participating with Jesus

The way of the cross always involves some form of self-denial. At the same time, the Way is where we become our most authentic selves, because we are living as God intended and participating in God's kingdom. We become more fully ourselves by letting go of ourselves. This paradox is challenging. Christians often disagree about how much we need to deny ourselves to follow Jesus, and they adopt different disciplines or methods of self-denial.

For example, Dietrich Bonhoeffer wrote that disciples "should keep on following Jesus, and should keep looking forward to him who is going before them, but not at themselves and what they are doing."[4] He believed Jesus' followers had to lose consciousness of themselves and their own motivations to pay attention to and follow Jesus. Bonhoeffer's friend and mentor, Karl Barth, criticized this as a kind of "sleepwalking." In support of Bonhoeffer, we remember Peter beginning to walk on water and then sinking into the sea at the moment he took his eyes from Jesus and thought of himself, or of a fearful Peter denying Jesus three times. With Barth, we remember a later Peter boldly proclaiming the Good News with full consciousness of his own journey with Jesus.

The goal, of course, is not self-denial. The goal is living with and following Jesus. The Way is neither active (doing it on our own) nor passive (letting Jesus work on us), but both. Following Jesus, like any act of love, is both active and passive. In an essay entitled, "Is Growth a Decision?"[5] Eugene Peterson describes the spiritual life in terms of living in middle voice. We typically use verbs in active voice or passive voice to describe the activities of our lives. I use active voice to describe an action that I do: "I counsel my friend." I use passive voice to describe an action that happens to me: "I am counseled by my friend." In middle voice, however, I both act and am acted upon: "I take counsel." In middle voice, one person "actively participates in the results of an action that another [person] initiates." Middle voice best describes our activities in intimate relationships, especially our relationship with God:

> Prayer and spirituality feature participation, the complex participation of God and the human, his will and our wills. We do not abandon ourselves to drown in the ocean of love, losing identity. We do not pull the strings that activate God's operations in our lives, subjecting God to our assertive identity. We neither manipulate God (active voice) nor are we manipulated by God (passive voice). We are involved in the action and participate in its results but do not control or define it (middle voice). Prayer takes place in the middle voice. . . .

We don't have enough (or any!) verbal experience in
this third voice, this voice that is fine-tuned to the
exquisitely and uniquely human venture of entering
into and responding to God. But no friendship, no love
affair, no marriage can exist with only active and passive
voices. Something else is required, a mode of willingness
that radiates into a thousand subtleties of participation
and intimacy, trust and forgiveness and grace.

Hearing and following Jesus—obedience—is an action in middle
voice. We desire to live and participate in actions God has originated.
Living in middle voice requires neither complete control nor complete
submission, but humility and boldness. Middle voice recognizes that we
are responding to a vocation, or calling, from God—not just with discernment, but also with the activities of our lives. Middle voice action
means that we co-create our lives and communities with and through
our relationships with God.

As disciples, we are not trying to lose ourselves, but to bring our lives
in concert with Jesus. We are trying to live in middle voice. To the extent we live in middle voice, we need not worry about how much of life
is controlled by God and how much of life is controlled by our choices;
both are the same.

Following the Way

Jesus proclaims and shares the Good News that a life lived with him
in God's kingdom is an entirely new way of life. Jesus comes into the
world to walk with us, and asks us to walk in a new path with him:

> *Come to me, all who are weary and heavy laden,*
> *and I will give you rest. Take my yoke upon you, and*
> *learn from me; for I am gentle and humble in heart,*
> *and you will find rest for your souls. For my yoke is*
> *easy, and my burden is light. (Matthew 11:28–30)*

When we live with Jesus, we experience life the way God created it
to be: gentle, humble, restful, and freed from burdens even when evil
and chaos surround us: "Even though I walk through the valley of the
shadow of death, I fear no evil; for you are with me" (Psalm 23).[6] When

we live in Jesus and Jesus lives in us, we are his disciples, we "bear much fruit," and his joy is in us and our joy is complete (John 15:1–11). When we live in relationship with Jesus and take that relationship into the world by sharing the Good News and serving others, each of us participates in God's kingdom and our joy is complete (1 John 1:4). People who walk with Jesus find themselves living in God's kingdom in an abundant life filled with peace, joy, love, and light (John 8:12).

Christians are "people who are so deeply in love with Jesus that they are ready to follow him wherever he guides them, always trusting that, with him, they will find life and find it abundantly."[7] This is how followers of Jesus can lose their lives and yet discover more loving, joyful, and fulfilled lives. This is how true discipleship can cost us everything, and yet we will gain something of immeasurably greater value—a special treasure and a bountiful harvest (Matthew 13:44–48).

Engaging Jesus

To continue engaging Jesus, read and reflect on Mark 1:30–45.

Questions for Personal Reflection:

1. Have you been called by Jesus? Have you answered Jesus' call? How?

2. When and how has Jesus helped you to answer his call?

3. What keeps you from following Jesus? How might these separations be overcome?

4. Are there times when you've had a real sense of what God wants for your life? What was that like?

5. Are there ways you particularly like to listen to God?

6. What types of questions do you ask God?
   What is OK to ask God?

7. Think of something that it would be helpful if God let you know. Can you ask God about this?

8. Do you feel that you have a unique relationship with God—a journey in which you participate with God in the creation of your life and identity?

9. Do you regularly reflect on the opportunities and choices you have in your life and listen for God's calling in them?

10. Are there important aspects of your life that you simply allow to happen as they may? What might be different if you took charge of them and asked for God's help?

11. How do you avoid being delayed or distracted from following Jesus?

12. Have you been led places you would rather not go? What happened?

13. How could you follow Jesus more closely?

Questions for Group Discussion:

1. The reading from Mark is full of miraculous healings. These miracles point to who Jesus is. Do you watch for signs, wonders, or miracles to suggest to you who you are or what God wants from you?

2. Why does Jesus leave?

3. How would Jesus (or God) feel when he hears, "Everyone is searching for you"? Why? (See, e.g., Deuteronomy 4:29, "From there you will seek the LORD your God, and you will find him if you search after him with all your heart and soul"; Jeremiah 29:13, "When you search for me, you will find me; if you seek me with all your heart." And Acts 17:26–27, "From one ancestor he made all nations to inhabit the whole earth, and he allotted the times of their existence and the boundaries of the places where they would live, so that they would search for God and perhaps grope for him and find him—though indeed he is not far from each one of us.")

4. In the King James Version, Jesus says "Therefore came I forth." What does Jesus say he came for? What is the message Jesus is proclaiming? (See, e.g., Matthew 4:17, Mark 1:14, Luke 8:1, Luke 10:9, Matthew 10:7.) What does this message have to do with listening to God?

5. What must the disciples have felt when Jesus essentially said, "I'm going on to preach rather than stick around and meet all of these people's needs"? Do you think they began to wonder whether he cared?

6. What would happen to Jesus' mission if Jesus let human needs alone determine his call? Can human desires to serve others prevent us from truly responding to God's call?

7. Does Jesus care? How does he treat the sick man?

8. Jesus has both a clear sense of what he is called to do and a deep, rich compassion. Where do these senses of calling and compassion come from? How does Jesus balance them?

9. How can we discover what we are being called to do so that we can respond with genuine generosity and compassion and care for the world?

10. Is Jesus' yoke easy?

11. What keeps people from following Jesus?

12. What are important steps to following Jesus?

13. How do we learn to trust in Jesus?

14. How important is self-denial in following the Way?

15. What is obedience?

16. What do we need to do to be Christians?

17. What do we need to do to help others follow the Way?

18. How could your church follow Jesus more closely?

1.4

Accepting God's Love

As we become disciples, we experience the compassion, love, and service Jesus has for people and the way that love attracts people to be part of God's family and kingdom. The experience that has the most profound impact on our individual characters and lives is God's love for each of us. A first challenge as disciples is personally accepting God's unconditional love for each of us: *"As the Father has loved me, so I have loved you; abide in my love"* (John 15:9).

As Christians, we can see God's love at work in infinite ways. We experience God's love and generosity in the gifts and blessings of our lives and opportunities and the world we live in. All that we are and all that we have are gifts from God in love. God is the source of everything we are, and God lovingly provides for us. We also know God's love for us in God's presence with us. We experience a security beyond our own reality in prayer and other encounters with God. We know God's love for us because God makes a gift of his Son, Jesus, to bring us closer to God. When we recognize God as our source and Jesus as coming from God as a means to love and serve and reconcile us with him (to overcome our separation from God), we begin to realize the magnitude and depth of God's love for us. We also know God's love for us by his invitation to share in the project of fulfilling God's kingdom. Jesus co-missions his followers to use their unique gifts in helping make disciples (Matthew 28:18–20) and feeding and tending his flock (John 21). Jesus invites us to participate in his mission of sharing God's love in the world. He recognizes and celebrates the value of each creature in the kingdom and encourages that value to be further realized to God's glory. And we know God's love for us is in the promise of eternal life.

The gift of incarnation

Jesus fully reveals God's love. The incarnational gift of Jesus—to bring us into closer, active, and eternal relationship with God—is astounding! Consider through the following parable that you are part of a deeply personal and never-ending love story with God:

> Once upon a time there lived a king who loved a poor maiden. The king was all-powerful in his land, and no one would dare to prevent his marriage to whomever he pleased, despite differences in class. But the maiden did not know the king or suspect his love for her.
>
> The king's love became a peculiar sort of tragedy. Because he desired the maiden and her true love and understanding, he could not approach his beloved as the king. For if he were to appear to the maiden as a king, she would be awed by the differences between them. She could worship and admire him for his power and status, but she could not forget that he was the king and that she was but a humble maiden. As a true lover, the king desired not to be glorified by the maiden, but to glorify her. He desired her true understanding and equality in love, and he knew true love could come only through his beloved's freedom, courage, and self-confidence. These all-important attributes of love would not blossom in the unequal relationship of king and subject. The differences between the king and the maiden would prevent either from being confident, understanding, or happy in their love.
>
> The king considered the possibility of elevating the maiden to his equal through secret gifts, transfiguring her to the joys of being a princess. But he quickly realized the folly of this approach. If the maiden accepted her good fortune, their love would be only a delusion created by the king. And, if the maiden were not completely deluded, in her heart she would suspect the deception and thereby recognize the differences between herself and the king. In either case, the elevation would be catastrophic if it changed the character

of the maiden. For the king loved her for herself! "It was harder for him to be her benefactor than to lose her," for he knew that "love does not alter the beloved, it alters itself."

The king grieved. How could he help his beloved to understand him as he wished to be understood, as a lover rather than as a king? "For this is the unfathomable nature of love, that it desires equality with the beloved, not in jest merely, but in earnest and truth." If their union could not be effected through the maiden's elevation to the king, it must be attempted through the king's "descent" to the maiden. The king realized he must "appear in the likeness of the humblest." He therefore had to appear as a servant, as one humble enough to serve others. So he clothed himself in a beggar's cloak and went out to meet the maiden.[1]

This simple love story is a metaphor that reveals how much God in the Person of Jesus loves each one of us, if we will only accept that love. The "Miracle" is this: For God so loved the world that God gave God's only Son. Of course, the analogy is too limited and imperfect. The author, Soren Kierkegaard, points out that God's servant form is "no mere outer garment, like the king's beggar cloak." Jesus is fully human and must suffer all human experience, even death. God's love is more genuine than the king's because God has fully assumed equal status with God's beloved. The analogy to God's love otherwise is true. For God so loved the world that God descended to human beings, in the form of these beloved creatures, so that God might preserve the dignity and freedom of God's people. And if a beloved human being chooses to love God, their union is based on true understanding engendered by true love.

The incomprehensible aspect of Christianity is God's love for each of us and God's coming to us. For God so loved the world that he sent Jesus himself into the world in our form and on our level to have a loving relationship with us and to be the way to relationship with God. God bridges the distances and the differences separating God from us. God equalizes sheer inequalities between God and human beings. By both descending to us and raising us up through the person of Jesus, God reconciles us to God and shows us his love for us.

Like the maiden in the story, our choice and challenge is to accept the love the king offers to each of us. We often have a very difficult time feeling and trusting in God's deep and unique personal love: *Is all this really God's personal gift to me? Does God really wish to have a personal relationship with me? Am I really in God's plans for his kingdom? Why would God love me or want to be part of my life?* Knowing God's personal love for each of us is an essential part of participating in his kingdom.[2] Our relationship with God, and our entire perspective and approach to life, changes completely if we truly accept ourselves as God's beloved daughters and sons.

Accepting God's love

God told Jesus at his baptism, "You are my Son, the Beloved; with you I am well pleased" (Mark 1:10–11). Knowing his identity as God's beloved made Jesus' mission and love possible. Jesus expects his followers to know this same unconditional love deeply and fully and with our whole being—emotionally and spiritually, not just intellectually. When Jesus speaks of being born anew, he means that we need to be born into the family of God (Luke 18:17, Mark 10:15). And as children of God, we also are beloved sons and daughters. As Henri Nouwen explains:

> Jesus' life is an invitation for us to believe, not primarily
> in him but in the *relationship* between [himself and his
> father, and] this very same *relationship* is uniquely available
> to each one of us. . . . Jesus never, never, never makes a
> distinction between his relationship with Unconditional
> Love and ours. . . . Jesus instead tells us, "All the things
> I've heard because of my communion with the Indwelling
> Beloved I tell you because I want you to have the same
> experience of knowing Love that I have." . . . Jesus
> came not simply to tell us about a loving Creator who
> is far away and who, from there, cares for us. Not at all!
> Jesus came to offer us the same full communion with
> the Spirit-Father-Mother-Lover that he enjoys, where
> he is in no way smaller than the One who sent him.[3]

Jesus wants each of us to experience the unconditional love God has for us as daughters and sons. In Luke 15:11–32, Jesus told the parable of the prodigal son to help us understand and accept God's love. This parable provides strong examples of human psychologies that keep us from accepting God's love. Most of us feel for any number of reasons that we do not deserve God's love. Then we mistakenly conclude that we do not or will not receive that love or that it is lost to us. The difficult aspect of God's love is that we can never deserve it or earn it, and yet God nevertheless gives love as pure gift, or grace.

At times, we may be like the younger son in the parable who wants independence and rejects his father's love to leave home and spend the father's estate in dissolute living. The younger son in the parable has, in his *rebellion,* effectively wished his father dead by asking for his inheritance. But the father continues to love him and to wait and watch for his return. Like this younger son, when we leave the father's home, we may allow our feelings of *guilt* about our independent actions to overwhelm us and feel that we could never return home and be pardoned. Unlike the prodigal son, however, we might not have sense enough to come home and to experience our father's forgiveness and love.

At other times, we may be more like the ethical, hardworking, and faithful elder son in the parable, and that may also prevent us from experiencing God's love. Like many of us, the elder son believes that he has to do something to *earn* his father's love and, perhaps, even that he has not received that love in return. He says, "Listen! For all these years I have been working like a slave for you, and I have never disobeyed your command; yet you have never given me even a young goat so that I might celebrate with my friends." In this attitude, the elder son "stayed home, worked hard, was obedient to the old father, and was faithful" and yet became a bitter, resentful, "frustrated, angry, and unhappy young man."[4] The resentment occurs because the elder son does not accept the gift of God's love but continually strives to earn it. He is unable to experience the loving truth of the father's statement, "Son, you are always with me, and all that is mine is yours."

We can neither earn God's love (the elder brother) nor can we lose it (the prodigal son). Like these brothers, many of us fear either that we have to earn God's love or that we could never earn it back. But that is not how God loves. God gives love freely, without regard to our righteousness or self-worth. When his children come home, God forgives and loves them. God does not require repentance before forgiveness.[5] A person, like the woman caught in adultery, might repent and "go and sin no more" (John 8:11), but she does not have to repent before she is loved and forgiven by Jesus. Nor does anyone else whom Jesus encounters and heals.[6]

The barriers to accepting God's love are within ourselves. And they are often complex, and psychologically and spiritually deep. We may need to peel back many layers in order to understand why we do not believe in and accept God's love.[7] Whether we are more like the rebellious and dissolute son or the reliable and resentful son, God our father loves us and wants us home:

> I believe the Giver of Life loves each of us as a daughter or son who is leaving and returning constantly. The more we become sensitive to our own journey the more we realize that we are leaving and coming back every day, every hour. Our minds wander away but eventually return; our hearts leave in search of affection and return sometimes broken; our bodies get carried away in their desires then sooner or later return. . . . It's normal, then, for us in growing up spiritually to live according to our nature. . . . The God in the parable is a personal, intimate, and loving Presence who lets each of us go and welcomes each one home, all in amazing generosity and forgiveness. This reflection isn't an intellectual exercise about right and wrong. More, it is an opening of ourselves to gradually let go of fear, to trust anew, and to make space for the love of the one who both blesses our leaving and waits to celebrate our return.[8]

Accepting the truth of the parable of the prodigal son that, like Jesus, I am God's beloved son or daughter does not happen once and for all. It is built gradually through a journey of a lifetime of leaving and returning to loving relationship with God:

> It's a real struggle to bring our whole selves home and it is best accomplished gently and gradually. Jesus tells us it is a narrow path, meaning that we slip off occasionally, and that is OK. The whole course of the spiritual life is falling off, and returning, slipping away from the truth

and turning back to it, leaving and returning. So in our leaving, as much as in our returning, we must try to remember that we are blessed, loved, cherished, and waited for by the One whose love doesn't change.[9]

Engaging Jesus

To continue engaging Jesus, read and reflect on Luke 15:11–32.

Questions for Personal Reflection:

1. Brennan Manning, the author of *The Ragamuffin Gospel*, often preached that he believed on Judgment Day each of us will be asked only one question by God: "Did you believe that I loved you?" How would you answer this question?

2. How do you experience God's personal love for you?

3. Is God's love hard for you to accept? Why?

4. Have you ever acted like the younger son, the older son, or the father in the parable of the prodigal son? How have you "left home" or felt separated from God's love? Can you return?

5. Do you abide in God's love? How?

6. If you considered a timeline of your life, when has God been part of it?

Questions for Group Discussion:

1. Were there things throughout your life that you thought could separate you from the love of God? Could they? What could? (Jesus speaks of only one unpardonable sin in Matthew 12:31–32.)

2. Do you have trouble believing that God is a person who loves you and wants to spend time with you? Which Bible verses say otherwise?

3. Reflect on the parable of the prodigal son:

  a. Why does the younger son want to leave? How would people hearing this in Jesus' time interpret his reasons for leaving?

  b. How does the father treat the younger son when he wants to leave?

  c. How does the younger son live on his own?

  d. Why does the younger son return home?

  e. What does the younger son expect upon his return home? What is his plan?

  f. How does the father receive the younger son?

  g. How is the father's welcome like the Christian love described in Romans 5:8 ("God proves his love for us in that while we still were sinners Christ died for us.") and 1 John 4:10 ("In this is love, not that we loved God but that he loved us and sent his Son to be the atoning sacrifice for our sins.")?

  h. How does the older son feel about this? Why?

  i. Who is God in the parable of the prodigal son? How is he described?

  j. Do we sometimes think of God more like the elder brother? How?

4. What is God like?

5. Why is it so hard for people to believe that God loves them unconditionally?

6. How does it make a difference to a person's life if they know God loves them?

7. Do leaders who understand God's unconditional love lead differently? How?

8. What opportunities do we have as a church community to share God's unconditional love with people?

9. How does sharing God's unconditional love change the world?

1.5

The Great Commission

The last words of Jesus in each gospel proclaim the same mission:

Go therefore and make disciples of all nations, baptizing them in the name of the Father and of the Son and of the Holy Spirit, and teaching them to obey everything that I have commanded you. (Matthew 28:18–19)

Go into all the world and proclaim the good news to the whole creation. (Mark 16:15)

You will receive power when the Holy Spirit has come upon you; and you will be my witnesses in Jerusalem, in all Judea and Samaria, and to the ends of the earth. (Acts 1:8)

Peace be with you. As the Father has sent me, so I send you. (John 20:21)

Follow me. (John 21:22)

Jesus tells his disciples to witness and proclaim his love and mercy to everyone. "God our Savior … desires everyone to be saved and to come to the knowledge of the truth" (1 Timothy 2:4). Every person we encounter needs our help in experiencing the possibility and presence of God's love. Jesus calls us to join him in sharing new life and hope. Like Jesus, Christians need to lovingly confront the world with the good news of God's love and of the new kingdom God is creating. Jesus will be with us, but his mission is now ours. It is this *co-mission* that we are asked to participate in as followers and leaders.

Our co-mission

In the introduction, I quoted Jesus saying, "Very truly, I tell you, the one who believes in me will also do the works that I do and, in fact, will do greater works than these, because I am going to the Father" (John 14:12). I wrote in Chapter 1.1, "Jesus calls his followers to follow him today in this life and he co-missions his disciples to live with him and continue his role in this world." In Chapter 1.2, I explained that "belief" in Jesus is putting our trust in Jesus to walk together with him into the kingdom of God. In speaking about following Jesus and living in "middle voice" in Chapter 1.3, I used the word "co-create" for our relationship with God. And yet, sometimes people ask, "Where does the Bible say, we are co-creators or partners with God?" This is a critical and foundational question. Behind this question may be an assumption that God is wholly self-sufficient, complete and static. But God is much more: God is wholly-loving and he brings us into the process of making a new creation so that we can become part of that creation. For we are not just followers, we are partners with God in the sharing and creation of God's kingdom of love. God partners with people to transform the world. We cannot become leaders in the Christian movement unless and until we accept that we truly are empowered to work with, for, and on behalf of God and other people. God is trying to bring new life into being, and he needs us for this work.

Christians must recognize and accept the tension that the kingdom of God is "already here" and that the kingdom is "not here yet." The kingdom of God is more fully revealed and realized by our participation in it. God created the world "very good" (Genesis 1:31) and created us in God's image (Genesis 1:26–27). God made us responsible for this world (Genesis 1:26, 28). When we had turned away from God, Jesus shared our humanity and came into the world to proclaim God's kingdom of love. And Jesus has redeemed us from separation and death once and for all and continues to bring us into closer relationship with God and one another.

Through his suffering, death, and resurrection, Jesus offers gifts of "justification" and "sanctification."[1] The sacrifice of Jesus "justifies" by pronouncing sinners free from sin and accepted by God, and including them in God's family once and for all. *You* are God's new creation, worthy of his love and loved by him. We are comforted that we can join in the resurrection and be welcomed into God's loving presence in everlasting life. As followers of Jesus, we are part of God's family and part of the fellowship of "saints" (Ephesians 2:19), which means "holy ones" or people set apart as God's own.[2] Through his redemption, Jesus makes it possible for us to leave our separation from God (exile in the Hebrew sense) and live as members of God's family in God's kingdom. This is the Good News.

We acknowledge that through justification we can be in real fellowship with all people who love what God loves and seek what God seeks. And yet God's reign is not fully realized. We can look at our world, our nation, our communities, our families, and our own hearts and see everywhere needs for healing, forgiveness, and reconciliation. God's redemptive work has not been completed. St. Paul says, "Not that I have already obtained this or have already reached the goal; but I press on to make it my own, because Christ Jesus has made me his own ... forgetting what lies behind and straining forward to what lies ahead, I press on toward the goal for the prize of the heavenly call of God in Christ Jesus" (Philippians 3:12–13). We are reminded that we are called to live today as God's people, on earth as in heaven. As saints, we need to pray for guidance and comfort, and strive to grow in faith, wisdom, and love until the "last day." Sanctification is an ongoing action by Jesus and the Holy Spirit, enabling us to faithfully continue to participate in God's kingdom. Disciples are called to participate with Jesus and the Holy Spirit in this process of sanctification.

Archbishop Desmond Tutu writes, "God *does* believe in us. God relies on us to help make this world all that God has dreamed of it being." He reminds us of the example of Mary, whom God partnered with to co-create his human Son, and of our other faith heroes like Moses:

> We are the agents of transformation that God uses to transfigure His world. In the Bible, when God wanted the children of Israel to be freed from bondage in Egypt, He could have done it on His own, but He wanted a human partner. We often forget that the patriarchs and matriarchs were flesh-and-blood humans, but the Bible reminds us

of this repeatedly. These people, with all their flaws, were able to be God's heroic partners. . . . Do you remember what God told Moses? He said, "I have seen the suffering of My people. I have heard their cry. I know their suffering and am come down to deliver them." Our God is a God who knows. Our God is a God who sees. Our God is a God who hears. Our God is a God who comes down to deliver. But the way that God delivers us is by using us as His partners, by calling on Moses, and on you and me.[3]

Christian leaders must be people who help change the world. And to do this, we must feel ourselves to be called and empowered to serve others as partners in creation. The kingdom of God is present with us; it is still opening and unfolding before us; and this is also happening through us. We are called to follow, to imitate, to share, to reveal so that others will see Jesus in our lives and also be drawn to him.

Evangelism

Successful evangelism—sharing the Good News of God's kingdom—follows the practices of Jesus as he invited his disciples to "come and see" by living in relationship with him. And it follows the training of his disciples for evangelism. When Jesus sent his disciples out on the practice missions described in Matthew 10 and Luke 10, he asked them to share both good deeds and Good News. Their service powerfully showed other people the presence and love of Jesus. In Luke, it's because people see the compassion of Jesus that they say, "God has come to help his people" (7:16b). When people see Christians serving others, they begin to trust them, and they want to know why Christians would want to help them. This opens the door for sharing the Good News of God's love.

In Matthew 9:35–38, "Jesus went about all the cities and villages, teaching in their synagogues, and proclaiming the Good News of the kingdom, and curing every disease and every sickness. When he saw the crowds, he had compassion for them, because they were harassed and helpless, like sheep without a shepherd. Then he said to his disciples, 'The harvest is plentiful, but the laborers are few; therefore ask the Lord of the harvest to send out laborers into his harvest.'" The chapter ends with a prayer for harvesters to be sent out into the field.

The next chapter, Matthew 10, begins by describing the answer to that prayer. The twelve disciples are commissioned to ministry, and Matthew uses the word "apostles" to describe them. The Jewish concept of apostle was much more than a person sent on a mission. It was an authorization to represent the person who sent them. The disciples are called to represent Jesus in his ministries: reinterpreting the Scriptures to focus on self-giving love and reaching out to the untouchables of their society.[4] The apostles are to risk confrontation with religious leaders to do God's will. The disciples' ministry is virtually identical to that of Jesus: proclaiming the Word and exercising power over unclean spirits, casting out demons, and healing every kind of sickness and disease.

The mission of disciples

Jesus gives his apostles specific instructions for this mission. On this first journey, the disciples are to go only to "the lost sheep of the house of Israel" or the "sheep without a shepherd" Jesus has compassion for. The disciples' shepherding ministry is patterned after the shepherding ministry of Jesus.

Christian ministry, both for the original Twelve and for disciples today, is based only on trusting God, without regard for payment. Jesus instructs his disciples to go without money, extra clothes or spare sandals, or even a staff for protection. Disciples carry no baggage that may get in the way of their ministry, and they do not have any other motives for their ministry. When we understand how generous God has been to us, we will be generous in giving our time and energies to ministry for him. If we try to provide ourselves with security, honor, or benefits, we destroy the total dependence on God that is the essence of the kingdom. If we become heavily invested materially in the outcome of ministry, it becomes difficult to serve others, and it also becomes more difficult to shake the dust off our feet and move on (and we may have the wrong motivation).

The disciples are told to seek worthy hosts in whatever town or village they enter. The host's worthiness will be determined by whether or not that host accepts and supports the ministry of the disciples. If the host accepts them, the disciples are to extend peace to the host. This peace refers to the blessings of the messianic age. If the would-be host refuses to accept and honor the message and messengers of Christ, the blessings of the messianic age will not be available. However, the disciples are not to judge or condemn the decisions of other people regarding the message of Christ. If they are rejected, they are to "shake off the dust of their feet" and move on to a more receptive audience.

Jesus sends his disciples into such a hostile environment that he characterizes this mission as sending sheep into the midst of wolves. He warns his disciples to be prepared for persecution and betrayal. This pattern began with opposition to Jesus himself. As Jesus was persecuted and people resisted his ministry, his followers are also persecuted and people resist their ministries. Jesus warns that people will hate them, families will be divided, and disciples will be handed over for legal proceedings, floggings, and trials before kings and governors. But we must witness if we are to be followers of Christ: "Everyone therefore who acknowledges me before others, I also will acknowledge before my Father in heaven; but whoever denies me before others, I also will deny before my Father in heaven" (Matthew 10:32–33). People who acknowledge Jesus are part of his kingdom: "Whoever does not take up the cross and follow me is not worthy of me. Those who find their life will lose it, and those who lose their life for my sake will find it" (Matthew 10:38–39). Sometimes, followers of Jesus may experience persecution as the validation of real discipleship and sharing in Christ's sufferings.

Jesus urges courage in the face of fear when betrayal and persecution come. He counsels his disciples to be wise as serpents and harmless as doves, requiring them to face persecution with a difficult combination of understanding and innocence. Followers of Jesus need to have enough insight about evil not to be surprised or taken in by it, and enough purity to respond differently and with love. Jesus also tells his followers not to worry about what they'll say when they're betrayed and persecuted, because God will provide the words through the Holy Spirit. This is not comfort that his followers will be able to defend themselves and their sufferings will be lessened or their lives will be preserved; they will, however, be enabled to hold onto and defend their faith in Jesus. Their saving relationship with God will endure, and disciples will find meaning and fulfillment in their allegiance to God; but discipleship is terribly hard because it requires hope, understanding, innocence, courage, and perseverance.

God's kingdom will prevail: "So have no fear of them; for nothing is covered up that will not be uncovered, and nothing secret that will not become known" (Matthew 10:26). The mission of the apostles is sometimes achieved. Some people welcome the apostles and, by welcoming them, also welcome Jesus himself into their lives. Bringing Jesus into others' lives is the most loving action disciples may offer, for Jesus brings these new family members more fully into the love of God's kingdom, so they too can share God's love (Matthew 10:40–42).[5]

Christians may look at Matthew 10, Luke 10, and Mark 6 as some of the most difficult chapters in the Bible—not because Jesus' instructions to his disciples are hard to understand, but because they are hard to do. We need to recognize that Jesus is asking disciples to do the same things he was already doing and that he was preparing them, using his own experiences, for what they would experience themselves. Jesus continually asks his disciples to follow where he leads and to do the things he does.

Sowing seeds

The Jesus movement, the Way, is a journey of continually living in closer relationship with God and other people. Because the kingdom of God is relational—it's all about love—we are responsible for co-creating it both by being drawn into God's love and by sharing it with others. Also because it is relational, it is never completed or achieved on earth.

Jesus uses the metaphor of a tree producing "good fruit" to describe the kingdom as a living and growing organism (Matthew 3:8–10, 7:17–19, 12:33; Luke 3:9, 6:44). Saint Paul writes that "the fruit of the Spirit is love, joy, peace, patience, kindness, generosity, faithfulness, gentleness, and self-control" (Galatians 5:22–23). The way that we bear good fruit is by living in relationship with Jesus and then taking that relationship into the world. "You did not choose me but I chose you. And I appointed you to go and bear fruit, fruit that will last" (John 15:16). Christians are called to sow the seeds of the kingdom in the world, and the eventual fruit from these seeds is a sign of healthy growth and productivity.[6]

Despite the travails of the Way and the many mistakes made by leaders who claimed to be followers of Jesus, enough seeds have been sown to continue the Jesus movement into our time. Contemporary leaders of this movement can have confidence that these seeds are being sown in our time for the next. At the same time, however, we do not know where seeds we sow will bear fruit, and we cannot prejudge them. When Peter denied Jesus, did he look like the next sower? Or did Paul, as he held the coats while his companions stoned Stephen?

Jesus says, "The kingdom of God is as if someone would scatter seed on the ground, and would sleep and rise night and day, and the seed would sprout and grow, he does not know how. The earth produces of itself, first the stalk, then the head, then the full grain in the head. But when the grain is ripe, at once he goes in with his sickle, because the harvest has come" (Mark 4:26–29). In Matthew 13:3–8 and 19–23, Jesus tells the parable of the sower and explains how seeds of God's kingdom are prevented from growing. When a person hears the word of the kingdom and does not understand it, the evil one comes and snatches it away like birds that eat seeds that fall on a path. When a person hears the word and immediately receives it with joy without becoming more grounded, the word withers away like seeds planted on rock that are growing in too-thin soil. When a person hears the word but still gives into the cares of the world and the lure of wealth, the word is choked like seeds falling in a thicket among thorns. "But as for what was sown on good soil, this is the one who hears the word and understands it, who indeed bears fruit and yields, in one case a hundredfold, in another sixty, and in another thirty." This parable causes its hearers to anxiously consider whether the seed of God's word is falling to them as to the belly of a bird, stony ground, shallow soil, or choking weeds—or as to good soil. Will it sprout forth like the mustard seed (Matthew 13:31–32)? Each of us may be a poorer or better receptacle at different times in our lives. But the followers of Jesus are not only good soil for his seeds; they will as leaders become the sower.

As the sower himself, Jesus poured out seed abundantly without worrying whether the soil that would receive it was good enough, pious enough, understanding enough, or deserving enough to receive it. Jesus shared with everyone his news of God's presence among us and God's love for us. Jesus let the seeds fall where they may and trusted that God would cause enough to grow for his purposes. And so each sower must generously pour out the bounty of love, and trust that those "who hear the word and understand" will be inspired to sow, and some of their listeners will also. The truth of the kingdom is that if we are generous with love, many will respond.

Engaging Jesus

To continue engaging Jesus, read and reflect on Matthew 10 (perhaps also comparing Luke 10).

Questions for Personal Reflection:

1. Are you on a mission for Jesus? How do you sow seeds of God's kingdom?

2. In Matthew 10, what are the disciples to take with them? What are they to leave behind? What does this mean in your own life?

3. Why, in Matthew 10:19, does Jesus command his disciples not to worry? In what way can you extend the promise of verse 20 to apply to circumstances of your life when you are tempted to worry?

4. What opportunities do you have to sow seeds for God's kingdom?

Questions for Group Discussion:

1. How does Jesus show his love for people? How do his disciples?

2. What is the mission Jesus gives his disciples?

3. What do disciples need to do (or not do) to follow Jesus' mission?

4. Who are the disciples to depend upon?

5. Jesus says he does not bring peace, but conflict. Why?

6. What warnings does Jesus give his disciples? Who are the disciples to fear? Who will protect them?

7. How can we be wise as serpents and harmless as doves? How would obedience to this look in our lives?

8. How are the disciples to treat those who reject them?

9. How is this mission daunting? How is it consoling?

10. How does hospitality work in Matthew 10? How is it different from what we might expect?

11. What rewards may disciples hope for?

12. How is our mission like that of the twelve apostles? How is it different?

13. "The kingdom of heaven has come near" may also be translated, "The kingdom of heaven is already here." Does this make our mission any different?

14. Why does Jesus use metaphors about organic growth to describe the kingdom of God?

15. Where does growth come from? What prevents growth for the seeds in the parable of the sower? For you personally?

16. How is your church doing with growing as a church community? What do you mean by growth?

17. How does your church community sow seeds of God's kingdom?

18. What opportunities does your church have to sow seeds for God's kingdom?

PART 2:

Sharing Christian Love

2.1

By Listening

The compassion of Jesus was shared in entering the world and responding to human needs to further reveal God's kingdom. Jesus did this not only in a universal sense, but in a personal way. Jesus has time for everyone and turns away no one. He spent time with all types of people, including the rich and important (the Pharisee Nicodemus, the tax collectors Levi and Zacchaeus, and the Centurion whose servant Jesus healed), as well as the poor and outcast (Matthew 11:19, Luke 15:1–2). He spoke with the Samaritan woman by the well (John 4) and the woman caught in adultery (John 8), saving and changing the lives of each in wholly unique and loving ways.

Listening to the needs of others

Jesus' compassion begins in his stopping and listening for the needs of others. In Mark 10:42–52, Jesus is traveling along when he hears cries for mercy by Bartimaeus, a blind beggar,[1] and calls him over. Jesus stands still and directs his full attention to this man who has interrupted his journey. Jesus, the Son of God, is bound for Jerusalem, and the action of the gospel journey is fast and furious, but Jesus stops and listens. Jesus always has time for us. Each of us matters to him. Imagine being Bartimaeus and hearing, "Take heart, get up, he is calling you." What comforting words! Take heart, the Lord has heard your cry. Take heart, you are no longer alone; you are not a despised beggar. You are heard and you are being summoned to Jesus to be saved and follow him "in the way" (Mark 10:52 KJV), to become his disciple.

When we approach, Jesus asks, "What do you want me to do for you?" He asks each of us to express our own needs. Why? He already sees into our hearts and knows our needs. But he wants each of us to understand our needs so that we can also recognize how God is meeting them. In the story, Jesus understands that Bartimaeus is asking, in referring to Jesus as teacher, both for physical sight and spiritual insight. Jesus says, "Go; your faith has made you well." Immediately, Bartimaeus regained his sight and followed Jesus on the Way.[2]

When Jesus stops and listens, he shows people his love, care, compassion, and welcome. Directing his attention to another person shows that he is setting aside his own needs and distractions to respond and that he personally values them. In each encounter, Jesus begins by accepting and honoring others just as they are, listening before making judgments about differing opinions, difficult behaviors, and irritating attitudes. When Jesus listens empathetically, he creates a trusting environment and provides an opportunity for troubled persons to talk about their deepest feelings and their meanings, and then mental, emotional, and spiritual growth can take place. The person receiving pastoral care from Jesus feels affirmed, acknowledged, and encouraged and experiences new insights, increased self-awareness, and changes in negative, self-defeating attitudes.

Listening is the foundation of compassion and service to others:

> The first service one owes to others in the community
> involves listening to them. Just as our love for God begins
> with listening to God's Word, the beginning of love for
> other Christians is learning to listen to them. God's love
> for us is shown by the fact that God not only gives us
> God's Word, but also lends us God's ear. We do God's work
> for our brothers and sisters when we learn to listen to
> them. So often Christians, especially preachers, think that
> their only service is always to have to "offer" something
> when they are together with other people. They forget
> that listening can be a greater service than speaking.[3]

The gift of listening is the power love has to give personal meaning, significance, and purpose to our lives. We realize our personal significance when we are touched by God or others. When they listen, this is an affirmation and an opportunity for acceptance and, in acceptance, for security and self-esteem. No other activity expresses as much value to us as when someone we respect and love listens, and thus shares our lives with us:

> Those who are unhappy have no need for anything in this world but people capable of giving them their attention. The capacity to give one's attention to a sufferer is a very rare and difficult thing; it is almost a miracle; it is a miracle. Nearly all of those who think they have this capacity do not possess it. Warmth of heart, impulsiveness, pity are not enough. ... The love of neighbor in all its fullness simply means being able to say to him: "What are you going through?"[4]

Listening takes us out of ourselves and makes it possible to love. Compassionate listeners have a willingness to serve others because others need to be listened to. Relationships come as we open our hearts. As with Jesus, this response to needs in the world shows people that God cares about each of his children more than we can imagine. In itself, the act of listening shows love, care, compassion, hospitality, and welcome.[5]

Inviting God into the conversation

In the heart of relationships, listening to others, God is able to use us and show his love through us. As we learn to really listen, we discover that compassionate listening is action that flows out of our relationship with God. Specific techniques or dos and don'ts may guide us, but effective caregiving is the result of our being touched by God within us. Loving listening begins with a choice to listen to God at the same time we are listening to another person who needs God's love. We listen most effectively when we remember that God cares more for the person we are listening to than we ever can, God knows what the person needs better than we ever will, and God wants to show his love through us in our response to the other person. To be more loving, we need to ask God through prayer to be part of our conversation with another person.

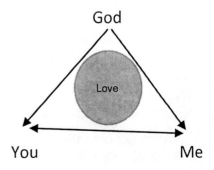

Interdependence

Ultimately, listening to another person is more loving if it is not about us but about God's love for that person. When Jesus sent his disciples into the world, he told them to take nothing with them (Matthew 10, Luke 10). We also need to leave our personal baggage behind. We need to go into the world unburdened, aware of the dangers and hopeful for the kingdom. We need to set aside our physical, psychological, and emotional distractions so we can concentrate on what another person needs and says.

To be in this frame of mind, we must interrupt our life patterns and change our ways of thinking and feeling to be more present to God and the other person. We must take the focus off ourselves and put it on God and the other person, perhaps through prayer (listening to God), preparation through reading Scripture, or other spiritual disciplines. And, because the conversation is not about us, we especially need, like Jesus, to accept and honor others just as they are, without being judgmental of differing opinions, difficult behaviors, and irritating attitudes.

These listening practices work for pastoral care relationships, and they also work to make all of our other relationships more loving. A simple way of beginning loving conversations is praying Mychal's Prayer:

> Lord, take me where you want me to go;
>
> Let me meet who you want me to meet;
>
> Tell me what you want me to say;
>
> And keep me out of your way.[6]

Deepening relationships

God asks us to extend our personal love as far and as truly as possible. By widening the circle of personal love, we prepare a place for an infinite and eternal love that we are not capable of creating on our own. Because of our natural skepticism, trust (or love) is not usually something that just happens; it has to be developed by choice and actions toward another person and their reciprocations.

We experience different levels of depth in our relationships with others. With someone we barely know, we engage in social conversation and conventions. We act the way we feel is expected when we begin to get to know the other person. As our relationship grows, we make small talk about the weather or noncontroversial current events. Our small talk begins to make us human to each other and opens channels between us for deeper discussions. Then we can begin to share ideas, perhaps even humor. To be successful in our working relationships, we have to progress at least to the level of sharing ideas so that we can interact with coworkers and share suggestions.

With most people, we go no further than sharing our ideas. We do not share our personal thoughts. Moving to a deeper relationship is tricky because it requires developing trust. In a deeper relationship, we take risks by asking for personal advice and even admitting personal mistakes. And the trust deepens if we experience intimate conversation, empathy, support, and encouragement. Often we aren't very good at trusting or communicating at an intimate level. We're afraid to be vulnerable to others. We frequently do not share with others because we want to avoid conflict, or we're afraid of "digging too deep" into our experiences or of confronting problems or of another's judgment. Talking about our feelings makes us uncomfortable. We fear other people's reactions to our own honesty and even expect them to take advantage of our openness. Thus, it becomes more difficult to build the trust we need to be intimate. We need to make ourselves vulnerable to each other in order to love, to become close; we need to be able to try our thoughts and feelings on another in order to take risks; we need others to complete the picture of who we are and affirm it. Notice, however, that intimate listening relationships will always require some personal self-disclosure as well.

Too frequently in our relationships we experience a lack of depth or of support, or we find criticism or censorship. We recognize that it is not safe to be intimate. Then our trust is shattered, and we move back to a safer relationship depth. Sometimes this failure to deepen our relationships is based on value differences. But we do not all need to share the same value systems to more deeply meet and respect other persons and to grow through our dialogue with them. To be a listener is to be nonjudgmental and supportive. Listening is about being present, and not about providing solutions.

From these patterns, we recognize that relationships grow deeper through mutual openness and mutual support. Both require us to be vulnerable to another person. We aren't looking so much for the intellectual sharing of our thoughts—an acknowledgment that what we think is true. We are looking for the experience of having another person actually wanting to share the activities of our life, including our thoughts, feelings, and choices. There is more value expressed to us personally in someone we respect and love sharing the time and experiences of our lives than in any other activity.

Today, there are many opportunities to follow Jesus by listening to those who need a loving ear. Some people need pastoral listening and care more obviously than others: those in hospitals, residential care facilities, and hospices who are sick, suffering, or lonely. But everyone needs love, and listening is always the first step.

Engaging Jesus

To continue engaging Jesus, read and reflect on Mark 10:46–52.

Questions for Personal Reflection:

1. How well do you really listen to your family, friends, coworkers, and people you meet on the street?

2. What keeps you from listening well to others?

3. What happens when you listen to others? What happens when you don't?

4. Think about your relationships. Who are the people you are closest to? Do you need to develop closer relationships? How?

5. Do you invite God into your relationships? How?

6. How do you share God's love by listening to people?

Questions for Group Discussion:

1. Can you think of examples when Jesus stopped to listen to people? How did they feel?

2. Why is listening to others so important?

3. What keeps us from listening well to others?

4. What are techniques that help you to listen? What are ways to show others you are listening to them? Should we be using them? How? Some examples:

Listening Technique	Purpose	Examples
Allowing appropriate silences	We are not there to solve a problem but to share our presence.	
Body language	Demonstrate that we are truly interested in the other person. Observe non-verbal cues from the care receivers that indicate something of their willingness to share.	Eye contact Leaning forward Touch Facial expressions Mirroring
Neutral, acknowledging responses	To convey that you are interested and listening. To encourage the person to continue talking.	"I see." "I understand." "Yes, I can see your point."

Invitation to say more		"Tell me about it." "I'd like to hear more." "I'm really interested in what you have to say about that."
Reflective responses (Distinguish between the facts the speaker expresses and the significance of those facts in the speaker's life.)	To show that you care about what the other is feeling or saying. To make sure you understand what the other person is saying. To identify meanings and feelings as well as facts. By listening for the emotional content in the conversation, we are able to "move from the superficial to real problems.	"You feel that ..." *Draw out feelings* "What was it like for you?" "How did you feel when you heard ... ?" *Encourage elaboration on needs and wants* "What do you want right now?" "What can you control and what can't you control?" *Help others discover things for themselves*
Restatement (or paraphrasing)	To check your meaning and interpretation with the other. To show you are listening and that you understand what the other has said.	"As I understand it, your plan ..." "Is this what you have decided to do ... ? And the reasons are ..."

Clarification (but use questions appropriately and sparingly)	To get additional facts. To help the person explore all sides of a problem.	"Can you clarify this?" "Do you mean this?" "Is this the problem as you see it now?" *Ask open-ended questions.* *Avoid asking "why" and "who."* *Avoid loaded questions.*
Summarizing	To show that you understand all that was said and not just individual points. To serve as a springboard to discussion of new aspects of the problem.	"These are the key ideas you have expressed …" "If I understand how you feel about the situation …"
Sharing experiences	Interpersonal relationships grow on both sides. God often uses our experiences to help others.	

5. How do you set aside your own physical, psychological, and emotional distractions so you can concentrate on what others are saying?

6. How does having a close relationship with God help us listen better?

7. What are some ways to get into a different attitude to listen more lovingly?

8. Try this exercise. Pair off with someone you don't know well and take turns talking about yourselves for two minutes within these constraints:

   - You may not talk about the weather or your achievements, including what you do for a living, where you vacation, what kind of schooling you've had or your children.

   - You may talk about:

     - childhood: what were you like as a child?

     - strengths: what are your personal strengths?

     - obstacles: what things hold you back, what things do you struggle with?

     - likes: what are the things you like to do (so long as they're not the achievements above, which you may not talk about)?

     - vision: what are your dreams about your life and future?

   What did you experience as you were doing this exercise?

9. Think about the culture that surrounds us every day, where achievement and success reign supreme. What are some of the ways we're evaluated in that culture? If the culture were based on character instead, what are some of the ways in which we would be evaluated? How do we operate in our daily lives with these very different paradigms?

10. How does your church community share God's love by listening to people (as in pastoral care or mentoring)?

By Healing and Forgiving

Jesus' compassion is especially evident in his healing of physically, emotionally, mentally, and spiritually disabled people: "Then Jesus went about all the cities and villages, teaching in their synagogues, and proclaiming the Good News of the kingdom, and curing every disease and every sickness" (Matthew 9:35). Once, a leper came to Jesus and knelt before him, saying, "Lord, if you choose, you can make me clean." Jesus stretched out his hand and touched him, saying, "I do choose. Be made clean!" (Matthew 8:2–3). Jesus consistently chose to heal people, even if it meant becoming ritually impure according to Jewish law. He healed a man with a withered arm and a man by a sacred pool who was unable to walk, even though this meant breaking laws against healing on the Sabbath. He restored sight to the blind and mental well-being to a soul possessed by demons. He brought Tabitha and Lazarus back to life. Even at the hardest times of his own life, he healed others. At his arrest, in the Garden of Gethsemane, he restored the ear of a slave Peter had attacked with his sword. On the cross, he gave comfort to the penitent thief crucified beside him, offering to see him in paradise.

Healing and new life

Jesus showed that God wants people to be whole in body, mind, and spirit—both actually and symbolically—with eyes that truly see and ears that truly hear. Jesus has come into the world because God does not want us to die:

> *God did not make death, and he does not delight in the death*
> *of the living. For he created all things so that they might*

exist; the generative forces of the world are wholesome, and
there is no destructive poison in them, and the dominion
of Hades is not on earth. For righteousness is immortal. . . .
For God created us for incorruption, and made us in the
image of his own eternity, but through the devil's envy death
entered the world, and those who belong to his company
experience it. (Wisdom of Solomon 1:13–15; 2:23–24)

Consider the story within a story in Mark 5:22–42. Jesus says to the woman who has reached out and touched him, "Daughter, your faith has made you well; go in peace, and be healed of your disease." First, he recognizes her as his child, a child of God. Then he commends her faith in coming to him for healing. He doesn't condemn her for reaching out and taking something of his; he gives freely and abundantly. And Jesus restores her not only to health but to community. For twelve years, she has been an outcast because of her ritual impurity; the crowd would not want her anywhere near them, much less touching them and making them impure as well. Jesus removes her affliction and isolation, just as he removes our sins and exile when we touch him in faith. And then Jesus goes and answers the prayers of the distressed father and raises the daughter from the dead. Jesus destroys sin and death that keep us from God's love and the love of friends, family, and community. God wants people to be whole.

Jesus says even death will not separate us from God's love: "Everything that the Father gives me will come to me, and anyone who comes to me I will never drive away; for I have come down from heaven, not to do my own will, but the will of him who sent me. And this is the will of him who sent me, that I should lose nothing of all that he has given me, but raise it up on the last day" (John 6:37–39). This why Saint Paul proclaims, "I am convinced that neither death, nor life, nor angels, nor rulers, nor things present, nor things to come, nor powers, nor height, nor depth, nor anything else in all creation, will be able to separate us from the love of God in Christ Jesus our Lord" (Romans 8:38–39).

Forgiveness and new life

In a culture which equated physical infirmities with moral ones, Jesus also cured people by forgiving their sins. This infuriated the scribes, who believed that only God could forgive sins and Jesus was blaspheming by making himself equal to God. Jesus pointed out the irony of their blindness to his healing power, saying,

> *For which is easier, to say, "Your sins are forgiven," or to say, "Stand up and walk"? But so that you may know that the Son of Man has authority on earth to forgive sins—he then said to the paralytic—"Stand up, take your bed and go to your home." (Matthew 9:5–6, Mark 2:9, Luke 5:23)*

This experience of healing and forgiveness was at the heart of the Good News for the apostle and evangelist Matthew. Jesus says "Follow me," and this tax collector gets up and follows him (Matthew 9:9–13).[1] As a tax collector employed by the civil authorities, Matthew collaborated with the oppressive Roman occupation of Israel. And tax collectors were commonly believed to be thieves because they collected more than they were entitled to and kept it for themselves. Although we might think of the disciples as good Jewish rabbinical students whom Jesus is teaching his Way, here Jesus is calling a Roman collaborator, possibly a thief, and an outcast to Jews. Clearly, this is someone who would have lived in direct conflict with some of the other disciples. But Jesus invites him into his community and offers him a new way of life. Matthew begins to see that if he can be called, no person is outside the reach of the love of Jesus. We begin to see how Matthew, the outcast, might begin to understand that this royal Messiah was calling not just the righteous, but everyone, into divine forgiveness and fellowship. And why Matthew might want to share this Good News.

The presence of this tax collector with Jesus presents a huge conflict for the Pharisees. The Pharisees ask, "Why does your teacher eat with tax collectors and sinners?" Eating not just with sinners but with thieves and oppressors violates the Pharisees' interpretation of the Law, and they are calling Jesus on this. Jesus responds to this legal charge of the Pharisees by saying that he comes as a physician to heal those who are sick. Presumably a doctor, out of mercy, might be able to go and help those who were ill and needed him. With this treatment, we begin to understand how Matthew, the outcast, might experience this royal Messiah standing up for him against Jewish authorities and saying that not just the righteous, but everyone, could participate in divine forgiveness and fellowship as a member of God's kingdom. And why Matthew might want to share this Good News.

Most people couldn't keep all of the laws placed on them by the Pharisees, and many gave up and felt separated from God. Sick people particularly felt alienated because it was widely believed that sickness was a sign that God had not forgiven a sinner. All of this was compounded by requirements of the Pharisees for repentance and good deeds *before* God's forgiveness could be granted. On the other hand, when Jesus healed people, he offered forgiveness freely, before they had repented and earned it according to the interpretations of the Pharisees. When Jesus said that people are called and healed not by righteousness but by mercy, he turned the legal world of the Pharisees completely upside down. Jesus proclaimed that the Pharisees had separated the Law from God's intent for the Law. From the beginning of his ministry, the Pharisees rejected any power and authority of Jesus to forgive sinners and heal the sick, and this conflict soon led to Jesus' crucifixion. For the Pharisees, forgiveness and healing could only occur according to their rules.

We can see why Matthew, this person who experienced the need for and power of God's forgiveness, would dedicate a whole chapter (23) to Jesus telling the Pharisees where they'd gone wrong, including words like this: "You snakes, you brood of vipers! How can you escape being sentenced to hell?" (v. 33). It was important to Matthew for everyone to know the availability of the divine forgiveness and fellowship he himself had received. And for Matthew, part of this good news was that Jesus would separate out anyone who would exclude anyone else from God's love, fellowship, and healing. Matthew's primary experience of Jesus was that people are healed not by becoming righteous but by being forgiven and invited to participate in God's family. And Matthew remembered and proclaimed this experience and good news, which is open to all.

The good news is that Jesus sees each person as uniquely valuable and worth saving, and his mission is to offer God's love to each person. Every person is significant and precious; no one is expendable. The Good Shepherd will leave ninety-nine sheep on the mountains and go in search of one that went astray because "it is not the will of your Father in heaven that one of these little ones should be lost" (Matthew 18:12–13, Luke 15:3–7). Jesus also compares God to a woman who loses a coin, searches everywhere, and rejoices when she finds it (Luke 15:8–9). Our Father will watch for and welcome back the most prodigal of sons (Luke

15:11–32). Remember, even for those who crucified him, Jesus asked, "Father, forgive them; for they do not know what they are doing" (Luke 23:34). Popular leadership writers Ken Blanchard and Phil Hodges remind us that God's love extends much further than we can imagine, and that we also have this responsibility in our relationships with one another:

> Grace extends unrestrained fellowship to others in celebration of their inherent dignity as being made in God's image and as the objects of His affection. Grace is at work in relationships when we are present for one another, accepting our mutual limitations and willing to exchange mutual efforts to enhance one another's well-being. It is only in intimacy that grace abounds. God has reached out in the most profound way to restore our intimate relationship with Him. Even when we walk away from Him in our sin, His grace abounds in that "while we were still sinners, Christ died for us" (Romans 5:8). During His season of leadership, Jesus constantly reached out in unrestrained fellowship and acceptance to heal and restore people to relationships of grace and acceptance. To lead like Jesus, we must come to understand the spiritual dynamics of our relationships as both leaders and followers so that we may be agents of grace in a like manner.[2]

Engaging Jesus

To continue engaging Jesus, read and reflect on Matthew 9:1–13.

Questions for Personal Reflection:

1. Where do you need healing and forgiveness in your life?

2. Where do you offer healing and forgiveness?

3. Whom do you need to forgive in order to restore a relationship?

4. How can you share God's love by offering healing and forgiveness?

Questions for Group Discussion:

1. In Eugene Peterson's beautiful paraphrase of 1 Corinthians
    12 in *The Message*, he writes:

    > By means of his one Spirit, we all said good-bye to our
    > partial and piecemeal lives. ... Each of us is now a part
    > of his resurrection body, refreshed and sustained at one
    > fountain—his Spirit—where we all come to drink. ...
    > I want you to think about how all this makes you more
    > significant, not less. A body isn't just a single part blown
    > up into something huge. It's all the different-but-similar
    > parts arranged and functioning together. ... What we
    > have is one body with many parts, each its proper size
    > and in its proper place. No part is important on its own.
    > ... The way God designed our bodies is a model for
    > understanding our lives together as a church: every part
    > dependent on every other part, the parts we mention
    > and the parts we don't, the parts we see and the parts we
    > don't. If one part hurts, every other part is involved in
    > the hurt, and in the healing. If one part flourishes, every
    > other part enters into the exuberance. You are Christ's
    > body—that's who you are! You must never forget this.

    If one part hurts, how are our other parts
    "involved in the hurt, and in the healing"?

2. Why is forgiveness important for healing?

3. How does your church community share God's love by
    offering healing and forgiveness?

4. What additional opportunities might your church
    community have to share God's love by offering healing and
    forgiveness?

By Shepherding

Jesus' compassion for people extends beyond listening, healing, and forgiveness to providing safety and guidance as the good leader of God's people. At Jesus' birth, the chief priests and scribes proclaimed the prophecy of Micah: "From Bethlehem shall come a ruler who is to shepherd my people Israel" (Matthew 2:6). The Bible has over sixty references to shepherds, over one hundred references to lambs, and over two hundred references to sheep. We are most familiar with the biblical models of good shepherds in Psalm 23, Ezekiel 34, and John 10.

We're removed from pastoral times and settings, and we tend to idealize them. The word "idyllic" comes from "idylls"—simple descriptive works either in prose or poetry that deal with rustic life or pastoral scenes or suggest a mood of peace and contentment. We picture livestock calmly grazing on beautiful grassy hills in the countryside, pleasingly peaceful and innocent. We romanticize the pastoral because we miss this feeling of peace and contentment. Some Bible verses portray the idyllic of the pastoral (e.g., Revelation 7:16–17). But the Biblical reality is that pastoral settings are idyllic only when a good shepherd is present. Without the good shepherd, sheep are in danger. Sheep are basically timid animals that have little protection from predators. Ezekiel says, "So they were scattered, because there was no shepherd; and scattered, they became food for all the wild animals" (34:5).

As independent people, we are not flattered by being compared to sheep. And yet the Psalmist proclaims, "Know that the LORD is God. It is he that made us, and we are his; we are his people, and the sheep of his pasture" (Psalm 100:3). The good shepherd metaphors remind us that people also are subject to going astray and that we also need guidance and protection: "When Jesus saw the crowds, he had compassion for them, because they were harassed and helpless, like sheep without a shepherd" (Matthew 9:36, Mark 6:34). As 1 Peter 2:25 says, "For you were going astray like sheep, but now you have returned to the shepherd and guardian of your souls."

Each of us is insecure until we are in Jesus' hands. Ezekiel tells us that good shepherds strengthen the weak, heal the sick, bind up the injured, bring back the strayed, and seek the lost. We have the same needs for a shepherd as sheep do. God says he will be the pastor because other shepherds failed:

> *For thus says the Lord God: I myself will search for my sheep,*
> *and will seek them out. As shepherds seek out their flocks*
> *when they are among their scattered sheep, so I will seek out*
> *my sheep. I will rescue them from all the places to which they*
> *have been scattered on a day of clouds and thick darkness. I*
> *will bring them out from the peoples and gather them from*
> *the countries, and will bring them into their own land; and I*
> *will feed them on the mountains of Israel, by the watercourses,*
> *and in all the inhabited parts of the land. (Ezekiel 34:11–13)*

And God fulfills this promise in Jesus. Jesus is the Shepherd who leaves his flock to go after one lost sheep, finds it, and brings it back to the fold (Matthew 18:12–14). Jesus says, "I came that they may have life, and have it abundantly. I am the good shepherd. The good shepherd lays down his life for the sheep" (John 10:10–11). Jesus is the person in whom we experience the peace and contentment of the pastoral. "They shall know that I, the LORD their God, am with them, and that they, the house of Israel, are my people, says the Lord God. You are my sheep, the sheep of my pasture and I am your God, says the Lord God" (Ezekiel 34:30–31). With Jesus, we can be free from fear, aware of God's forgiveness and abundant love. We hear the Good Shepherd's voice and find security. As vulnerable as we are, we cannot be snatched away.

When Jesus commissions Peter as the first leader of the church in John 21, he is sharing the responsibility for his flock. This commission applies not only to Peter, but also to every apostle and every church that wishes to serve others for Christ.

The context of the commission Jesus gives Peter is important. After Jesus' death and resurrection, the disciples have gone fishing in Galilee. All night they fish in their own strength and catch nothing. Then in simple obedience to Christ, they take in a huge and miraculous draught of fish. As soon as they listen to Jesus' instruction and learn to depend on his strength, they discover an abundant catch. Of course, this also hearkens back to the story of Peter's first calling into discipleship (Luke 5:1–11). Once the disciples recognize Jesus and return to shore, Jesus invites them to a meal he has prepared. Jesus is about to send the disciples on their great apostolic mission, but first he gives them nourishment. After breakfast, Jesus asks three times whether Peter loves him and restores Peter to the ministry Peter rejected by his three denials (John 18:17–27). Jesus shows his love in commissioning Peter for a new ministry. Jesus exhorts Peter to "follow me," even though people and troubles will take him where he does not want to be.

Jesus commissions Peter to do three things—feed my lambs, tend my sheep, and feed my sheep.[1] In Jesus' first instruction to "feed my lambs," the Greek words mean "feed or nourish" my "little lambs."[2] We especially need to help spiritually nourish those who are new to Christ and help them realize that they are an important part of God's family. A verse that speaks to this is Isaiah 40:11: "[The Lord God] will feed his flock like a shepherd; he will gather the lambs in his arms, and carry them in his bosom, and gently lead the mother sheep."

The second instruction by Jesus is "tend my sheep." The Greek word for tend means not only to feed, but to take care of, guide, govern, guard, etc. Phillip Keller, an experienced shepherd, wrote about the shepherd's responsibility of tending to his sheep:

> He will go to no end of trouble and labor to supply them
> with the finest grazing, the richest pasturage, ample winter
> feed and clean water. He will spare himself no pains to
> provide shelter from storms, protection from ruthless
> enemies and the diseases and parasites to which sheep are
> so susceptible. . . . From early dawn until late at night this
> utterly self-less shepherd is alert to the welfare of His flock.
> For the diligent sheepman rises early and goes out first
> thing every morning without fail to look over his flock. It

is the initial, intimate contact of the day. With a practiced, searching, sympathetic eye he examines the sheep to see that they are fit and content and able to be on their feet. In an instant he can tell if they have been molested during the night—whether any are ill or if there are some which require special attention. Repeatedly throughout the day he casts his eye over the flock to make sure that all is well. Nor even at night is he oblivious to their needs. He sleeps as it were "with one eye and both ears open" ready at the least sign of trouble to leap up and protect his own.[3]

Jesus is the Good Shepherd (Psalm 23, 2 Samuel 7:7, Zechariah 11:4–17, Ezekiel 34, John 10:1–16), and he commissions his disciples to also act as good shepherds. For Jesus, this includes feeding the hungry, clothing the naked, tending the sick, visiting the prisoner, and sheltering the stranger (Matthew 25:31–46).

Jesus' third instruction to Peter and the church is "feed my sheep." We must be willing to not only tend the flock, but also feed it with spiritual food. Jesus' disciples will be the shepherds of Jeremiah 3:15: "I will give you shepherds after my own heart, who will feed you with knowledge and understanding." Taking care of people's needs without spiritually feeding them is not enough.[4]

Jesus commissions Peter to do three things—feed my lambs, tend my sheep, and feed my sheep. People at different stages of their journeys have different needs, and we are commissioned to shepherd them appropriately. Shepherding is not taking people where we want to go and treating them as we wish; it is loving and serving the Good Shepherd's flock in the Good Shepherd's Way.

Engaging Jesus

To continue engaging Jesus, read and reflect on John 21.

Questions for Personal Reflection:

1. Why does Jesus ask Peter three times, "Do you love me?"

2. When have you denied Jesus?

3. Do you love Jesus?

4. Is Jesus calling you to nourish his little lambs or to tend or feed his sheep? How?

5. What opportunities do you have to follow Jesus by tending and feeding God's flock?

Questions for Group Discussion:

1. In John 21, what is Jesus asking Peter to do?

2. Why does Jesus use different words for each answer?

3. What does it mean to tend?

4. Who are the sheep to be tended? How do we tend them?

5. How are people fed?

6. What other verses speak to this?

7. What do these verses tell us about Jesus' expectations for the church's ministry to new Christians, to the community and to church members? How are his expectations different for people at different places in their spiritual journey?

8. What are people looking for when they come to church?

9. What do people want from church? How do people's desires match up with Jesus' expectations?

10. How are we doing in our community in nurturing God's people?

11. Who is responsible for this? How can we lead in these areas?

12. What opportunities does your church have to follow Jesus by tending and feeding God's flock?

2.4

By Serving

Jesus reminds us in Matthew 25:31–46 that how we respond to the needs of others has eternal significance:

> *Come, you that are blessed by my Father, inherit the kingdom prepared for you from the foundation of the world; for I was hungry and you gave me food, I was thirsty and you gave me something to drink, I was a stranger and you welcomed me, I was naked and you gave me clothing, I was sick and you took care of me, I was in prison and you visited me. . . . Truly I tell you, just as you did it to one of the least of these who are members of my family, you did it to me.*

The surprise is that Jesus receives our gifts. When we love and serve others, we give Jesus food, bring Jesus water, give Jesus clothes, and seek Jesus out in prison and when he is ill. Each person is a beloved child of God whom God wants to love through disciples. We begin to experience a life of love in God's kingdom when we visit the sick or the imprisoned or provide food, drink, or clothing to those in need, or welcome a stranger. Serving others is also integral with living in the kingdom of God today in several ways.

Our service responds to God's concerns for his children.

God's perspectives of the kingdom are not only personal, but familial, communal, societal, global, and universal. God cares for each person, and especially for people on the margins: the sick, poor, widowed, orphaned, disabled, immigrants, and prisoners. Jesus shows us that God wants all people to experience his love, mercy, compassion, healing, forgiveness, and justice. Responding to all of the needs of God's children is important to God. Individual Christians and churches who serve are vital to the well-being of their communities and can be effective at changing and improving the world. We are serving God to respond to the needs of God's children and to change the world to more closely reflect God's kingdom.

Our service helps others experience and discover God's love.

When we share our love, people can see how the kingdom of God works. Our first impact is being present with the anguished, the lonely, the hungry, and the sick, just to let them know that they're not alone—they're children of a loving family. For people to overcome their loneliness and separation from God and other people, they need to experience that they are loved. And love is only shared when we let ourselves go and go to them. The exact actions vary:

- Feed the hungry.

- Give the thirsty something to drink.

- Welcome the stranger or outcast.

- Clothe the naked.

- Heal the sick.

- Comfort the bereaved.

- Visit the prisoner.

- Give to the poor.

- Shelter the orphan and the refugee.

- Help the wounded victims of domestic, social, political, or international violence (battered women, victims of crime, terror or oppression, wounded soldiers).

- Respect and protect each and every child of God.

- Share what you have.

- Wash one another's filthy feet.

- Forgive the trespasses of others.

- Help people begin anew.

- Seek peace and reconciliation.

- Treat every person in need as though you are that person.

- Share and care for God's creation.

- Do justice, love mercy, and walk humbly with God (Micah 6:8).

If these actions are to show forth God's love and our love for one another as members of God's family, they must be personal actions, actions in twos and threes, actions of a local church community. Each one needs a human face in the image of God: the face of Jesus now in a follower of Jesus. Jesus teaches his disciples both to continue praying for this kingdom to come and to help in revealing and living into it. He teaches his disciples prayer and personal involvement. And from this personal involvement, people will also unite to address larger concerns about justice and peace. Jesus gives his disciples immense responsibility and power to reveal and share God's love throughout the world.

The kingdom of God happens when the love of God is poured out in us and through us, when we experience God's love and reveal God's love to others. Christians are sent on the same mission as Jesus was (Matthew 10), to share God's love for the world and to show that the kingdom of God is at hand. The real Good News is not just this message but the presence and revelation of God's love. Christians help bring real love into the world through concerted action with God. Through this love, God is revealed.

Our service helps God's kingdom grow.

People begin to see the kingdom as a place where people love one another and their needs are met. In *The Externally-Focused Church*, Rick Rusaw and Eric Swanson share examples of how a church can serve others and then describe what happens: "As we have entered into the life of the city through service, we have had the opportunity to engage with people from whom we normally would be isolated. We are seeing relationships formed and people taking steps toward God and his church as never before." Service becomes a bridge to evangelism:

> Increasingly we have found that ... we are now being invited to serve and that service has become a bridge to salvation. It is "God's kindness" that leads to repentance (Rom 2:4), not the threat of God's judgment. Barriers to the gospel melt away when people are served and blessed. It's been said, "There's only one way to God and that is through Jesus. But there are a thousand ways to Jesus." By creating a thousand entry points into the community, we create a thousand opportunities to show the love and share the Good News with the city.
>
> "Service" is the only location that encompasses the needs and dreams of the city, the mandates and desires of God, and the calling and capacity of the church. Service is the "sweet spot" where all three interests come together. Service is something the community needs, God desires, and the church has the capacity to do. The community may not care much about salvation, but it does have needs. It is in meeting those needs through service that meaningful relationships develop, and out of relationships come endless opportunities to share the love of Christ and the gospel of salvation. The early church grew because its people loved and served. We believe servants can go anywhere. Service gives us access not only to places of need but also to places of influence.[1]

The Great Commission, given to disciples, is not just proclaiming this Good News as truth or doctrine (as often seemed to have been the primary motive of the modern church), but actually sharing God's love. This is the basis of the reminder, attributed in various forms to Saint Francis, to share the gospel at all times and, if necessary, to use words.

Our service prepares us to live in God's kingdom.

We become Christians by loving and serving others. Ministering and serving are the normal expressions of Christian living. Our faith does not just grow by what we think or believe but by what we do and experience. As Jesus says in John 17:7, people learn the way and the truth and the life by following it: "Anyone who resolves to do the will of God will know whether the teaching is from God or whether I am speaking on my own." Christians can learn through good instruction, but they really can't grow if they remain uninvolved in ministry and service. Christians grow best when they are serving and giving themselves away to others. This is where people most meet and experience Jesus.[2]

We don't do this through a process or a program but by offering our own lives directly for others:

> As Jesus ministers, so he wants us to minister. He wants Peter to feed his sheep and care for them, not as "professionals" who know their clients' problems and take care of them, but as vulnerable brothers and sisters who know and are known, who care and are cared for, who forgive and are being forgiven, who love and are being loved. ... How can we lay down our life for those with whom we are not even allowed to enter into a deep personal relationship? Laying down your life means making your own faith and doubt, hope and despair, joy and sadness, courage and fear available to others as ways of getting in touch with the Lord of life. We are not the healers, we are not the reconcilers, we are not the givers of life. We are sinful, broken, vulnerable people who need as much care as anyone we care for. The mystery of ministry is that we have been chosen to make our own limited and very conditional love the gateway for the unlimited and unconditional love of God.[3]

To live within the kingdom of God, we need to love God and love others. We need to turn outward from ourselves to God and other people. This turning outward is a form of "repentance" that turns us away from "sin"[4] and prepares us to participate in God's kingdom. This repentance through loving and serving others is a way of believing in Jesus. Because, at the heart of everything, that is what God wants to do to, with, and through us. In this way, we are saved not just for everlasting life but, as we share God's love with other people, we ourselves also discover and are transformed by that love. Ministry to others is especially important to our spiritual growth. "For we are what he has made us, created in Christ Jesus for good works, which God prepared beforehand to be our way of life" (Ephesians 2:10).

A paradox in God's kingdom is the reciprocal effect of serving others. Jeremiah 29:7 says, "Seek the welfare of the city where I have sent you into exile, and pray to the LORD on its behalf, for in its welfare you will find your welfare." Or as Jesus says, seek your life and lose it; lose your life in God's service and find it (Matthew 10:39, 16:25; Mark 8:35; Luke 9:24, 17:33; John 12:25).

Engaging Jesus

To continue engaging Jesus, read and reflect on Matthew 25:31–46.

Questions for Personal Reflection:

1. Do you believe that you can make a difference in the world? How?

2. If you are involved in pastoral care or service activities, how are they making a difference in your life?

3. How do you feel God is calling you to respond in love? How do you feel Christ might be calling you to serve him?

4. What are opportunities for you to follow Jesus by loving and serving others?

Questions for Group Discussion:

1. In Matthew 25, when do the "righteous sheep" realize they are doing ministry? How do we help others recognize when they are ministering to others and celebrate and support those ministries?

2. Why is it important to serve others?

3. What are ways to serve others? How do we prepare to serve others in these ways?

4. Where are we serving others in our community? Who are we serving?

5. How are we doing in serving God's people?

6. Who is responsible for this? How can we lead in these areas?

7. What are opportunities for your church to follow Jesus by loving and serving others?

2.5

By Reconciling

T aking up the cross and following Jesus requires courage, confrontation, and suffering to reveal God's love for each person. This is an Amish community praying for and forgiving the killer who entered their school and murdered their children. This is Martin Luther King Jr. walking into an angry mob, knowing that someone may kill him.[1] How is it possible for Christians to go this far with Jesus?

Dying to ourselves

Jesus always wants to reveal God's love for us and to reconcile us to God and one another to make that love possible. Among all of the ways Jesus shows his love for others, he demonstrates his greatest love as our savior: "No one has greater love than this, to lay down one's life for one's friends" (John 15:13). By his death and resurrection, Jesus bore our sins, suffered rejection, anguish, and death for us; redeemed us from sin; and conquered our death and separation from God and other people (Isaiah 52:13–53:12; Romans 4:25, 5:6–11, 6:3–10).

Jesus calls each of his followers also to "take up their cross" with the same purpose of revealing God's love for each person and reconciling people to God and one another (Mark 8:34–35). We are called to love one another as Jesus loved us: "We know love by this: that he laid down his life for us—and we ought to lay down our lives for one another" (1 John 3:16; see also John 13:34–35, 15:12). We participate in God's reconciling work because Jesus makes us part of sharing God's love for all of the other people he wants to bring into relationship with him, and the Holy Spirit empowers us and acts through us in sharing God's love. It is by our love and through our love that we help make possible God's love in the world.

Like Jesus, all of our actions must show love for others and reveal God's love. As disciples (followers) or apostles (sent people), we don't save or redeem the world in the way God did by sending Jesus or in the way Jesus did by dying on the cross. Disciples don't take up their crosses, bear the sins of others, and die to free others from sin in the same way Jesus does. But Christians do put others first and carry their burdens to free them from alienation from God and other people and to help them experience God's love. In this world, the kingdom of God is revealed by our offering the hope, listening, forgiveness, reconciliation, healing, and love God has for each person and helping each person live more fully into loving relationships.

This is not an easy path. Following Jesus to the cross requires Christians to take God's love for every person to the farthest extreme: "Love your enemies, do good to those who hate you, bless those who curse you, pray for those who abuse you. . . . Do to others as you would have them do to you. . . . Be merciful, just as your Father is merciful. Do not judge, and you will not be judged; do not condemn, and you will not be condemned" (Luke 6:27–37).[2] Disciples are not even permitted to get angry with another person. Jesus says, "If you are angry with a brother or sister, you will be liable to judgment; and if you insult a brother or sister, you will be liable to the council; and if you say, 'You fool,' you will be liable to the hell of fire" (Matthew 5:22). Anger keeps us from respecting the other person as God's child, loving and forgiving a brother or sister, and sharing God's love. If I become angry or insult or curse another person, I have placed myself above that person and failed to treat him or her as a child God loves as much as he loves me.

Jesus reveals that God is love and that life in God's kingdom is love. God's kingdom is near; but violence, conflict, anger, judgment, and even the disrespect of calling a brother or sister a fool takes us out of the loving relationships of that kingdom. Whenever anger is a natural reaction or harming someone is an option, we need to consider the eternal significance of Jesus' love for each person and what it means for Jesus to say, "While I was with them, I protected them in your name that you have given me. I guarded them, and not one of them was lost" (John 17:12). In God's kingdom, we are responsible for caring for everyone else. Each person is a child of God, none of us is better than anyone else, and each of us must support the worth and dignity of every person.[3]

Because the Way of Jesus is a path of love, it will often lead to humiliation and suffering. Jesus says, "Blessed are you when people revile you and persecute you and utter all kinds of evil against you falsely on my account" (Matthew 5:11, Luke 6:22). Jesus expects his followers to love and serve as he does, even to the extreme of suffering for others. When Jesus says "You have heard that it was said, 'An eye for an eye and a tooth for a tooth.' But I say to you, Do not resist an evildoer" (Matthew 5:38–39), he means "Do not strike back at or harm one who has done you evil" or "Do not retaliate against violence with violence." Jesus' followers may be subject to violence for their loving Way of life, but they are to act and respond lovingly and not violently to accomplish their mission. As Dietrich Bonhoeffer wrote, "Jesus' disciples maintain peace by choosing to suffer instead of causing others to suffer. They preserve community when others destroy it."[4]

This will bring about God's kingdom of love in a more lasting way. And this is how Christians "die to themselves" and find their lives by losing them.[5] We take up our crosses and die to ourselves when we are willing to show that love is always more important than our own righteousness or well-being. We suffer and bear the burdens of others for the sake of Jesus and the full expression of God's love. As Jesus offers reconciliation and love to all, so must those who would follow him. Disciples take up their crosses and follow Jesus without giving in to anger or hatred or violence. Instead, they choose a means to reconciliation.

Lovingly confronting others

This Christian path of love and nonviolence is often confused with passivity, submission, or surrender. Acting with love and without violence does not mean giving in to, or running away from, suffering or injustice. Because we love others, we cannot accept their sufferings, whether from famine, poverty, disease, captivity, social alienation or exclusion, torture, war, or other evils. We must hate injustice and fight against it. We need to pray, to directly serve others, and to engage all kinds of social, economic, and political wrongs. At the same time, our response—like Jesus'—must always be loving and reconciling, never destructive, never harming other creatures we are sent to serve. In his desire to persuade others to live in God's kingdom, Jesus was wholly willing to disturb, but not to harm.[6]

When Jesus says "Do not react violently against the one who is evil," he does not mean "be passive" or "do not confront oppression." Seminary professor and activist Walter Wink explains how Jesus uses three colorful examples of "experiences of being belittled, insulted, or dispossessed" to encourage his followers to surprise and "seize the initiative from the oppressor" and force "him or her to believe in your power and perhaps even to recognize your humanity."[7] When Jesus tells his followers, "turn the other cheek" (Matthew 5:39, Luke 6:29), "give your shirt as well" (Matthew 5:40, Luke 6:29), and "go also the second mile" (Matthew 5:41), he gives examples of directly confronting and resisting people who don't love and respect others. By turning the other cheek, a person who has been struck shames her attacker with "Try again. You failed to demean me."[8] A person who also gives up his shirt embarrasses his creditor by revealing, "You've taken everything and you're even leaving me naked."[9] And the person who carries a Roman soldier's heavy pack for more than the required mile reminds the oppressor that he is mistreating a human being and not just a slave.[10] Jesus wants his followers to take nonviolent actions that creatively cause people who are engaged in oppressive acts to be uncomfortable with their actions and repent. Acts of nonviolent resistance are calculated to spotlight, confront, challenge, and counteract injustice and to change the hearts of others so that they will cease to oppress and begin to love others. In this way, nonviolent disturbances can sometimes make an unloving person think and change and even reconcile with others.

As a Christian leader, Martin Luther King Jr. used creative types of nonviolent direct confrontations—such as marches, sit-ins, boycotts, freedom rides, and being jailed—to create life-changing disturbances for the civil rights movement in the United States. He used these disturbances "to create a crisis and foster a tension . . . to dramatize the issue so that it can no longer be ignored."[11] He pointed out that a nonviolent resister "is constantly seeking to persuade his opponent that he is wrong" and this action works both on the oppressor and the resister and leads to reconciliation. Nonviolent confrontation disturbs the oppressor and arouses a sense of shame as it works on the oppressor's "conscience [so that] he does not know what to do." At the same time, acting nonviolently "does something to the hearts and souls of those committed to it. It gives them new self-respect; it calls up resources of strength and courage that they did not know they had." Nonviolence is able to bring about both real change and reconciliation because its purpose is not "to defeat or humiliate the opponent—but to win his friendship and understanding," or to "bring about a transformation and change of heart." The purpose of nonviolent confrontations is to "defeat the unjust system, rather than the individuals who are caught in that system."[12] Over time, nonviolence attracts attention and empathy, works to change attitudes, and helps people begin to envision new relationships. This is a far more loving way and a better means of persuasion and progress than either the hopelessness of acquiescence or the tragedies of violence.[13]

Jesus encourages his followers to take nonviolent direct actions that are both confrontational and loving. Christians must be courageous enough to confront others without conflict or violence because these confrontations are not about us, but about revealing God's love through our own love. Confrontation is the opposite of passivity or avoidance; confrontation means simply "meeting face-to-face" or addressing. Thus, confrontations can and should be positive. When we address a problem or a challenge with another person, we often can reconcile with that person. Most of us are uncomfortable with confrontations. We may avoid dealing with a challenge or problem just because we dislike confronting another person—especially if this means making ourselves vulnerable or putting ourselves at risk. And yet, confrontations are necessary for moving forward. Failing to confront often means failing to raise awareness or solve problems. If we can't lovingly dialogue with one another, we can't avoid polarization and learn and grow together. Confrontations are required in any successful relationship, especially love. Without confrontations, we give up on relationships. But we can never give up on relationships—because the heart of God's kingdom is love.[14]

Jesus tries to change people's hearts, thinking, and actions so that they are prepared to live in God's kingdom. By no means is he a passive person or a pushover; he will die to bring us to God's love. Jesus will always confront any unloving actions and secure the dignity and worth of each person as God's beloved child. But his loving actions encourage and persuade rather than compel people to live his Way.[15] Followers of Jesus respond with love rather than force: "Whoever wishes to be first among you must be slave of all for the Son of Man came not to be served but to serve, and to give his life a ransom for many" (Mark 10:42–45).

Revealing God's love

The kingdom of God is love and can never come out of polarization, coercion, or violence. Martin Luther King Jr. frequently reminded people that coercion and violence bring about more hatred and violence, not love. He said, "Along the way of life, someone must have sense enough and morality enough to cut off the chain of hate and evil. The greatest way to do that is through love."[16] Similarly, antiapartheid leader Desmond Tutu reminds us, "In the act of forgiveness we are declaring our faith in the future of a relationship and in the capacity of the wrongdoer to change. We are saying here is a chance to make a new beginning. According to Jesus, we should be ready to do this not just once, not just seven times, but seventy times seven, without limit."[17]

A disciple's courage and suffering confronts the world with a love the world cannot understand, but which can transform it:

> During a demonstration in Selma, Alabama, [Martin Luther King, Jr. was] spat upon and cursed unmercifully. As his group of protesters approached the Selma courthouse, they were met by more than three hundred angry white segregationists. Fearing for Martin's safety, Andrew Young pulled up in a car and asked him to get in. "No," came the reply. "I'm going to walk." Hosea Williams recalled what happened next: "You know that man turned around to leave, and he went dead toward that mob. He got about three or four feet away, and you could hear the breathing. They got just as quiet as a mouse. And Dr. King smiled and said, 'Excuse me, please.' And the line just opened up. He walked right on up through them and got on the sidewalk. The line just opened up as he went along and closed behind him. And not one of them touched him. They got so quiet, it was like they were all spellbound, I guess, that the man who they were all raving about would come and submit his body to them. They didn't touch him."[18]

This is the same way Jesus responds to the angry mob from the synagogue at Nazareth: "When they heard this, all in the synagogue were filled with rage. They got up, drove him out of the town, and led him to the brow of the hill on which their town was built, so that they might hurl him off the cliff. But he passed through the midst of them and went on his way" (Luke 4:28–30). We love by making ourselves vulnerable to others as Jesus did—from washing people's feet, to healing lepers, to walking into an angry mob, to crucifixion—and that vulnerability reveals our love. In the kingdom of God, loving confrontation—through humiliation, suffering, and even death—actually overcomes evil with love.[19] We overcome our enemies by loving them. This paradox is proven when resurrection and new life follows crucifixion, and it is also revealed by bringing kingdom love—rather than greater violence—into this world.

We are not naïve enough to think this always works or that it works immediately. During just the last century, people committed genocides in the Soviet Union, Nazi Germany, Rwanda, Somalia, Bosnia, and more than a dozen other countries. But we are realistic enough to know that nonviolent loving confrontation is a better way of sharing God's love and is often very effective. Also during the last century, we have also experienced movements for civil rights, for the elimination of apartheid, for women's and children's rights, for gay and lesbian rights, and for freedom and democracy in many places.[20]

Of course, this way of Christian suffering and reconciliation is not just for overcoming evil and injustice and "loving our enemies." It is also for creating loving relationships and bringing divine love into every human interaction; it applies to our friends, our families, our marriages, our church communities, and to every person we meet. While it is often challenging or painful, we each have greater abilities to effect relationships with people we know personally than we have to fight the injustices of the world. In our partnerships, in our marriages, with our natural and adoptive siblings, we can insist together not to let any bond become just another broken human relationship, and we can insist that we treat one another with the love of Jesus (Galatians 5:13–14, 6:2).

Christian confrontations and reconciliations are never about what we believe to be right or good for ourselves; they must be about revealing God's love for each person. The Christian Way is not a belief, an ideology, or a cause, but an activity of sharing love for God and one another as fully as possible. We must develop loving relationships in the kingdom of God by meeting each person face to face—without polarization, coercion or violence—to accept and love and learn and grow together:

> One way to begin cultivating this ability to love is to
> see yourself internally as a center of love, as an oasis
> of peace, as a pool of serenity with ripples going out
> to all those around you. . . . If more of us could serve
> as centers of love and oases of peace, we might just
> be able to turn around a great deal of the conflict, the
> hatred, the jealousies, and the violence. This is a way
> that we can take on the suffering and transform it.[21]

Engaging Jesus

To continue engaging Jesus, read and reflect on Luke 6:27–37.

Questions for Personal Reflection:

1. Is reconciliation hard for you? Why?

2. When you face conflict, how do you keep in mind that "everything Jesus does is an attempt to change people's hearts, thinking, and actions so that they are prepared to live in God's kingdom"?

3. Are there opportunities in your life to use appropriate creative, loving, nonviolent direct confrontation? How would that work?

4. How might you think about reconciliation in all of your encounters and relationships?

5. What opportunities do you have to follow Jesus by reconciling people and helping them to grow together?

Questions for Group Discussion:

1. What does Jesus mean by "love your enemies"?

2. How does this way of life give additional meaning to Jesus' call to his disciples, "If any want to become my followers,

let them deny themselves and take up their cross daily and follow me" (Luke 9:23, 14:27; Matthew 10:38; Mark 8:34)?

3. How is nonviolent confrontation effective to change people's hearts, thinking, and actions?

4. Jesus gives three examples of loving, nonviolent confrontation: "turn the other cheek" (Matthew 5:39, Luke 6:29), "give your cloak as well" (Matthew 5:40), and "go also the second mile" (Matthew 5:41). What happens when people try to treat these as universal moral principles rather than just as specific instructional examples? Is this what Jesus intended?[22]

5. Nonviolent direct action requires creativity. Jesus, Gandhi, and Martin Luther King Jr. have only given us a few examples of specific techniques. How can we think of creative ways to resist oppression in circumstances we face?

6. Consider this quote from *Lead Like Jesus: Lessons from the Greatest Leadership Role Model of All Time*: "Jesus spent significant time interacting in positive ways with people who disagreed with Him. He did not isolate Himself from those who disagreed; He embraced those who disagreed. He did not change His message to gain approval, but He continued to love those who did not accept His message."[23] What does nonviolence teach us about how to argue with one another (either within or Christian community or in other contexts)? Who today uses this approach?

7. What injustices need to be confronted nonviolently today? Why?

8. What does God require of us in response to the needs of others?

9. How can we participate in the struggle of the oppressed for a more just world?

10. What opportunities does your church have to follow Jesus by reconciling people and helping them to grow together?

2.6

The Great Commandment

A lawyer asked Jesus a question: "Teacher, which commandment in the law is the greatest?" Jesus answered, "You shall love the Lord your God with all your heart, and with all your soul, and with all your mind.' This is the greatest and first commandment. And a second is like it: 'You shall love your neighbor as yourself.' On these two commandments hang all the law and the prophets" (Matthew 22:35–40).[1]

The author of 1 John carefully examines the Great Commandment. He reminds us that "God is love, and those who abide in love abide in God, and God abides in them" (1 John 4:16). We are to love God not from fear but because God "first loved us" (1 John 4:19). In the kingdom of God, we respond to God's love by loving God; and by loving one another because we are all children of God. If we do not love one another, we cannot see or love God. "Beloved, let us love one another, because love is from God; everyone who loves is born of God and knows God" (1 John 4:7). When Jesus says that the first and second commandments are alike, he means that both loves are needed to live in God's kingdom.

When the lawyer paraphrases the Great Commandment in the Gospel of Mark, Jesus says to him, "You are not far from the kingdom of God" (Mark 12:34). Jesus' statement includes two very important points. First, when we live the Great Commandment, we are participating in the kingdom of God. The second point is that we are not there yet. It is not enough just to know and state this reality conceptually as the lawyer does. We need to live it with our whole being: all of our hearts, all of our souls, all of our minds, all of our strength.

How to live in God's Kingdom

It is significant that Jesus is speaking to a lawyer, because Jesus is not just summarizing the law or putting forth the ethical principle the lawyer wanted. For Jesus, this is not a moral law, but the way to life as God designed it. Jesus isn't saying "Do this to be righteous" or "Do this so you can go to heaven." He's saying "Do this because it's part of the reality of living in the kingdom of heaven (right now)." Or "Do this because you'll have an opportunity to experience living in the way you are made to be." Or "Do this because it's who you really are." Christians believe we are created and called by God, and that it is therefore possible to live in loving relationships with God and one another in the kingdom of God.

In Luke, when the lawyer asks how to live in God's kingdom, Jesus tells the parable of the Good Samaritan to illustrate how we are to love others (Luke 10:25–37). The lawyer who asks Jesus "Who is my neighbor?" is asking how we can go about living in the kingdom of heaven, where we love God and love one another day by day as Jesus did. The lawyer is also looking for some boundary to the Great Commandment, but there is none. God's love is boundless, so there really are no limits to the love God asks disciples to share. Disciples do not let even personal concerns (food, clothing, lodging, dangers, or fear) get in the way of sharing God's love (Matthew 10). Every boundary must be crossed for the sake of love.

The parable is well known: A man on the way from Jerusalem to Jericho was robbed and severely beaten. A priest and a Levite came along, saw him, and passed by on the other side of the road. A Samaritan came along, saw him, was moved with pity, and took care of him. The Good Samaritan's response required getting involved, getting his hands into the mess, taking his time, using his resources. It required vulnerability and intimacy. Unlike others on the road, he put aside his fears: fear of strangers or those who are different, fear of being inconvenienced or harmed, fear of making things worse. The Samaritan touched the man. He washed, cleaned, and dressed the man's wounds. He acted; Jesus tells the lawyer both "do this" and "go and do likewise." Love requires action.

Rick Warren has described the actions of the Good Samaritan as four practical steps to taking action to serve the needs of others the way Jesus would:

1. See the needs around you: "Don't think only of your own good. Think of other Christians and what is best for them" (1 Corinthians 10:24, NLT).

2. Sympathize with people's pain: "He comforts us in all our troubles so that we can comfort others. When others are troubled, we will be able to give them the same comfort God has given us" (2 Corinthians 1:4, NLT).

3. Seize the moment to meet the need: "Never walk away from someone who deserves help; your hand is God's hand for that person. Don't tell your neighbor, 'Maybe some other time' or, 'Try me tomorrow,' when the money's right there in your pocket" (Proverbs 3:27–28, MSG).

4. Spend whatever it takes: "Therefore, as we have opportunity, let us do good to all people, especially to those who belong to the family of believers" (Galatians 6:10, NIV).[2]

Each of these steps recognizes our own limits or excuses to loving others: blindness, lack of caring, hesitation, weighing the cost—all elements of selfishness. We need to overcome these barriers to love by "confronting" others, dying to ourselves, putting others first, and sharing God's love.

If we're blind or unsympathetic, perhaps it is because we have chosen to be isolated from others. In the pursuit of happiness as a way of life, many of us have lived toward a misguided ideal of cocooning (separation, isolation) and acquiring comfort and possessions (security, selfishness). As postmodern people, we're beginning to feel dissatisfaction and restlessness with the alienated, solipsistic, and nihilistic lives we've made.

If we are not seizing the moment, perhaps it is because we are unprepared to act. We might want to act like the Good Samaritan but, if we come upon an injured person by the side of the road and we do not know first aid, the best we are going to do is call 911. We will be scared that we do not know how to help or that we might even make things worse. We are going to miss an opportunity and leave it to the professionals. So, if we are to become the missionaries Jesus commissions us to be, we need to prepare ourselves as best we can for mission, and then we need to step forward and act whenever we're confronted with need.

If we are weighing the cost, perhaps it's because we have not recognized what we have already received. Although those who serve God's kingdom may be motivated to find love, personal transformation, and everlasting life, loving actions are never really about personal salvation or getting ourselves together or getting it right; Jesus has already taken care of all that. We should be thankful, and our true motivation should be to show and share God's love, without hesitation, by responding to real needs of God's children.

Jesus asks us to begin loving those in close proximity. He asks disciples to love one another and then to love our neighbors as ourselves. Jesus asks us to extend our personal love as far and as truly as possible. If everyone did this well, the world would be an entirely different place. By widening the circle of personal love, we prepare a place for an infinite and eternal love that we are not capable of creating on our own.

One of the hard realizations is that even in the power of discipleship, we can't solve all of the world's problems. We would like to be in control, to "do things, show things, prove things, build things," but we need to become "completely vulnerable, open to receive and give love regardless of any accomplishments."[3] We will never complete this work or fulfill God's kingdom ourselves, and only God will fully accomplish a new heaven and a new earth (Revelation 21, Romans 8, 1 Corinthians 15).

Jesus tells his followers that the rewards of this journey are experiencing life and light in the kingdom of love, and the alternative is living in the "outer darkness." People are not authentically following Jesus on the Way (and being transformed into disciples) unless they are on a primary journey of loving God and loving others. The light we experience is in relation to the love we share. The Christian life choice is not simply a difference in belief, but making a difference in responding love.

Becoming a blessing for others

A friend who was teaching Sunday school asked her class, "Do you think God can be everywhere?" A young boy answered, "I don't think God can be everywhere. That's why he needs each of us to help." In fact, God is everywhere and he could do everything, but he has chosen us to act with him. That's the nature of a kingdom of relationships, a kingdom of love: to love we must be engaged with one another.

The Great Commandment proclaims that God has a different plan for us, one of belonging (loving relationships) and purpose (meaning and action). Christianity offers a better Way, but we will need to change our habits and our lives by going outside ourselves and living with and serving others. We are limited in our ability to love, but always less limited than we claim.

When Peter identifies Jesus as the Messiah, or the "liberating king promised by God," Jesus tries to explain what this really means: "Then he began to teach them that the Son of Man must undergo great suffering, and be rejected ... and ... killed, and after three days rise again" (Mark 8:31). Jesus twice tries to tell his disciples that he is the person who manifests God's love by coming into the world, suffering, dying, and rising again—all to reconcile each one of us to live *in loving relationships*, with God and one another.

Then Jesus asks his disciples to also take up their cross. Jesus wants to bring every person into God's kingdom. He wants *us* to help do that, too, by caring for others—by listening to them, accepting them, forgiving them, journeying with them, serving them, reducing their suffering or loneliness, reconciling with them, loving them. Jesus expects his followers to love and serve as he does: making ourselves vulnerable to others, even giving up our time, possessions, or well-being for the sake of others. In this way, disciples become a blessing for others.

Rob Bell describes a community of disciples that follows the Great Commandment as a "blessing machine." He writes:

> Jesus teaches his disciples that the greatest in his kingdom are the ones who serve (John 13). For Jesus, everything is upside down. The best and greatest and most important are the ones who humble themselves, set their needs and desires aside, and selflessly serve others. So what is a group of people living this way called? That's the church. The church doesn't exist for itself; it exists to serve the world. It is not ultimately about the church; it's about all the people God wants to bless through the church. When the church loses sight of this, it loses its heart. ... We reclaim the church as a blessing machine. ... It is when the church gives itself away in radical acts of service and compassion,

expecting nothing in return, that the way of Jesus is most vividly put on display. . . . Jesus commanded us to love our neighbor, and our neighbor can be anybody. We are all created in the image of God, and we are all sacred, valuable creations of God (Genesis 1:26–27). Everybody matters. . . .

To be this kind of person—the kind who selflessly serves—takes everything a person has. It is . . . difficult. It is going out of our way to be more generous and disciplined and loving and free. It is refusing to escape and become numb to and check out of this broken, fractured world. And so we are embracing the high demands of Jesus' call to be one of his disciples.[4]

Christians listen to people the way Jesus does. They stop like Jesus and give their full attention to those in need: a tax collector, a woman at a well, a woman caught in adultery, a blind beggar. They don't judge them; they spend time with them and show that someone loves them, cares about their pain, and wants them to be OK.

Christians heal people the way Jesus does. Like Jesus, they ask each person what their deepest needs are and how they can help. They ask, "What do you want me to do for you?" (Matthew 20:32). Then they believe what Jesus says: "Very truly, I tell you, the one who believes in me will also do the works that I do and, in fact, will do greater works than these" (John 14:12). They work to reduce suffering, or help people walk or see or hear, or be less lonely, or grieve less.

Christians forgive people the way Jesus does. Forgiveness brings us back into relationship and community with God and one another, and we are given this power either to reconcile or to exclude: "If you forgive the sins of any, they are forgiven them" (John 20:23). We look for ways to welcome others home and bring them into our family and community.

Christians serve people the way Jesus does. Jesus reminds us that we serve him and show God's love and our love for one another as members of God's family by taking care of others' physical needs such as food, drink, shelter, and clothing (Matthew 25) and spiritual needs (John 21).

Christians reconcile with all people the way Jesus does: loving and never harming other people we are sent to care for, even to the extreme of suffering for others.

Christians try to follow Jesus by keeping him in sight and caring for people in the same ways he does. Christians help extend God's love farther and farther, to more and more people—people who need acceptance and love:

> Transfiguration of our world comes from even the most unlikely places and people. You are the indispensable agent of change. You should not be daunted by the magnitude of the task before you. Your contribution can inspire others, embolden others who are timid, to stand up for the truth in the midst of a welter of distortion, propaganda, and deceit; stand up for human rights where these are being violated with impunity; stand up for justice, freedom, and love where they are trampled underfoot by injustice, oppression, hatred, and harsh cruelty; stand up for human dignity and decency at times when these are in desperately short supply. God calls on us to be his partners to work for a new kind of society where people count; where people matter more than things, more than possessions; where human life is not just respected but positively revered; where people will be secure and not suffer from the fear of hunger, from ignorance, from disease; where there will be more gentleness, more caring, more sharing, more compassion, more laughter; where there is peace and not war.[5]

Engaging Jesus

To continue engaging Jesus, read and reflect on Luke 10:25–37.

Questions for Personal Reflection:

1. With which of the four steps to serving identified by Rick Warren do you most identify? Which is the most challenging for you?

2. How do you love God?

3. How do you love other people?

4. What opportunities do you have to share God's love with those near to you?

Questions for Group Discussion:

1. What are some ways to love God?

2. What are some ways to love others?

3. When are the first and second commandments the same?

4. Is it significant that the person who helped the man in need was a Samaritan or that those who did not help were religious leaders?

5. Why did the Samaritan go out of his way to help the man in need?

6. What personal resources did the Good Samaritan use to love a person in need?

7. What are reasons the Samaritan could have come up with for not helping the man in need? Why do many people walk right by opportunities to serve others? Why is it often difficult for us to show genuine concern for others and put their interests ahead of our own?

8. How committed is your church community to reaching out together in social ministries to serve brothers and sisters who are struggling or suffering, advocating for justice, or seeking peace? How involved are members in these activities?

9. How is your church a "blessing machine"? What are blessings you offer to your community?

10. List outreach and pastoral care ministries and identify whether they (a) are church sponsored, led, or managed, (b) are partnerships with other agencies or churches, (c) are served by church members, or (d) use church money,

facilities, or other resources. What are your church's principal outreach ministries?

11. What unmet needs in this community might your church help with? How could your church become more of a "blessing machine"? (How can you support people in the Way?)

12. What resources do you need to offer these blessings?

13. How are you doing as a church in having members participate in ministries beyond attending worship services? What expectations does your church or ministry area have for people?

14. How can you as leaders help prepare people for serving others?

15. What are ways to connect more people to service ministries? Some examples are (a) getting each ministry group to define itself, celebrate and witness to the opportunities for involvement, and make individual invitations, (b) spotlighting key ministries during worship services three or four times per year, and (c) highlighting ministries in the bulletin, through ministry day or a gift fair, and an opportunity booklet.

PART 3:

Becoming Disciples in Community

3.1

Helping People Experience the Way of Jesus

Journeying in community

Jesus came to teach us, by word and example, that loving relationships with God and other people are possible and that loving relationships transform our lives. Because the kingdom of God is comprised of loving relationships, we cannot live in it on our own. Church communities are truly needed to proclaim and help people experience and participate in God's kingdom by living the Way of Jesus. We are often separated from God and other people unless we live together and journey together.

Church communities can participate with Jesus in helping make new and stronger disciples—people who live in close relationship with Jesus, follow Jesus along the Way and become more like Jesus—and in sharing and showing forth God's love to the world. The church is at its best when it is *incarnational* (showing forth God's love for people and creation), *discipling* (helping people live into the loving relationships of God's kingdom), and *apostolic* (sending people to love and serve God and other people in the world).

The church community grows out of our efforts to create and support true, transforming relationships with God and other people. The most loving action we can take is to draw someone into a deeper relationship with God. The way that Jesus showed his greatest love for people was by helping them become his disciples. The church helps spread God's kingdom by going, baptizing, teaching, and sharing the living presence of Jesus. A faith community helps affirm God's presence in our lives and activities.

The church community helps people grow spiritually. The church strives to provide an atmosphere where people can love one another and witness to one another about God's love. We are with one another to listen and to encourage and to share (Romans 1:11–12). We grow more than we could ever imagine, and we are blessed with a greater awareness of God's presence as we work together (1 Corinthians 14:12). The gifts God gives each of us are for building up the body of Christ, and our faith matures as we use our gifts (Ephesians 4:11–13). Loving relationships in church communities profoundly transform individual lives: "Everything we do, beloved, is for the sake of building you up" (2 Corinthians 12:19). In the process, we discover more permanent relationships, relationships that do not fail us, relationships with and through God.

The church community that genuinely strives to follow Jesus is a gift from God, not only to the members of that community but to the world. Christians work together in and through loving Christian communities to more fully realize God's kingdom. At the same time, the church strives to improve human beings' relationships with one another. The church exists not for itself but for the kingdom, to love and serve God and other people.[1]

An authentic church is a community of people trying to love in all these ways. In a Christian community, we praise God; make a joyful noise; share in the Eucharist; pray for one another; care for others; are formed and transformed, supported, challenged, loved, and sent into the world to serve God. In these ways, the church keeps alive the message and practice of God's love for a world that intensely needs that love. It would be awfully difficult to live and journey in this kingdom of loving relationships without the presence and help of other people in community.

Experiencing Jesus in community

Frankly, many people who come to churches today do not find such ideal loving Christian communities. They do not find Jesus. Although Jesus adopted the practice of supportive community in the rabbinical tradition of discipleship, he did not minister to the world through a church organization. During his ministry, Jesus taught in the temple (e.g., Mark 12:35, Luke 19:47, John 7:14), and people knew they could find him there: "The blind and the lame came to him in the temple, and he cured them" (Matthew 21:14). But Jesus was not a priest, scribe, or elder within the temple system, and they did not want him there. Jesus rejected the temple system. He challenged and contradicted church leaders and highlighted how the institution did not serve God's kingdom. It is not coincidental that Mark makes Jesus' striking down of the fig tree and driving the money changers from the temple immediate events (Mark 11:13–17; see also Matthew 21:12–13, Luke 19:45, John 2:14–17). The temple was not bearing fruit for the kingdom, so Jesus said, "The kingdom of God will be taken away from you and given to a people that produces the fruits of the kingdom." Matthew notes that "the chief priests and the Pharisees . . . realized that he was speaking about them" (Matthew 21:42–45). After the ascension of Jesus, his disciples returned to the temple to bless God and pray (Luke 24:53, Acts 2:46), but it was not the center of Christian life.

Jesus predicted the destruction of the temple: "You see all these [buildings of the temple], do you not? Truly I tell you, not one stone will be left here upon another; all will be thrown down" (Matthew 24:2, Mark 13:2, Luke 25:5–6). Jesus didn't say he would destroy the temple, as his accusers claimed (Matthew 26:61, Mark 14:58), but he said that when the temple was destroyed, he would replace it. In speaking of destroying and rebuilding the temple in three days, Jesus meant that this would occur through his own death and resurrection (John 2:19–22).

Jesus does not need the temple to bring about God's kingdom. Jesus said, "I tell you, something greater than the temple is here" (Matthew 12:6). The kingdom of God is not where the temple is, but where Jesus is. That does not mean he must be physically there, as he explains: "where two or three are gathered in my name, I am there among them" (Matthew 18:20). The temple is no longer God's dwelling place and the place of forgiveness, reconciliation, and salvation. That place is a person, Jesus: "I saw no temple in the city, for its temple is the Lord God the Almighty and the Lamb" (Revelation 21:22). The Good News does not happen in a "faithful" remnant or temple but wherever Jesus goes forth through his people to show love to the world. Jesus himself is a new foundation (Matthew 7:24–27). And the religion Jesus brings with him into the world is kingdom love. We need always to put loving relationships before the ministry tasks, programs, operations, or structures of the church. And we can always do better in our loving relationships.

Loving one another

In John 13:34–35, Jesus says, "I give you a *new* commandment, that you love one another. Just as I have loved you, you also should love one another. By this everyone will know that you are my disciples, if you have love for one another." Jesus repeats his new commandment in John 15:12. The Great Commandment, the law of God's kingdom, is to love God and one's neighbor as oneself. The new commandment is to love as Jesus has loved us, to love as fully and completely "as I have loved you." A church community shows forth God's love to the world when that love is experienced, shared, and manifested within the community itself. "See how they love one another!" affirms the reality of Christian community, and "See how poorly they treat each other!" denies it.[2]

Living into loving relationships in Christian community is an introduction to living into God's kingdom. Loving relationship is not easy or natural, but it is essential, "for we are members of one another" (Ephesians 4:25, 1 Corinthians 12:25–27). To begin, we might ask several questions:

Do we live in harmony? Harmony is different notes played together to create a chord, and New Testament writers frequently write about the concept and its importance, even if they don't use that exact word: "Be at peace with one another" (Mark 9:50). "Live in harmony with one another" (Romans 12:16). "Lead a life worthy of the calling to which you have been called, with all humility and gentleness, with patience, bearing with one another in love, making every effort to maintain the unity of the Spirit in the bond of peace" (Ephesians 4:1).

Do we treat one another as we would like to be treated? Christians may think of the Golden Rule as uniquely Christian (Matthew 7:12; Luke 6:31, 10:25–28), but this rule of reciprocal respect for all people is found in many religions and moral philosophies, including Judaism (Leviticus 19:18), Buddhism, and Confucianism.[3] Jesus extends the reach of our love to everyone, even to our enemies and those who persecute us (Matthew 5:43–48; see also Luke 6:35).

Do we avoid judging others? "Be merciful, just as your Father is merciful. Do not judge, and you will not be judged; do not condemn, and you will not be condemned" (Luke 6:36–37). Rather than constantly critiquing others, we need to search for the value and worth of each person and show compassion and forgiveness, which also encourages others to a better way of life.[4] As the accusers of the woman caught in adultery were reminded, none of us is without sin (John 8:3–11). Even when sin breaks community with God and other people, we can forgive and restore community.[5]

Do we reconcile with one another? Jesus came to bring us from estrangement into a closer relationship with God and other people. To reestablish a close relationship with another person or group, we may need to accept, resolve, or forgive differences. This brings us back into the kinds of relationships God wants among members of his family, but it is often very hard. Jesus reminds us that reconciliation is needed not only for God's kingdom, but also for our own health and safety. He warns that we might ourselves be wrong, lose our dispute, and be imprisoned: "Come to terms quickly with your accuser while you are on the way to court with him, or your accuser may hand you over to the judge, and the judge to the guard, and you will be thrown into prison. Truly I tell you, you will never get out until you have paid the last penny" (Matthew 5:25–26). Beyond this very tangible warning is the deeper truth that we are personally and spiritually imprisoned and destroyed by our hatred and resentment.

Do we confront one another? Remember that "confrontation" means simply "meeting face-to-face," or addressing. Confrontations are required in any successful relationship, especially when love is involved. When we address a problem or a challenge with another person, we often can reconcile with that person or reveal more of God's love to them. Jesus always lovingly confronts people. Confrontations with the Samaritan woman at the well and the woman caught in adultery seem gentle, while confrontations with the Syrophoenician woman (Mark 7:25–29) and the Pharisees seem harsh.[6]

Conflict results when our desires, expectations, fears, or wants collide with the desires, expectations, fears, or wants of others. We are told in James 4:1–3 that we fight and quarrel within the church because of the desires that battle within us for the things we want and do not ask God for or the things we ask God for and do not receive because we have wrong motives. These often come down to issues of control. Other times, conflict comes from differences in values or perspectives. Conflict and unresolved tensions destroy community in multiple ways, including a lack of spiritual growth, a drain of the church's resources, diminished ministry opportunities, decreased church attendance, voluntary or involuntary leadership separations, congregation division, and sometimes church splits.

When conflicts are ignored, perhaps for the sake of peace, they can become unhealthy behavior patterns. Churches sometimes have "old issues" or conflicts which were never fully resolved and tend to resurface in unsettled times. A congregation needs to be released from any inappropriate or crippling power of the past in order to move forward. A process of loving confrontation around these unresolved issues can help a congregation improve structurally, emotionally, psychologically, and spiritually to help members enter into stronger relationships with one another.

Leaders need to encourage, facilitate, and mediate confrontations that may help the community make better decisions about questions that do not have clear answers and solutions. Jesus specifically describes how we need to confront one another when there are disagreements:

> "If another member of the church sins against you, go
> and point out the fault when the two of you are alone. If
> the member listens to you, you have regained that one.
> But if you are not listened to, take one or two others
> along with you, so that every word may be confirmed
> by the evidence of two or three witnesses. If the member
> refuses to listen to them, tell it to the church; and if the
> offender refuses to listen even to the church, let such a
> one be to you as a Gentile and a tax collector. . . ."

> Then Peter came and said to him, "Lord, if another member
> of the church sins against me, how often should I forgive? As
> many as seven times?" Jesus said to him, "Not seven times,
> but, I tell you, seventy-seven times." (Matthew 18:15–22)

Do we confess to one another? "Therefore confess your sins to one another, and pray for one another, so that you may be healed" (James 5:16). "If we confess our sins, he who is faithful and just will forgive us our sins and cleanse us from all unrighteousness" (1 John 1:9). In confession to another member of Christian community, a sinner is no longer alone and separated from God and community, but truthfully reveals his or her sins and experiences the presence of God in another person. In the humiliation of the confession, we take our sins to Jesus, who will bear them and free us from them. When there is a break from sin, there is a breakthrough to new life and there is conversion. And confession is the beginning of discipleship because "as the first disciples left everything behind and followed Jesus' call, so in confession the Christian gives up everything and follows. . . . In confession, Christians begin to renounce their sins. The power of sin is broken. From now on, the Christian gains one victory after another."[7]

Do we forgive one another? Saint Paul instructs, "Be kind to one another, tenderhearted, forgiving one another, as God in Christ has forgiven you" (Ephesians 4:32). And Jesus repeatedly emphasizes the importance of forgiveness: "Forgive, and you will be forgiven" (Luke 6:38); "If you forgive the sins of any, they are forgiven them" (John 20:23; see also Mark 11:25, Matthew 6:14–15, and Matthew 18:21–22). Forgiveness frees us to live in closer relationship with God and with other people.

Do we encourage one another? We need to inspire one another with kind words, to "build up" one another, to give each other courage and hope to stimulate action: "Let us consider how to provoke one another to love and good deeds, not neglecting to meet together, as is the habit of some, but encouraging one another, and all the more as you see the Day approaching" (Hebrews 10:24). "Therefore encourage one another and build up each other, as indeed you are doing" (1 Thessalonians 5:11).

Do we worship God together? A Christian church needs to express its love for God in all of its activities, and we begin by placing God first and at the center of all we do. Our worship may share and celebrate God's living presence (positively and enthusiastically), give hope and meaning to our lives, and send us out into the world to serve and proclaim. We mistake worship if we think there is a particular style that it must follow. Inspiring worship is not preserving a tradition or completing a duty; it is honoring God and transforming our lives to offer them in response to God's love; ultimately, it is not what we do but what the Holy Spirit does. We need to make room for God's Spirit, as 1 Thessalonians 5:16–19 says: "Rejoice always, pray without ceasing, give thanks in all circumstances; for this is the will of God in Christ Jesus for you. Do not quench the Spirit." In our worship we strive to remain alive to God's presence and to avoid extinguishing the Spirit's fire.

Do we pray for one another? "Therefore confess your sins to one another, and pray for one another, so that you may be healed. The prayer of the righteous is powerful and effective" (James 5:16). When we pray for one another, we ask God to take care of the other person, and this is the greatest care we can offer. "And this is the boldness we have in him, that if we ask anything according to his will, he hears us. And if we know that he hears us in whatever we ask, we know that we have obtained the requests made of him" (1 John 5:14–15).

Do we welcome others? "Welcome one another, therefore, just as Christ has welcomed you, for the glory of God" (Romans 15:7). A church community glorifies God by being a place of hospitality and generosity to members and visitors. This happens more in our personal relationships than in programs or processes, so small groups, like Bible studies and prayer groups, may be more invitational than corporate worship, because they support close relationships with one another where we may share our true feelings, support each other, and grow in humility and love.

Do we proclaim the Good News? A church community worships God by telling others about God. A worshiping community does not keep God's love a secret but continually shares the gospel and welcomes new people into the body of Christ. Paul says in 2 Corinthians 4:19 that as God's grace brings more and more people to Christ, God will receive more and more glory.

Do we teach one another? Unlike judgment, advice and guidance is "useful for building up, as there is need, so that your words may give grace to those who hear" (Ephesians 4:29). A church community worships God by coming to know God better. "Let the word of Christ dwell in you richly; teach and admonish one another in all wisdom" (Colossians 3:16). In God's family, God wants us to grow into spiritual maturity, to become like Jesus in the way we think, feel, and act. Paul says as the Spirit of the Lord works within us, we become more like Jesus and reflect his glory even more (2 Corinthians 3:18). Again, small groups, which offer intimate opportunities for people to experience fellowship and love as well as learning, may be a foundation for strengthening personal relationships with God and helping a church community love one another.

Do we help one another to grow along our Christian spiritual paths? We are called to love others by helping Jesus make new and stronger disciples (Matthew 28:19–20). In *The Road Less-Traveled*, Scott Peck says love is helping another person to grow spiritually. The way that Jesus showed his greatest love for people was by helping them become his disciples and drawing them into deeper relationship with him: "Jesus, looking at him, loved him and said … 'Come, follow me'" (Mark 10:21).

Do we encourage one another to use our spiritual gifts? 1 Peter says that we glorify God when we serve one another with whatever gift each of us has received and with the strength that God supplies (4:10-11). A strong and effective mutual ministry happens best as each person is encouraged to recognize and use his or her unique gifts "for the work of ministry, for building up the body of Christ" and to accept and celebrate his or her role as part of the body of Christ.

Do we follow a way of living together that helps us treat one another with love? Creating a culture of love means intentionally creating the types of relationships we want to have. This means mutually defining and agreeing about the ways we want to treat each other. More than a moral rule book, this "covenant" is an agreement about attitudes, approaches, boundaries, and processes that support mutual love and respect. A good example is the Mennonite peace covenant, "Agreeing or Disagreeing in Love."[8] Beyond the covenant, we may want to discuss means of calling one another to accountability and reconciliation when the covenant is broken.[9]

Does our community depend on God? It is in all these ways that a Christian community loves God and loves one another and lives into the reality of God's kingdom. The key question is: *Do we care for and serve one another in all these ways?*

The fundamental realization must be that this way of community is impossible for us by ourselves. It is not a human venture, and if we venture it outside of relationship with God, we will fail. What Jesus says is true for our Christian life is also true for our Christian lives together in community: "For mortals it is impossible, but not for God; for God all things are possible" (Mark 10:27; see also Matthew 19:26; Luke 1:37, 18:27). How much we are able to do these things will depend upon our awareness of and response to God's presence with us. In the short Christian classic *Life Together*, Dietrich Bonhoeffer reminds disciples: "Christ opened up the way to God and to one another. Now Christians can live with each other in peace; they can love and serve one another; they can become one. But they can continue to do so only through Jesus Christ. Only in Jesus Christ are we one; only through him are we bound together."[10] Whether the church community is described as the body of Christ (1 Corinthians 12), branches on a vine or an olive tree (John 15:1–8, Romans 11:17–24), a field or building (1 Corinthians 3:6–9), or a house (Hebrews 3:6, 1 Peter 2:5), its life only comes through active relationship with God and loving one another.

Engaging Jesus

To continue engaging Jesus, read and reflect on Romans 12.

Questions for Personal Reflection:

1. Reflect on your personal relationships with others. On a scale of one to ten, how would you rate yourself on each of the questions above?

2. Where are your areas of strength and areas for improvement?

3. Who do you love well?

4. Who could you love better?

5. How can God and members of your community help you?

Questions for Group Discussion:

1. The quality of healthy churches that is the fruit and the genesis of all the others is *loving relationships*. Most of us consider our church a loving community (or we wouldn't belong). Yet, Schwarz and Schalk conclude from their studies of over five thousand Christian churches that this is the area where most churches "extravagantly overestimate" their strength.[11] Many churches have developed cliques that seem comfortable, warm, and open to regular members but

are inaccessible to newcomers. How is your church doing in answering each of the questions in this chapter?

2. Which of these loving practices seem contradictory?

3. Why is forgiveness more important than judgment, self-righteousness, or condemnation?

4. How is a community centered in God different from human communities?

5. Does your church reflect unity in Christ? Why or why not?

6. What does the kingdom of God described in the Great Commandment look like? Can it be reflected in church community?

3.2

Helping People Connect to Community

F inding ways to connect with and invite people to share the Christian journey in loving community is especially important now. A post-Christendom challenge is that non-church people do not feel inclined or comfortable coming to church to see what it might be about. Churches today can no longer rely on people simply coming to church on their own.

This challenge should not be surprising, and it is not even unique to Christian communities. Health clubs, country clubs, fraternal clubs (such as Lions, Elks, Rotary, or Kiwanis), and other social organizations have similar challenges in reaching new members. I was interested in a conversation about the challenges of declining classical concert attendance between two music professors. Of course, traditional audiences are getting older and younger audiences are not replacing them. This art is challenged because fewer people are gaining an appreciation, much less a passion, for the music and for the live experiences. Fewer people experience the music in performance and find it meaningfully touching them—emotionally, intellectually, spiritually, or collectively. Fewer people hear the music at home or come to concerts with their friends, parents, or grandparents. Who—on his or her own—is going to plan ahead, find a concert, buy a ticket, drive through traffic, find parking, enter a concert hall (where they know no one), and listen to music they know little about and feel uncomfortable with? Does this sound familiar?

Abandoning Christendom

Many people have never even experienced a church community. Others are disillusioned by what they perceive church organizations have become. With more people today rejecting "church," Christian leaders face greater challenges in leading Christian communities and helping people become disciples who love and serve others. If it has not always been this way, how have we reached this point where many people reject belonging to church communities?

In the early Christian church described in Acts, Christians were engaged in preaching, teaching, taking care of those in need, visiting the sick, praying, and breaking bread together (Acts 2:42–47). Early Christians were united by a deep *trust in the person of Jesus* and by their faith in the dawning of a new era of freedom, healing, and compassion—especially for the poor, the outcast, and the marginalized. In the fourth century, however, a different form of church emerged. Constantine made Christianity the established religion of the Roman Empire. A new clerical class patterned on the ruling structure of Rome received authority over a new, institutional Christendom. The church held councils and adopted creeds to obtain common agreement about unifying religious beliefs. For many people, church came to be more about accepting a *set of beliefs about Jesus* than trusting in, or walking with, Jesus. More people joined the church because it was "the thing to do" when political, economic, and religious cultures were aligned. People were expected to attend church to be accepted in their communities.

In many ways, this authoritative and institutional church continued right into the twentieth century. At least by the Middle Ages and on into the 1960's, the church in Western settings could largely depend on a "cathedral" or "field of dreams" model of evangelism: Build it and they will come because it is the most amazing thing and the center of community. With the cathedral model, churches would not have to go out and reach people, because people would seek to be part of the church spectacle and community. An attractive church (with good preaching, music, Sunday school, and social activities) could essentially wait for people to come to its building and then serve them where it was. In another classical model of church, the "monastery" became a spiritual home, refuge from the world, and place of pilgrimage, setting an example for life in the world. People would participate in these communities as places of safety, learning, and transformation, but also because they too were accepted centers of community. As with cathedrals, people were "attracted" to monasteries.[1]

Since the fourth century, we've primarily looked to the church to help people see Jesus and learn how to walk with him; we would bring people to live in Christian community or to participate in church programs. Many contemporary churches still attempt "attraction" models of evangelism. The cathedral model is employed by creating new and different ministry tools or sensations—often besides buildings—to capture interest; but many churches discover that their buildings or ministries are not attractive enough to create a "buzz" and bring in people on their own.[2] The monastery model is employed by people who support a return to hospitality and spiritual practices, and, while these activities clearly help form disciples and strengthen spiritual communities, they do not in themselves seem to "attract" many new members.

In just three generations, churches have lost their general acceptance as social and religious institutions. During the last forty-five years, more and more people did not feel a spiritual need or social requirement to attend church and either never came (so-called "unchurched" people) or stopped coming (so-called "dechurched" people). Between 1991 and 2004 (less than one third of this forty-five-year period), the number of these "non-church" people in the United States grew from thirty-nine million to seventy-five million. Only one in six people seek direction in their spiritual life from a local church, and less than one in ten attended church last weekend. When seven out of ten Americans still identify themselves as Christians, this means that many consider themselves "spiritual but not religious": they believe that they can be Christian without being part of community. A substantial portion of the population is "post-Christian" and "post-seeker" in terms of the Christian church; these people are not looking for a church community as a possible way of life. Church members who say that others will eventually "come back" to church forget that ever-greater numbers of people either have never been to church or were dissatisfied with church and left to look for something else.

We can identify a myriad of reasons why "non-church" people might feel that a church would not meet their social or spiritual needs. For one, people beyond the church often see the authoritative and institutional church as more concerned with rules, processes, and politics (preserving rituals, programs, and structures in the name of orthodoxy) than with spiritual life or healing relationships. While these things may support our conceptual understanding of Christianity or Christendom and give us comfort, we should not be surprised that an ideological or procedural way of life does not satisfy contemporary spiritual hunger to walk together with Jesus. These things do not help the church look or act much like Jesus.

We need to remember how Jesus taught his disciples to get the Word out: "By this everyone will know that you are my disciples, if you have love for one another" (John 13:35). When non-church people encounter "Christians" or "Christian communities," they often do not describe them as sharing this kind of love. Our contemporaries, while often desiring a spiritual life, have become wary of encountering the collective church. Because they have either no experiences or bad experiences with church communities, they will not come on their own, and they are reluctant to come at all. This is especially true for people who are "spiritual but not religious," and various barriers need to be recognized and removed in trying to invite them into church communities.

The fields are ripe for harvest

Although the Christian church has declined, more people are seeking spiritual direction. They are not at all interested in finding a church, but they hunger for loving relationships and life-transforming experiences of God. They're looking for spiritual guidance somewhere other than in Christian community. Most people desire loving community, but they lack the time it takes to develop relationships. Building community is difficult in a time when people are more individualistic and less community oriented. People want to be spiritual but not religious, focusing on personal spirituality and personal salvation. Unfortunately, Christianity doesn't work this way, and people's real needs are not met.

Over half of the people in the United States are not actively and happily involved in the life of any church. The need to share the love of Jesus with the world is growing. Jesus' words are as true now as ever: "I tell you, look around you, and see how the fields are ripe for harvesting" (John 4:35). We cannot simply accept the decline of church communities. We need to recreate, revitalize, or reshape—in a word, change—the way we "do" church to follow and serve Jesus on the Way into the kingdom.

Where churches are no longer central to the culture or sought for their values in spiritual growth and support, Christians need to find other models for "reaching" people. We need to do more than develop an attractive church (cathedral) or community (monastery); we actually need to find people and bring them into our activities. We cannot simply "attract" people to churches; we need to "reach" them. We need to go out and meet people and bring them into community.

This can happen through the growth or revitalization of existing congregations, or it may occur through planting new churches. Numerous church studies show a direct link between the rate of church growth or decline and the rate of starting new churches.[3] This may be because new churches immediately focus on reaching more people and are often more open. New churches are free to try new styles of worship, new methods of education, new music, and other "nontraditional" ways to reach new groups of people. New churches may seem more inclusive in terms of racial or ethnic background, generations or age levels, socio-economic class, theological views, and liturgical styles. So, in various ways, new churches provide opportunities to connect and build relationships differently with non-church people who aren't drawn to existing churches or who dropped out of church some time ago.

Not only is there growth in new churches themselves, but churches that start new churches also grow significantly. Helping start new churches teaches us how to reach and engage new members rather than passively waiting for new people to come through our doors. And while existing churches may fear competition, they discover that there is lots more room for other churches. The most effective churches do a few ministries very well and reach only up to three percent of the local population. Few churches have all of the resources or skills to serve everyone in an area. Every Christian church community needs to consider helping to plant new church communities as one of its priorities for building up the body of Christ.

Begin with relationships

At the same time we are thinking about revitalizing or starting churches, we need to remember that non-church people are not coming to church. We need to think about both new expressions of faith communities and new connecting points and relational connections to faith communities. Evangelism is most effective when we begin with existing, trusting relationships—our friends, relatives, neighbors, coworkers, and so on. Three Biblical stories of people inviting others to come and see Jesus are exemplary: the stories of Andrew (John 1:35–42), Philip (John 1:43–51), and the woman at the well (John 4:7–30). Each of these people simply shared Christ with people they already knew. Similarly, the vast majority of people who come to a church community and stay come on the arm of someone they know. Our primary connecting points are our relationships (not our beliefs, our purposes, our buildings, our activities, or anything else).[4] Although inviting friends into church activities may feel more difficult than inviting them to a classical concert, this is often the only way our friends will come to either activity.

A traditional response when church communities ask members to invite their friends was, "All of my friends already have a church home." Statistics suggest that is less likely today. Because many people do not feel they need a church community, and fewer people are seeking one, we need to actually connect with people in contemporary society. This requires some form of "missionary" or "relational" model of going into the world and living with others who need God's healing love. We need in "post-Christendom" society to go out and find people, develop trusting relationships, and bring them into the Kingdom and into the church as a supporting community. To do this, we need to have connecting points—*places* where we can meet people and *activities* we can bring them into.

Create connecting points

We need to be aware of the connecting *places* with our church community. Traditional connecting points with churches include bringing people to church for social events, inspiring worship experiences, and quality learning opportunities (such as Christian formation for all ages designed to help people become stronger disciples and apostles). Less traditional connecting points include inviting people into small group relationships,[5] support groups for people with different interests or challenges or at different stages of life (such as youth groups or vacation Bible school), or outreach projects. These less traditional activities often happen beyond church walls and connect people to one another and begin to serve their needs before they directly connect people to a church community. And even less traditional connecting points are farther afield. They include any opportunities to meet people where they are—at home, at work, in a hospital or bar—listen, connect, and begin responding to their needs for friendship and love (belonging) and a meaningful spiritual journey (purpose).

Churches often focus on opportunities to invite guests to their facilities or activities. Traditionally, the primary invitation was to worship. Unfortunately, it has become more difficult to invite non-church people to rituals and assemblies they may be unfamiliar or uncomfortable with. Non-church people feel like strangers when church language (whether Biblical or creedal, in prayers or in sermons), customs (liturgy), and sometimes even dress are foreign to them. Bringing a person directly into a foreign culture and making them feel welcome and at home is difficult. Moreover, worship services are limited points of connection. Unless a church building is very large, it may have one, two, or three worship services. Often these aren't very diverse in style. Perhaps there is a service without music for people who like more silence and a more traditional liturgy. Depending on service time and day, these experiences seem to connect more with the silent generation (born 1925–1945) or millennials (born 1980–2000). There may also be a service with "contemporary" rock music that seems to connect more with baby boomers (born 1946–1964). And often there is a "traditional" service with a traditional choir and organ, and hymns and "classical" music favored through several generations of people who grew up in church. In any of these services, there exists a need for a newcomer to adapt to the particular worship culture. An individual or a family may find all kinds of reasons not to connect besides differences in musical styles or inconvenient service times.[6]

People may be more comfortable if they come with friends, if they are invited to activities in a non-church setting, or if they are invited to activities in a church setting that are not church related (for example, use of the church's facilities by community groups or for social activities or performances). Notice that sharing a facility or providing space for a group or activity builds awareness of a community, but it requires more to make an actual relational connection. Without that connection, it is simply an unspoken invitation to something more. Similarly, in today's world, church events, workshops, classes, small groups, outreach projects, programs, services, or ministries are only connecting points if someone invites and brings someone to them! Stretching beyond the walls of our churches might begin as simply as enjoying Bible study with friends at the local pizzeria or holding a Bible study online with friends across the Internet. We need to create communities of faith beyond, or parallel to, our church doors for people who don't make it to our doors or inside them. We need to have a new or different type of visibility in society, even if this does not feel "politically correct" today.

Churches need to integrate more places of connection into evangelism efforts. George Hunter has described how Saint Patrick and his companions used two different places of connection for evangelization during the fifth century in Ireland: (i) a monastic community welcoming seekers as guests, and (ii) missionary teams from the monastic community visiting settlements for weeks or months.[7] One model brings people to live in Christian community; the other goes to people in their own setting, becomes part of that community, and serves it so that people can experience Christian life. Traditional churches often avoid a "missionary" model of going into the world and living with others who need God's healing love, unless they are sending gifted specialists to do this work. However, going beyond church walls opens up far more possibilities for new relationships and activities. If needs are nearby, sometimes a church can become a community center and bring people in to serve them. But more often, missions will need to go and serve people where they are.

Connecting *activities* care for others or serve others through a church's community center or mission. Lyle Schaller gives useful examples of ways church communities use intentional ministries to meet people where they are. First is the powerful witness of outreach ministries such as working in nursing homes, calling on shut-ins, feeding the hungry, sheltering the homeless, visiting those in prison, caring for needy children, crusading for world peace, assisting in hospice for the terminally ill, and other acts of Christian mercy. Second are off-campus worship, teaching or service ministries in "storefronts, nursing homes, college dormitories, large apartment buildings, mobile home courts, vacation centers, or new sites . . . to meet people on their turf." And third are offerings that meet people's needs at particular life stages, such as retreats and support groups for newly engaged couples or newlyweds (in their first or subsequent marriages), parents with children at various developmental stages, empty nesters, people in the process of divorce, or people recently widowed. Other examples are Christian nursery schools and day schools.[8]

We certainly need to turn away from a wholly congregational focus and direct our focus intently upon the community in which God's placed us. We need to become missionaries in the most positive sense of sharing God's love and Good News. As we care, comfort, heal, empower, and share hospitality, safety, and hope with our neighbors, we will also find new life in our church communities and ourselves. The question is not "How can we get more people to join our church?" but "How can we move beyond our church walls to live with Jesus and serve, love, and learn from God's people living around us?" Whether we are starting a new church, revitalizing a church, or extending faith communities in new ways, we need to help people belong to community, help people with physical, psychological, emotional, or spiritual needs, nurture people in faith, and send them out to love and serve others.

Ministry activities often make better connections than communities can make in the aggregate through corporate worship or large events. This is true both for people who are served by ministries and for people who are engaged in ministries. A connecting point is inviting people to help us with our service ministries. For example, if church members invite friends to help with a meal program or tutoring or Habitat for Humanity, this helps their friends get involved and feel really good about both themselves and the people they work with in the church community. They choose to participate in activities that meet their needs and are meaningful to them at their life stage or place on a spiritual journey. These relationships will take time to develop, and it may be some time before people feel comfortable participating in other church activities or being brought to church, but they are probably already on the Way. And they are much more likely to eventually come to a church community with their friends.

Ministries extend the reach of the community by meeting people both inside and outside the church, at more connecting points, and with experiences which are more intimate, personal, and engaging. An individual has a better likelihood of connecting through a ministry activity with a diversity of leaders and members—some of whom might relate better to an individual's needs than a single pastor or the collective church. People connect directly with others who are not strangers, are less foreign and are more like them. Ministries require engaged participants, not just "spectators" or "fans," and more than learning "about" the Way, people actually live and experience the Way. So the success of ministries comes not from just offering a variety of choices for people to connect with, but in meeting important needs. Nevertheless, offering a variety of connecting points connects more people and helps connect more strongly with them.

In *The Purpose Driven Church*,[9] Rick Warren discusses the need to use both attraction ("come and see") and reaching ("go and tell") evangelism strategies as connecting points, and he describes the hybrid strategies Saddleback Church has used. Beginning in the living room of his condo with his realtor as his first "member," Saddleback worshiped in seventy-nine different facilities in fifteen years as it grew to ten thousand members without its own building. Saddleback offered worship services geared toward seekers.[10] And it grew to offer over seventy targeted ministries to meet people's specific needs, including "Hope for the Separated" for couples trying to save their marriage, "Empty Arms" for couples dealing with miscarriages and stillbirths, "Lifelines" for troubled teenagers, "Peacemakers" for people in law enforcement, and "Recovery" for people struggling with alcohol or drug dependency.[11] Dr. Warren says, "Anybody can be won to Christ if you discover the key to his or her heart,"[12] and he believes that most people have the same emotional and relational needs:

> These include the need for love, acceptance, forgiveness, meaning, self-expression, and a purpose for living. People are also looking for freedom from fear, guilt, worry, resentment, discouragement, and loneliness. If your church is meeting these kinds of needs, you won't have to worry about advertising your services. Changed lives are a church's greatest advertisement. Wherever needs are being met and lives are being changed the word quickly gets out into a community.[13]

At the root, Dr. Warren identifies "the most overlooked key to growing a church: We must love unbelievers the way Jesus did."[14]

Build connecting relationships

Connecting points are opportunities to build relationships. Once we create connecting points, we must consider how well we do in making, sustaining, and building actual connections. For many people, the order of their connecting experiences is important. A faith community invites us to "come and see" what God is doing and will do in our lives. Most often that begins through developing loving and supportive relationships with authentic Christians; this is important so that others can experience the kingdom. As a loving Christian community manifests God's love, new people may wish to become part of the community and its activities without fully understanding why. Then Christians share experiences and encourage behaviors that open people to a new personal awareness of the living Jesus Christ, the power of the presence of the Holy Spirit, and faithful trust in the love of God. Once a person is welcomed into community and begins to experience and learn about the community's way of life, he or she may also choose to journey along the Way.

People generally enter into community relationships and then grow in faith. Some churches approach community building in the wrong order. Teaching people in community to worship, to pray, to study scripture, and to participate in the sacraments are important activities for the Christian life, but they often are not very effective until a person chooses to live in relationship with other people and with God. Churches make a difference in people's lives by offering loving relationships that truly reach into human lives before developing personal knowledge, beliefs, or new habits.

This is also why so many people cringe when they think of evangelism: they think of the confrontational process George Hunter calls the "Roman" model of evangelism, based on this approach:

Presentation. The evangelist presents the Christian message to the nonbeliever and explains the gospel.

Decision. The evangelist invites the nonbeliever to believe in Christ and to become a Christian.

Fellowship and Assimilation. If the nonbeliever accepts the message, he or she is welcomed into the fellowship of the church and trained in its ways.[15]

Sometimes, the Roman method of evangelism works. (The Holy Spirit can work through all kinds of opportunities.) Peter seems to have this kind of success in Acts 2. Another example is Philip and the Ethiopian eunuch in Acts 8:27–39, when Philip interpreted Isaiah and the eunuch asked, "Look, here is water! What is to prevent me from being baptized?" Although the Roman way of evangelism is a logical process, it is not an effective approach to evangelize everyone. People who are not already seeking or not under some kind of compulsion often feel put off by this approach.

In contrast to the Roman process, Professor Hunter describes a more gentle, experiential, and loving way of coming to Christian community and religious faith as the "Celtic" or relational way of evangelism. The steps in the Celtic, or hospitality, process of evangelism are as follows:

Fellowship. An evangelistic community practices hospitality by bringing people into the fellowship of faith or meeting and serving them in their own community. In Ireland, during the fifth through tenth centuries, Christians evangelized through monastic communities that offered openness and hospitality.[16] People in monastic communities experienced care and compassion and a sense of belonging: "The monastic communities produced a less individualistic and more community-oriented approach to the Christian life. ... The people supported each other, pulled together, prayed for each other, worked out their salvation together, and lived out the Christian life together. Every person had multiple role models for living as a Christian, and ... Irish Christians knew what it meant to be a Christian family or tribe."[17] At the same time, hospitality meant affirming the feelings, imagination, and creativity of seekers, refugees, and other guests and not compelling them first to accept the beliefs or practices of the community.[18] This required the evangelistic community to seek to understand and appreciate the indigenous language, culture, and concerns of another community and how to minister accordingly. "When you understand the people, you will often know what to say and do, and how. When the people know that the Christians understand them, they infer that maybe the High God understands them too."[19]

Ministry and conversations. Within the fellowship of community, the evangelistic team engages in conversation, ministry, prayer, and worship. Celtic Christianity focused not just on heaven, the sacred, or the transcendent, but on the pressing problems of daily life: "the questions of the uncertainty of the near future, the crises of present life, and the unknowns of the past." "Their Christian faith and community addressed their life as a whole ... and helped common people to live and cope as Christians day by day in the face of poverty, enemies, evil forces, nature's uncertainties, and frequent threats from many quarters."[20] The Celtic evangelists engaged people in a way that sounds very much like Jesus:

> The "apostolic" (in the sense of the Greek word meaning "sent on mission") team would meet the people, engage them in conversation and in ministry, and look for people who appeared receptive. They would pray for sick people, and for possessed people, and they would counsel people and mediate conflicts. ... They would engage in some open-air speaking, probably employing parable, story, poetry, song, visual symbols, visual arts and, perhaps, drama to engage the Celtic people's remarkable imaginations. ... The apostolic band would probably welcome people into their group fellowship to worship with them, pray with them, minister to them, converse with them, and break bread together.[21]

Belief and Invitation to Commitment. In time, as the people welcomed in hospitality discover that they believe in the Way of Jesus, they are asked to commit to the Way. An experience of fellowship enables belief and commitment.[22]

The Celtic or hospitality model of evangelism recognizes that Christianity is "caught more than taught" and people experience "belonging before believing."[23] Another summary of the Celtic way of evangelism is "Go to the People. Live among them. Learn from them. Love them. Start with what they know. Build on what they have."[24] In the Celtic way of evangelism, the evangelist must be flexible and adaptable, walking a path with people, and sometimes guiding but not directing the journey. People accept this process because of the practice of hospitality in genuinely welcoming people into the kingdom of God. Evangelism through church community is not really an independent activity as much as an activity that makes use of the other people and activities of the community to introduce people to God and God's family and begin to support them in their walk with God.[25]

The Celtic process of bringing people to the Way is similar to the model taught in relational evangelism of making friends, introducing them to our church friends and introducing God into our conversations.

Making Friends. If we wish to bring people we know to church, a first step is simply making friends. We generally make friends by spending time together and sharing activities—like playing golf or having a barbecue. These activities do not need to be at church or church-related. Most of us already can think of friends or acquaintances who do not know Jesus and who should. We need to start praying for these people, make them a bigger part of our lives, and see what happens. We are not trying to convert people to a theology; we are simply making friends.

Introducing them to our community. If we want our friends to become part of our church community, we need to introduce them to our church friends. A second step in inviting people to church is including our church friends in small group activities with our non-church friends. This is really important because people who do not go to church have one main concern about church: "Are these people normal?" You can see why people might have this concern from the way Christians are portrayed on television and in movies. Many of our contemporaries, while often desiring a spiritual life, are initially wary of encountering the collective church. But if a person likes you and you genuinely like them, the person may be agreeable to visiting your church.

Introducing God into our relationships. In addition to making friends and introducing them to our church friends, we need to introduce God into our relationships. This third step may make us uncomfortable, but we will have opportunities to do this. When our friends are sick or have sick friends or relatives, we can ask if we may pray for them. When we share a meal, we may offer a blessing. Or we may share our own faith experiences at an appropriate time. If we pray for our friends to find Jesus, God often makes us part of this process. The Holy Spirit gives us opportunities to share our faith with our friends. Eventually, some of us will invite our mutual friends to church and to participate in our church community.

This discussion of relationship building steps shows that evangelism must be an intentional process. We need to pay attention to how we make and strengthen our relationships. A huge part of a positive experience is relational—not what we tell people but whether we show hospitality and care for them. And it is much more than inviting, welcoming, and fellowship—the discreet steps churches often focus on. We certainly do not want people to leave because they do not feel connected. But we need to ask, connected for what? When we understand a person's needs, we can invite them to take a next step on a spiritual path—not our program or path, but his or hers. As a missionary church community, we are initially a companion or support group for people on their spiritual journeys. As we begin to connect with people, a first step in hospitality and welcoming is listening for the needs of the person and then making an appropriate invitation or introduction. We might ask: What has brought you here? What are you most excited about? What can we help you learn or do? What would you like to see us doing? How can we support you? Effective evangelism is more than having interesting and high quality programs or activities and depends on how we engage and empower and support the person's growth and development.

Part of this is helping people understand what it means to belong to the community and the broader body of Christ and what opportunities are available, so they know where they can go next, one step at a time. When we both understand the person's needs and know what we might have to offer in response, we can invite the individual to take another step on a spiritual path. Churches tend to do this pretty well initially with visitors or new members who actually come to church but not carry it on with everyone. Greeters make handoffs to the newcomers committee to the introductory course to the Christian formation process to small groups to outreach, etc. The path isn't linear; a person may step in many directions but often needs ideas, encouragement, and help with discernment (shepherding and mentoring). It is never enough to make an invitation to a new activity without making a true personal connection and another invitation into further relationship. When people are personally invited, become actively engaged, and journey together with one another, they truly find a place in community.

Our church communities need to fully embrace the mission and adventure of reaching the ever-increasing number of non-church yet deeply spiritual people that live all around us. Few will come to church on their own. We are called to leave the comfort of our buildings and practices and journey to meet and serve the majority of people around us who may not have a spiritual home. The process of strengthening relationships is very personal. We would like to have evangelism done for us through some tool or method, but evangelism is nothing less than offering love, building trust, and personally engaging people in the Way; and that requires caring, personal relationships.

Engaging Jesus

To continue engaging Jesus, read and reflect on Luke 5:17–26.

Questions for Personal Reflection:

1. Have you ever acted like the friends in Luke 5:17–26? How could you be more like this?

2. What brought you to your congregation originally?

3. What activities have you been involved with?

4. Were you ever frustrated by what people in your church community expect of you?

5. To whom are you accountable?

Questions for Group Discussion:

1. Reflect on Luke 5:17–26:

   a. Why did these friends carry this man to Jesus?

   b. What did Jesus do?

   c. How do we act like these friends?

2. Have you ever been alienated from others because you confronted them with the gospel or the church's practices? How did that happen?

3. How do people come to your church community?

4. Does your church have a model for evangelism? Is it more of a cathedral, monastery, or missionary model? More of a Roman or Celtic style? How is this working?

5. What are some "missional" churches' approaches to evangelism?

6. To whom is God sending us? Do we have a sense of urgency about reaching these people? Why or why not?

7. What are the connecting points for newcomers into the life of your congregation? How effectively are connections made?

8. What are the processes in your church community for connecting and assimilating new people? How effective are they?

Building Community
through Small Groups and Ministry Teams

While Jesus did not create formal organizations, he used a small group to support and prepare his disciples for mission. Long before the cathedral or the monastery, small groups were the basic building blocks of the early church. "Day by day, as they spent much time together in the temple, they broke bread at home and ate their food with glad and generous hearts, praising God and having the goodwill of all the people. And day by day the Lord added to their number those who were being saved" (Acts 2:46–47). By the fourth century, however, the focus of the church had moved from home meetings to programs centered in a building. Some people became more of an audience than active participants in the body of Christ. In this larger setting, love, community, relationships, ministry, and evangelism spring up less naturally, personally, and powerfully than in small groups.

The power of small groups

Small groups are powerful because "where two or three are gathered" in Jesus' name, he is present (Matthew 18:20). Small groups support discipleship in much the same way as the first Christian small group Jesus led and, because Jesus comes to be present with us, we can be transformed into disciples.

In small groups, we can have much the same experience as two early disciples did on the Road to Emmaus (Luke 24:13–35). On the first Easter, two disciples were going to Emmaus, and as they were discussing Jesus and the disturbing reports that he was alive, Jesus himself came and went with them. They did not recognize Jesus, but he interpreted the prophecies about himself in the Scriptures for them. As they came to

Emmaus, they asked him to stay with them. Then:

> *When he was at the table with them, he took bread, blessed*
> *and broke it, and gave it to them. Then their eyes were*
> *opened, and they recognized him; and he vanished from*
> *their sight. They said to each other, "Were not our hearts*
> *burning within us while he was talking to us on the road,*
> *while he was opening the scriptures to us?" That same hour*
> *they got up and returned to Jerusalem; and they found*
> *the eleven and their companions. Then they told what had*
> *happened on the road, and how he had been made known*
> *to them in the breaking of the bread. (Luke 24:30–35)*

Disciples have "hearts burning, eyes opened" experiences of God's powerful presence in their lives. In this story, we see a process of meeting Jesus, going along with him, listening to him, asking him to stay, recognizing him, and proclaiming him. These experiences can also happen in small groups. We recognize Jesus in a shared journey. And we need to bring ourselves and other people into other activities of the journey to go along with Jesus, recognize him in our presence, and proclaim him. We help people have "eyes opened, hearts burning" experiences by journeying together with Jesus and one another and meeting Jesus (incarnation), recognizing and knowing Jesus (discipling), and going out to serve Jesus (apostleship). As Christian leaders, we want to lead and support the important activities of this spiritual journey.

Many of us have experienced the power of small groups by joining in regular Bible studies, prayer groups, pastoral care groups, or other small church groups. A small group usually is six to twelve people who meet regularly for spiritual support and encourage one another through worship, prayer, outreach activities, and the application of the Bible's message to life. In small groups, individuals may discover the love of a supportive community, become rooted in the gospel and Scriptures, center their lives in prayer, experience the power of God's presence in their lives, discern and follow their unique vocations, and, eventually, gain experience in witness and ministry.

In an effective small group, we can truly experience God's love. A group of friends meets regularly to consider God's part in our lives. Our friends in these groups are not trying to change one another, but to help each of us be more aware of God's presence. We listen to one another's concerns and challenge each other with the deepest, most personal and loving question: Where is God in your life these days? Perhaps we read the Bible together. We talk about how our personal stories might fit into God's story. This is not as simple as finding and following certain prescribed rules; it is about being more aware of God and our own responses. Our discussions are not academic, and we are not looking to pluck verses out of the Bible and take them as universal statements of absolute truth. The personal faith experiences members share give glimpses of what God is trying to do in each of our lives, the lives of others, and the world around us, and how to possibly respond to that.[1] We pray for one another over time and see God working amid the joys and sorrows of the experiences we have prayed about.

Small group experiences help reveal God's presence and affirm, equip, and support members in their faith journeys and ministries. Small groups are best known for offering quality learning opportunities (such as preparation for baptism or confirmation, youth groups, or Bible and book studies), for serving as support groups for people with different interests or challenges or at different stages of life, or for operating pastoral care teams or outreach projects. People connect with a small group because the group meets some of their needs or the needs of others or, best of all, both.

As small groups help members relate their faith to their life experiences, they encourage us to recognize God in daily life and to use life more for God's purposes in the world. A natural response is loving, accepting, and working to help the world around us. Small groups help us see our everyday roles—as friend, child, sibling, parent, and worker—as part of a Christian vocation and as opportunities to help and serve God in the world. Small groups also help us develop practical skills for loving others. They improve our skills in being present with and listening to others as children of God, and with God as a part of the conversation. With practice, we can become more compassionate, open, and nonjudgmental so that we can offer comfort to one another around the deepest concerns of our lives. As we become more aware of and able to share our own faith stories, we also become better at seeing and saying how God might work in other situations. We hope we get better at seeing and responding to some of the physically, emotionally, and spiritually hurting people around us and ask God to work through us.

Small groups serve as vehicles for evangelizing, connecting, pastoring, equipping, and ministering. In ministering, a church community's ministry teams work best if they operate like small groups. Connection and engagement work much better with ministry teams than with church committees. In many churches, committees are assigned to oversee ministry areas. They make decisions and find separate volunteers or resources to do the ministry and then supervise them. This is a less engaging, top down approach. Self-directed ministry teams actually do the ministry for the community. There is no Christian education committee, for example. Sunday school teachers run the Sunday school. Youth leaders bring together the youth small group activities and ministry projects. This example for one ministry area can work for any ministry area. And the ministry teams will be stronger and more effective if they try to operate like successful small groups (e.g., incorporating prayer, Bible study, and formation with their ministry activities).

Small groups are wonderful settings for the goals outlined below.

Developing relationships: Individuals in small groups discover the love of a supportive community.

Providing pastoral care: If each member of a church belongs to a small group, the church is assured that a small community of faithful people is looking after the spiritual and pastoral needs of each member. The church can grow without sacrificing responsibility and accountability to individual members.

Promoting discipleship: We grow together and support and encourage one another in walking in relationship with Jesus. Christians grow together through faith sharing, becoming rooted in the gospel and Scriptures, and centering their lives in prayer. We become more disciplined by becoming accountable to one another for our faith journeys.

Reaching out in evangelism and witnessing: Active small groups tend to not just focus inward on their members. Their excitement in their faith causes them to ask, "Whom do we know who would enjoy being part of a group like ours?" As we develop true community with each other, we are also enabled to reach out together to others in the world. When small group members are committed to incorporating new people, the group can multiply and divide into new cells as the group grows;

this is why small groups are sometimes called "cell" groups. Small groups thus help the church grow. If most church members belong to a small group of about six members, and if each small group adds one person per year who also becomes a church member, a church will double in size within five years.

Growing the body of Christ: Small groups affirm that all Christians are ministers and that the work of ministry is performed by each of us. The groups provide opportunities for leadership development and gaining experience in witness and ministry.

Discerning spiritual gifts and answering God's call: Small groups are excellent settings for helping individuals identify and follow their unique vocations, use each of their spiritual gifts to help others, and live out faith in everyday life.

Building a strong foundation for the church: When small groups are strong, a church can survive and even grow and thrive in spite of any political, economic, social, or internal turmoil. This was true of first century churches and many others since.

Small groups are truly where we experience what Paul is calling us to in Ephesians 4: "all humility and gentleness, with patience, bearing with one another in love, making every effort to maintain the unity of the Spirit in the bond of peace" (Ephesians 4:2–3). Small groups are a foundation to becoming part of the body of Christ and loving God and one another. With each person who becomes involved in a small group—whether it's a Bible study, pastoral care group, prayer group, gifts course, or outreach ministry—a church becomes stronger in its worship and mission.

How small groups and ministry teams form connecting relationships

Small groups and ministry teams can create deeper relational connections with people—beyond social conversation and social conventions to really begin to get to know and care for the other person, involving more intimate conversation, empathy, support, and encouragement—as in pastoral care. In our own spiritual journeys, we have had experiences of belonging and purpose through community, and this is why our church community is so important to us.

The essentials of creating deep relational connections involve community, worship, and action, as outlined in this table:

Essentials of Effective Connecting Relationships
(Belonging + Purpose)

Community	Listening	
	Caring	
	Deep Conversation	
	Prayer	Worship
	Openness/Permeability	
	Leadership	
Action	Ministry	
	Stewardship	

Jesus shows us how to truly engage people. First, he genuinely shows that he loves them. He doesn't ask them to first believe a certain way or to do certain things (like going to church or doing things for the church or giving money). Jesus goes out and meets them where they are and truly cares for them. He does this in infinite ways, and we can also begin to do this by remembering to ask three questions that Jesus asks people he meets.

First, Jesus asks the individuals he meets what they are going through. We have more deeply considered the importance of listening to others in Chapter 2.1. When we experience people asking what we're going through—without judging us or offering quick solutions—we have this miracle of someone who truly cares. This kind of listening goes far beyond superficial conversation (about the weather, sports, jobs, children, vacations, etc.) and into deeper conversations (about hopes, dreams, aspirations, challenges, grief, suffering). These deeper conversations require vulnerability on our own part and the other person's. This is the level where we may begin to share the stories of our lives and to talk about Jesus. Through our caring, another person may begin to experience that God also cares.[2] This is what is revealed to people like Bartimaeus (Mark 10:46–52) who are surprised that Jesus is paying attention to them.

Second, Jesus asks individuals he meets what they want him to do for them. For us, this is really the same as asking what we need to pray about. At a deeper level, we connect closely, develop trust, and can introduce God into the conversation, asking "May I pray for you?" Making time for sharing and praying for one another's thanksgivings and concerns makes room for a deeper intimacy and revelation.

Third, Jesus asks the groups of people he is with, "Who isn't here who needs to be here?" Jesus is not exclusive, and he keeps inviting and welcoming others into relationship—especially, of course, the ones other people see as outcasts or "sinners." This openness or permeability seems to be hard for most groups because people are hesitant to add new people to groups they feel comfortable in. They naturally feel that they cannot trust others and be vulnerable in their conversations. But members of successful groups discover this just is not true. They continue to invite others into relationship. A group that continually invites and welcomes new members continues to grow and to create strong relational connections and ultimately may need to replicate and divide group ministries to continue to grow.

If you look at some of the examples where Christian communities are engaging new people in different ways today, you'll notice that they include these important elements of loving relationships and that they often are involved in purposeful ministries or tasks. The actual activities that groups or communities choose differ depending on particular needs they're trying to meet. In some places, we see a new focus on activities going on beyond church walls, like pub theology or community gardens or knitting ministries or grief groups or social justice or outreach teams. But at the heart of each new group or community, they first help create close, deep, and caring relationships.

Small group and ministry team practices

To successfully accomplish these objectives, small groups or ministry teams need good leadership. This leadership involves providing some structure and direction and, most importantly, creating a safe space for the members to interact. Leaders convene the group and make sure everyone participates. Leaders encourage every person to experience love, support, and spiritual development. These leaders need to help the group develop pastoral skills and an atmosphere of prayer, openness, faith sharing, trust, safety, honest respect, tolerance, and love.

To support a small group, it is always a good idea to have designated co-leaders so the group is covered when the leader is absent and so a second leader develops to lead future groups. In order to structure small groups successfully, make sure you can answer the questions *who, what, when, where,* and *how.*

Who? A small group should start with at least three to five members and a plan to grow to nine to twelve members during the period it meets by inviting other friends who might benefit.

What? People's needs vary, and more people are reached through small group ministries when a church varies the choices of small groups. Groups are stronger when they are called together based on a focus, topic, or shared need or interest rather than just being social groups. Co-leaders need to choose a focus or project they are excited about. Their enthusiasm and energy will help attract and encourage other members. Then the leaders need to be clear about the focus so that it can be described and people know what they're choosing (i.e., not just "fellowship" or "Bible study").

Making relational connections requires intentionality. We need to identify specific people we can reach and serve ("mission fields" from Matthew 9:38 and Luke 10:2) and make relational connections. Without understanding who we are trying to make relational connections with, we don't learn where and how to best make personal connections, and we are not aware of their needs and what to offer. Too often, we try to get people to want what we have rather than respond to where they are. Moreover, we need to intentionally identify people who feel called to missionary work in one of these fields. Their gifts and passions help determine who to reach; their passions match the needs of the particular mission field.

There are almost unlimited opportunities for small groups or ministry teams. They may begin by considering how to reach a particular mission field and then actually making efforts to reach people. Or they may begin by starting a mission (e.g., outreach or pastoral care) and inviting others to join in. Or they may even grow from adding a relational (small group) focus to existing ministry teams and inviting others to participate and experience this ministry. Specific groups often center around life stages (youth, young parents, seniors, grief groups), conversations (small groups, pub theology, shared activities) or ministries (pastoral care, outreach, prayer, community garden).

When? Hold meetings at a regular and convenient time during the week and not less often than twice per month—so people do not lose touch with one another even if they occasionally miss a meeting. Decide on a period for the discussion or project (often six to twelve weeks) so people know what their commitment is up front, attention is focused on the group's purpose for a concentrated period, and groups can regularly re-form and invite new members or make handoffs to and from other groups to support each individual's spiritual development. This will mean regularly starting some new small groups.

Where? Consider meeting outside the church—perhaps in someone's home or a coffee shop or restaurant or library or wherever people are served—and where people who don't feel comfortable going to church may feel at home.

How? Members of small groups need to have fun together, to share their needs, hurts, and encouragements and to pray for one another. Each small group needs primarily to be relationally oriented rather than program or agenda oriented; for example, the emphasis in a small group Bible study is more properly on application and action than on theory and knowledge.[3] A typical outline of a one-and-a-half-hour formational small group session is (i) greeting one another (five minutes); (ii) opening prayer; (iii) a video, reading, or introductory discussion (ten to twenty minutes); (iv) facilitated group discussion with outline (forty-five minutes); (v) identification of roles for next meeting (prayers, discussion facilitator, refreshments); (vi) group prayer time (sharing and praying for one another's thanksgivings and concerns); and (vii) social time and refreshments.

We ask the following of all participants:

Be open. Make room for God to do something new in your life.

Be transparent. As you openly share your hopes, fears, successes, and failures, God will use your life experiences to build faith and courage in the lives of others.

Be available to God and to each other. Get to know other members of the group. Keep your eyes open for opportunities to encourage and pray for one another.

Create a safe environment. Make the group a community where people can be heard and feel loved (no quick answers, snap judgments, or simple fixes), and keep discussions confidential among group members.

Be committed. Take this opportunity and commit yourself to make your group life a priority by attending meetings and keeping up with daily readings. Bring your study materials and Bible to each meeting.

Invite and welcome newcomers. Be clear that we are always open and welcoming and looking for people to join us on the Way. Be permeable to new members; we can always learn from others, wherever they are on their spiritual journey, and being part of a clique does not really make us safe or help us share with one another or grow. We are committed to incorporating new people and to multiplying and dividing into new cells or groups as our group grows.

Keep your focus on God and your faith. Resist the temptation to make discussions a critical and intellectual enterprise; listen for what God is doing and wants to do in your life.

Consider becoming a small group leader and trying your hand at facilitation. The strongest groups trade off responsibilities so that people can learn new roles. Remember, Jesus prepared his disciples to eventually go and confidently lead others. This kind of leadership is not limited to "experts" or specially gifted individuals. Small groups grow the way Christianity has: start the first group, invite potential lay leaders and show them how to lead, and eventually ask these members to co-lead another group. Steps of invitation, apprenticeship, training, experience, and encouragement lead to success and confidence. Over time, each group needs to select and develop apprentice leaders who are trained through experience to lead groups of their own. The effective small group model lends itself very well to the development of church leaders.

Small groups today

A small group experience might happen something like this:

Chris didn't have much time in his life for God, but he was troubled by the way his life was going. A friend stopped to listen and asked if it was OK if she prayed for him. She gently told Chris not to forget that

God wants to be part of his life, even when it's not going well.

In time, Chris and his friend returned to this discussion. She invited Chris to get together with a group of friends that regularly considered God's part in their lives. They read the Bible together. The discussion wasn't academic, and they weren't looking to pluck verses out of the Bible to understand as universal statements of absolute truth. They talked about how their personal stories might fit into God's story. This wasn't as simple as finding and following certain prescribed rules; it was about being more aware of God and their own responses. At the end of each meeting, they prayed. Chris wasn't too uncomfortable because someone just asked about his concerns and thanksgivings before beginning to pray for them. Within a few weeks, Chris saw God working amid the joys and sorrows of the experiences people prayed about. This group only met for a few weeks, and Chris hated to miss any meetings; he was glad when he was invited to join another group.

Chris found that his new friends in these groups weren't trying to change him, but to help him be more aware of God's presence. They listened to his concerns and challenged him with the deepest, most personal and loving question: Where is God in your life these days? The personal faith experiences they talked about gave him glimpses of what God was trying to do in his life, the lives of others, and the world around us, and how Chris might respond to that. Chris still had trouble believing that anyone would care about him, much less love him. These friends welcomed him, with all of his faults and differences (even things Chris felt he'd done wrong and things about him they disagreed with), and reminded him that God wanted Chris—just as he was—to have a close, loving relationship with him. Jesus wasn't waiting for Chris to do something good to earn his favor; he became human to show his love and to bridge the gap between us at any cost. Chris still found it hard to understand and accept God's love for him.

Eventually some of these friends brought Chris to Sunday worship at their church. It was different from what Chris expected. The words that came from the Bible and the pulpit spoke to his daily life as a Christian. The liturgy, music, and prayers touched him deeply and helped him experience God's presence. Chris began treating worship as a joyful response to finding God present in his life and the world, not just a place where God is present on Sundays outside the real world.

Chris accepted a new way of life with baptism. He was certain that God was calling him to surrender his life to Christ, and that would mean a new lifestyle more dependent on God. The church community welcomed Chris as a member and committed to helping him live into the role of a Christian in the world.

Chris brought other members of his family along to church, and his church friends affirmed and supported them too. Youth leaders connected with his children and encouraged them to learn about God and be aware of his presence, and to reach out to others in fellowship and service. The family even began to pray together and discuss their faith at the dinner table.

Today, Chris says his church helps reveal God's presence and affirms, equips, and supports him in his faith journey and ministry. He spends some time in spiritual practices of praying, reading the Bible, and worshiping, and sometimes he attends retreats or conferences. He continues to participate in small groups that help him relate his faith to his life experiences. Of course Chris helps out in church, but he doesn't feel his church is concentrating so much on what happens within the organization. His friends remind him that they aren't only to focus on holiness or the church, but on loving, accepting, and working to help the world around us. They encourage him to recognize God in his daily life and to use his life more for God's purposes in the world. Chris recognizes that he needs to integrate his faith into his daily life, rather than just balancing his ordinary life with his church life so that he can become a more active church member.

Chris realizes that church isn't enough and he needs to do the work of Christian ministry in his own life. His everyday roles as friend, child, sibling, parent, and worker are part of his Christian vocation and are opportunities to help and serve God in the world. Chris understands that Jesus and his church friends expect him to learn to live and serve as a priest in his everyday world. To do that, Chris needs to continue learning and practicing new approaches and skills.

Chris has discovered that the skills he needs are not just spiritual practices or knowledge and that he can't get them just by focusing on a particular topic like evangelism or Bible study or ethics or organizational development. He needs practical skills for loving others. Chris needs to improve his skills in being present with and listening to others as children of God, and with God as a part of the conversation. He wants to become more compassionate, open, and nonjudgmental so that he can offer comfort to others around the deepest concerns of their lives. He feels he even needs to understand basic first aid and counseling skills, and to know where people can find more skilled assistance with physical, emotional, psychological, or spiritual problems. As Chris is more aware of and able to share his own faith story, he is also becoming better at seeing and saying how God might work in other situations. Chris asks God to work through him, and he tries to trust and permit God to help him take greater risks and do more than he is capable of doing himself when he reaches out to others.

Chris feels he's getting better at seeing and responding to some of the hurting people around him. Sometimes, with God's help, he risks reaching out to them. Not long ago, he spent time with a coworker and empathetically listened to her story of the challenges she was facing with a serious disease; he asked if he could pray for her and her family and gently told her not to forget that God wants to be part of her life, even when it's not going well.[4]

Building community through small groups

Church growth statistics show that today it is even more important for individuals to be involved in small groups that apply Christian messages to daily life than to attend corporate worship. Small groups are building blocks of church communities because they involve people more personally and more fully than full corporate community activities. Attendance is better in small groups than in corporate worship; attendance in small groups also improves attendance in corporate worship. Each of us needs the inspiration, instruction, and universal vision of the larger church; and each of us needs to integrate and express our relationships with God and one another through a closer interaction with other growing Christians. Small groups are an essential part of our Christian journey.

Small groups or ministry teams are much more simple, flexible, adaptable, and accountable than the larger community. Small groups or ministry teams can come and go—form for a purpose, develop for a ministry, disperse more easily when that ministry is completed or loses energy, and reform in new configurations for other compelling purposes. Ideally, a group of people focuses on its task together, takes care of one another, and gets a job done. The whole community does not have to be brought along to do everything. Two or three people who are passionate about a ministry bring in other passionate people to help them. Of course, this requires shared ministry, new structures of authority, and intentional and effective development of small group and ministry team leaders.

Small groups and ministry teams are effective ways to build community because they can connect with people at more points and directly involve them in the Christian Way from meeting Jesus (evangelization, incarnation) to coming to know Jesus (formation, discipleship) to serving Jesus in active ministry (outreach, apostleship). Sometimes these activities can occur more naturally and be integrated more effectively right in ministry team activities instead of trying to balance the full range of separate church activities (evangelizing, connecting, forming or training, preparing and sending into ministry) in different functions. Small groups and ministry teams create enduring friendships, encounters and closer relationships with God, personal and team challenges, learning and growth, and a sense of significance and satisfaction. However, this requires excellent leadership at the ministry team or small group level.

These connecting relationships no longer happen, as they have for centuries, primarily through place or programs. The social, political, and religious expectations that brought people to church no longer exist. That's fine and gives us the opportunity to live more like first century Christians in this twenty-first century. When we begin to set goals for our church community, we need to think about how to create these connecting relationships.

Engaging Jesus

To continue engaging Jesus, read and reflect on Luke 24:13–35.

Questions for Personal Reflection:

1. Has Jesus appeared in your life at unexpected times or in an unexpected manner?

2. Do you see Jesus in each person you happen to walk down a path with in your day-to-day life? When you look at another person, do you see someone who is worthy of Christ's message? Someone whom God loves beyond measure? Do you see Jesus himself, lost, hurting, and alone? Or do you see just another person?

3. How has your congregation or small group nourished your personal spiritual journey?

Questions for Group Discussion:

1. In Luke 24:13–35, there are two instances of Jesus appearing when two or three are gathered (Matthew 18:20). Does this still happen? When?

2. Two friends, people who had known Jesus—who had walked with him, talked with him, and eaten meals with him—didn't recognize him even on a seven-mile walk. There is a difference between seeing and recognizing. The disciples were looking at a man who happened to be traveling along the same road they were. They did not see Jesus because they did not expect to see Jesus. How do we recognize Jesus? How do we help others to see him?

3. What is the importance of asking Jesus to stay?

4. What is the experience disciples have when Jesus is revealed?

5. What is the experience of "eyes opened, hearts burning" like? How and where do people experience it?

6. How do people have "eyes opened, hearts burning" experiences through your church community?

7. Describe an activity in your church community when you personally felt most touched, excited, or transformed. How did it feel? What did you learn? Why was it special?

8. Where is the greatest energy in your community right now?

9. How might we support more "eyes opened, hearts burning" experiences?

10. Where do we feel God's presence?

11. Many of you have experienced the Holy Spirit's presence in small groups. What do small groups offer their members? What have you experienced in small groups such as Bible studies and prayer groups? Begin a list of the important things that happen in small groups.

12. Why are small groups important?

13. What kinds of small groups does your community have?

14. Which ministries does your community operate through committees? Ministry teams?

15. How could your ministry teams act more like small groups?

16. Are your small groups integrating experiences of meeting Jesus (evangelization, incarnation), coming to know Jesus (formation, discipleship) and serving Jesus in active ministry (outreach, apostleship)? Are individuals in small groups loving God and loving other people with aspects of our whole being (mind—knowledge, heart—passion, soul—spiritual growth, and strength—doing)?

3.4

Helping People Act
from Their Giftedness

A church cannot function as the body of Christ (Romans 12, 1 Corinthians 12, Colossians 1) without involving each person. Christianity requires our involvement. This tells us something important about our mission as congregations: If we want to help people become stronger Christians and we want to have healthier communities, we need to get individuals in our church communities involved in serving others.

Each person is most authentic—and most joyful—when he or she uses the gifts God has given to become the unique person God calls him or her to be.[1] One of the wonders of our faith is that we discover even greater spiritual gifts by using our gifts (1 Corinthians 14:12).[2] We experience what it means to be part of the body of Christ and to grow more and more into that body (Ephesians 4). God has made each of us and made us each uniquely to love and serve God and one another. For the church to become more of the body of Christ, each person needs to bring and use their special gifts in the community of faith. A church community has all of the gifts it needs to become the body of Christ. Often the greatest challenge is that those gifts are not being opened—they are not being unwrapped—and used. Sadly, many Christians either are not involved in a ministry or participate in a ministry that does not match their gifts. This happens when people are not fully encouraged and helped to discover and use their gifts in community.

Understanding the variety of gifts

Christian communities are more successful when they bring a variety of gifts to meet needs in different and effective ways. Gordon T. Smith, the dean of a Presbyterian seminary in Canada, offers a metaphor to show how people with different competencies or callings feel the need to respond in different ways to the brokenness of the world and how each gift is needed. His example considers the seven diverse expressions of giftedness described by Saint Paul in Romans 12: prophecy, teaching, service, encouragement, giving, leading, mercy. Smith describes how each of these different gifts might be used to respond to problems in a hospital emergency room.

As each gifted person enters the emergency room of a hospital, they immediately encounter a dark, discouraging, and unhealthy place. Hurting people are lying there unattended. Members of the nursing staff are outside smoking. People with each different gift will respond differently in identifying what has gone wrong and what needs to happen to make it go right.

Prophecy: The prophet's instinct is not so much to foretell the future but to call people back to God. A prophet says the problem with this world is that people know better, but they are not doing what they know they should be doing. So a prophet calls people back to that which they know is true. "You know this is true, but look at your behavior: it's not consistent with what you believe." You can see why prophets are not the most popular people; they say things we would not like to hear. The prophet's response to the emergency room situation is to say the medical staff know what they should do and we need to call them back to that.

Teaching: A teacher identifies the problem as not that people understand and do not function properly, but that people do not understand. The remedy is through education and learning. The teacher's response to the emergency room situation is to say the medical staff needs training—perhaps a workshop or a seminar.

Service: A servant believes that we will be able to respond to the deep needs of this world through practical tangible helps. People who think they'll fix world problems through words are crazy. Practical things need to be done, and a servant responds by seeing what needs to be done and doing it. A service-oriented person's response to the emergency room situation is to say you can't just go talk to or teach the medical staff; there's work that needs to be done. The servant would immediately start cleaning up and fixing things, doing the practical things that need to be done to make this hospital work.

Encouragement: The problem is not that people do not know what's wrong with this world (or this emergency room) or are not responding to it, the problem is that they've lost hope. The problem needs to be turned around through the restoration of courage or the restoration of hope. So some people will want to find words or actions of encouragement. Encouragers might support what people are doing in the hospital or brighten the space up and make it more cheery. They would use the right words or actions to animate others, to bring them hope in the midst of the darkness.

Giving: Givers are people who generously contribute to the needs of others. God gives people the gift to make or raise money and to generously give it away in a way that makes it possible for crucial institutions to survive, to thrive, and to make a difference. Givers are inclined to say the only way this hospital will work is with more and better resources. And they know where to raise money and how to make improvements. We may not equate this gift with the other gifts. We see these people leaving the hospital and wonder where they are going. They are going to respond to the situation in a practical way.

Administration: A good manager solves the problems of this world (and this hospital) by coordinating activities so the work of various people contributes to a common goal. An administrator walks into this hospital and says, "I know where to find superb doctors and nurses and supervisors. I can get people to make this space an enlivening, animating, healthy space. I can find people to help fund all this."

Mercy: People with the gift of mercy respond to the people who are actually hurting by showing mercy and compassion. These people offer pastoral care by being present with people, empathizing with them, and bearing their burdens. This is the role of the chaplain in the emergency room, and pastoring to and praying with people helps them heal.

Each of these seven responses to the world has an implicit perspective on the world. Each gift sees the world and feels the world differently, and each gift responds to the brokenness of the world in unique ways. Each of these gifts turns out to be an essential part of God's redemptive power in this world. We need them all to complete the body of Christ.

Using everyone's gifts

At the root of the church becoming the body of Christ is a belief in people's potentials and a conviction that each person brings special gifts that are to be used in the community of faith. In *Leadership is an Art*, Max DePree envisions a community with a great deal of trust: "We need to be able to count on the other person's special competence. ... We can see that without each individual, we are not going to go very far as a group. By ourselves we suffer serious limitations. Together we can be something wonderful."[3]

In some communities, improper distinctions are made between "gifts" of clergy and laity. This is not just the fault of the clergy. Many lay people today do not see the spiritual life of the church as their responsibility and leave it up to professional clergy. Lay people may resist taking significant responsibilities for evangelism, for forming disciples, for pastoral care and outreach, for stewardship, for oversight, for building up the church. There are churches without clergy simply waiting for a priest or pastor. There are churches with clergy measuring their progress in terms of what the priest or pastor does. There are parishioners who say, "We can't start a Bible study or prayer group without clergy." Why not?

There is too much of a pastor-centered consumer mentality in many churches. The priest or pastor is idealized as a "speaker, counselor, academic, public relations specialist, organizer, social worker, evangelist, master of ceremonies, teacher and competent at everything else, except perhaps walking on water."[4] Dennis Campbell tells of a time when he asked parishioners to list his functions as their priest. Four pages into the list, a "saint" remarked that it would be impossible for anyone to do everything listed. Dennis replied, "Yes, it is impossible, and that is why we need everyone to minister. I can't even oversee all of this ministry alone. That's why there have to be some of you who are willing to serve as leaders and share that responsibility."[5] Adopting a paradigm of strong lay involvement in ministry became a turning point in that congregation: "It was a pivotal moment in our life together when, as a congregation, we learned a new understanding of what ministry can and should be."[6]

Christian Schwarz reminds readers both that the Reformation criticized the view of clergy as especially holy because they administered sacraments and that clergy are not spiritual gurus simply by virtue of their positions as leaders.[7] He warns that a priest or pastor is often condemned to mediocrity and ineffectiveness because he or she is not gifted in all these areas. Our priests and pastors have special gifts—as each of us do—and we need to discover them and share them in the body of Christ. No spiritual gifts are exclusive to clergy, and no cleric has all of the gifts needed in the body of Christ. Lay members are not simply helpers to the priest or pastor who cannot do all of the tasks a priest "should" perform. We need to celebrate each other's particular gifts and support each other with the diversity of our gifts. As we are all servants, ministry in a congregation is collaborative, not hierarchical; it is based more on using all individual gifts than on any position or authority.[8]

We are each critically important to achieving our purposes, and we each need to receive and accept meaningful assignments we can successfully achieve. This means that each of us needs to find tasks for which we are gifted. The body of Christ will be unbalanced unless all of its members grow.

Discerning spiritual gifts

Many churches have an effective process for discerning gifts for ordained ministry and need to further develop a discernment process in contemplation of sending all people into the world to minister. Healthy churches adopt systems to meet people and help them identify their gifts and passions and then provide affirmation, training, coaching, and resources for individuals to live into their ministries. It is not enough to operate in an organizational model of volunteerism, asking people to volunteer for various activities without first identifying their gifts or desires for those particular ministries.

Discernment helps with an understanding of vocation, identification of spiritual gifts, and application of gifts within the body of Christ. Like Jesus, we have come from God, and God is the source of each of our lives and who we are. With abundant love for each one of us, God makes every person as unique and special as an individual fingerprint. Each of us has our own origins, personalities, skills, perspectives, passions, and roles in God's kingdom. We each also have a need to understand how God has uniquely made us and who God is calling us to be. Each individual has a unique mission to respond to God's calling in the world. A person can't simply measure himself or herself against some third-party objective standard of who they "should" be. Rather than thinking that there is a single way to serve God, each individual needs to be aware of his or her unique context and personality and hear God's particular call.

Because God has made us, God knows us better than we know ourselves. And we are our most authentic selves when we respond to who God has made us to be or is calling us to become. What God is calling you to do, your "vocation," will be the same as your true identity and your most genuine self. You are most authentic and most fulfilled when you use the life God gives you to become the person God calls you to be. If you know your true purpose from God, you can more easily decide which paths you are called to take on your spiritual journey. We must each respond to our unique lives and identities in order to hear and understand God's call.

Discernment is challenging because it requires us to distinguish between God's call for us and other distracting calls from our egos, our careers, our culture, and so on. Each act of spiritual discovery is as unique and individual as our personal gifts (1 Corinthians 12:4–7). Each of us is responsible for discovering the uniqueness of God's love for us: the special gifts God gives us and the individual purpose to which God calls us. We can't look to some objective standard to discover the direction of our personal spiritual journey; discernment is much more than a one-time personality or career test and much more than a regular procedure that reaches a specific result.[9] Discernment needs to be intentional, deliberate, and spiritual; it is truly a wonderful process during which we take time to listen to our deepest natures. Discernment occurs not just through individual creativity but through deeper relationships with God; that means we need to follow spiritual practices, such as prayer, that help us spend time with God (Luke 11:9–10). We often wonder what we are to do to have a closer relationship with God. But there are also times when we feel a sense of purpose, a sense of direction to a new activity or destination. That sense tends to be unique and individual, and we tend to recognize it as our deepest personal nature. This sense of purpose is *vocation*. As we discover a vocation, or calling, we recognize God's call to use unique gifts God has given us for God's purposes.

Discernment is not just finding out information (on our own or from God or other people) and making a decision. Our discernment is actually a revelation of ourselves in relationship with God and the family of God. Closer relationships and improving awareness are the fruits of an open and ongoing life process. Discernment flows from an endeavor of living our lives with

- an *awareness* of God's presence in them;

- a *trust* that God will take us where he wants us to go, but that he will also give us choices of how we wish to follow;

- a *practice* of careful listening for opportunities God is offering and perhaps calling us to; and

- a *reliance* on God that allows us to be less concerned about our material well-being and more concerned about what we'll create in relationship with him.

Real discernment is ongoing in relationship with God and one another, not just a process of planning and decision making. When we have a better sense of how God has made us and what he is calling us to do, we can be faithful to God's creation and calling.

Discernment for ministry often occurs best in community (Matthew 18:19–20). Our ministries are not just our own; they are from and for the community as well, and others will support us and enable us in our ministries. Our own perspectives are limited, and we learn better as we lovingly and respectfully share our thoughts and gain insights from others. Leaders may particularly help a person grow into a particular ministry (Jeremiah 3:15; see also chapter 5.4). But we need to receive insights from others critically, recognizing the possibilities for error even in Christian community and taking personal responsibility (Philippians 2:12–13). So how do we begin to discern in community? One beginning is with confirmation and baptismal preparation programs. Other good resources are gifts discernment courses.[10] Several people may support one another to mutually discern and to learn particular skills at the same time in training sessions.

Each of us needs—as we look around at others in our church community—to recognize each person's special gifts, passions, abilities, personalities, and experiences.[11] We need to remember that God has brought each one into community for a purpose, because of his or her uniqueness and interdependence (incompleteness without one another).

One of the greatest responsibilities is helping adult Christians mature in their faith (Ephesians 4) by discovering and using their spiritual gifts in service to God and other people. We can always do better at identifying gifts and desires for particular ministries, developing our gifts to serve others, and supporting people in serving others. Practical steps include the following:

> *Help people identify ministries.* This includes sharing our stories, especially about our ministries, what different people do in them, and how to participate. This is an important description of our common identity as well as the basis for making specific invitations to participate.

> *Help people identify their own skills, spiritual gifts and passions for ministry* (possibly through a spiritual gifts course, if not less formally). Here the caution is to base invitations to ministry on discernment of personal gifts, not just needs or a "volunteerism" model.

> *Bless people by inviting them into ministry.* (Too often we rely on clergy for this.) All leaders need to be aware and make invitations—not necessarily just from our own needs, but broadly—so that everyone feels connected. Many people do not feel invited unless they receive personal invitations.

> *Help people to be successful in ministries* through mentoring, training, or apprenticeship. This is needed in simple outreach opportunities and even more so in the development of people who will minister in more complicated roles such as pastoral care or small groups.

> *Support and follow up with people* to check in, deal with (emotional) ministry challenges and celebrate successes. Sometimes this involves helping people find their next ministry or a better fit.

A key role in Christian growth and church development is helping Christians find the place in community and the world where God calls them to serve. Any act of giving more of our lives to God is an act of stewardship and self-discovery and helps us learn to live in a closer relationship with God and with a sense of grace, blessing, and joy:

- We turn our attention to God in a way very like prayer.

- We appreciate the blessings we have received and express our gratitude.

- We experience more keenly our dependence on God for everything and begin to understand that everything we are and have comes from God.

- We respond to God by offering something back to God for God's use and service.

- We let God begin to transform us by reprioritizing our lives to pay attention to him and by becoming more aware of his presence.

- We experience joy from giving God a greater part in our lives as we purposefully use our gifts and undergo transformation.

A paradox of God's kingdom is that we find meaning, purpose, and fulfillment not by getting something more but by using what we have received in God's service. God has given us gifts of time, talent, and treasure, and we have an opportunity to give some of these back and to find fulfillment in serving God. When we take a small risk, when we make ourselves the least bit vulnerable, we allow God to work in our lives and to use us. Sometimes what God calls us to do will cost a whole lot, but most of the time, it will be something smaller, something that is just enough for us to feel our dependence on God and to show God and ourselves that we trust and need him. If we risk something, we really discover where the gifts have come from. And we show our trust in our God who furiously loves us and wants to provide even more for us—especially the opportunity to participate in God's kingdom.

Engaging Jesus

To continue engaging Jesus, read and reflect on 1 Corinthians 12.

Questions for Personal Reflection:

1. Do you feel that you have a unique relationship with God—a journey in which you participate with God in the creation of your life and identity?

2. Are there important aspects of your life that you simply allow to happen as they may? What might be different if you took charge of them and asked for God's help?

3. Do you regularly reflect on the opportunities and choices you have in your life and listen for God's calling in them?

4. Are you more likely to listen for God when you're happy or troubled or in between?

5. Try to answer the following questions:

    What brings me joy? What are the desires of my heart? What am I passionate about? What motivates, energizes, animates me? What do I long for? Would I grieve if I didn't do this?

    What are the talents and abilities that God has given me? What can I do well and in a way that pleases God? What are talents, competencies, and capacities might I make available to God and nurture by education and practice?

    What is my unique situation, and what are the opportunities that I have? Where am I in the world? Where can I go from here? What are my background and experiences? What limitations, responsibilities, and possibilities do I have?

    What is my personality? What is my way of acting and responding to others, to my world, and to myself?

    What are my spiritual gifts? God gives us spiritual gifts to support our ministries.

One way to identify our gifts is by understanding how we feel the need to respond to the brokenness of the world. Perhaps you feel that what the world needs most is prayer or hope or teaching or prophecy or faith or giving or encouragement or leadership or service. Of course, the world needs all of these gifts, but you have been given a particular gift to add.

6. Can you identify ways in which your gifts and vocations draw you more closely into relationship with God?

7. "Discernment does not imply fully comprehending God's will, but rather it raises the question, What is the next step God wants me to take?"[12] What is a next step God might want you to take?

Questions for Group Discussion:

1. Why does Paul compare spiritual gifts to the body?

2. Why is it important for each of us to identify our spiritual gifts and participate in the body of Christ?

3. How are spiritual gifts unique? What does this say about our necessity to the body?

4. How are we each incomplete? What does that say about our need for unity and love? (What Bible chapter follows this one, and how are they related?)

5. How does knowing oneself support humility? Why is humility important to the spiritual life? How does humility bring us closer to God?

6. How can identifying your gifts help you with discernment?

7. How could overemphasizing your gifts prevent discernment?

8. How is your church applying 1 Peter 4:10 ("Like good stewards of the manifold grace of God, serve one another

with whatever gift each of you has received")? Have you moved from a model of "volunteerism" to a model of gifts discernment and call?

9. How do we identify and use people's special gifts? (Also consider Romans 12 and Ephesians 4.)

10. Why is it important for each of us to discover our gifts and vocation and participate in the body of Christ?

11. Are there different roles for lay or clergy? What is ordained ministry?

12. What does this mean for our roles in the church and the world?

13. Are lay people in this church fully involved, or do they tend to leave the clergy with much of the responsibility?

14. Are people in the church getting the practical help they need to discover their spiritual gifts and to develop an appropriate ministry?

15. How might we help others discover their special gifts and encourage them to use them?

16. How could we support a more involved laity?

17. What are you passionate about doing together as a church community? What gifts do you have, and how will you contribute?

18. According to Paul, what holds the body of Christ together?

19. How do we want our ministry and mission to happen?

20. Has your church started to fall into some of the traps of the clergy dominance paradigm?

21. How do we empower others for ministry and mission?

22. What do we need to do differently to empower all members of the body of Christ?

23. Can we look at each of our congregation's goals as mutual ministry opportunities?

24. Are we prepared to make good handoffs in formation and ministry? Who is responsible for supporting each person's spiritual journey?

3.5

Supporting Holistic Life in Community

A significant challenge we have as Christians and as Christian communities is including and supporting the seemingly diverse aspects of community life into a Christian way that simply follows Jesus. How do we do this when church communities have so many activities or processes to manage? How do we do this as individuals who want to pray, learn, worship, and serve? How do we keep the main thing—walking with Jesus—the main thing? We need to intentionally choose and structure activities of our church community to balance or integrate them in a Way that follows Jesus.

A church that follows Jesus strives to be

- *incarnational* by showing forth God's love for people and creation;

- *discipling* by helping people live into the loving relationships of God's kingdom; and

- *apostolic* by sending people to love and serve God and other people in the world.

In other words, we invite people to *come and see Jesus*, to *come and know Jesus*, and to *come and serve Jesus*—all to experience and share the depth and breadth of God's love. A church community needs to be a "crucible" for growth, not focused just on single aspects of the Christian journey but on bringing people into a holistic Christian way of life. A

crucible is a vessel, place, or event for transformation to occur.[1] In God's kingdom, this transformation occurs through sharing loving actions. A church community is thus a crucible for us to become more actively and more fully loving. In this sense, the incarnational, discipling, and apostolic activities of the church are the same. We are being transformed by being loved and by loving God and other people with our whole hearts, minds, strengths, and souls. To the greatest extent possible, church communities need to engage people on the Way with holistic experiences of connection, growth, and service.

Church communities with a purpose of connecting and forming people in relationship with God experience greater vitality. When these churches speak of "building up the body of Christ," they aren't speaking of building the organization or facilities or even the community of the church. They are speaking of building up the people of God who are called and formed to experience God's kingdom. Formational activities of a church community include sacraments and celebrations, social activities, nurturance and education, and discernment of vocation and spiritual gifts—that often happen within church buildings. All of this is important to community and discipleship. Vitality comes from connecting with others in community and coming to know Jesus. People experience life with Jesus and with one another. The church community is not losing sight of Jesus as it helps people begin to live into God's kingdom.

Nevertheless, something vital may still be missing from effective discipling or "shepherding" communities. A challenge for church communities is that so many of our efforts may center around building community or preparing people for ministry that we neglect the kingdom purpose of sharing the gospel with the world. Living into Jesus' Way takes more than developing lifelong learners in a secular sense; people must learn to participate in God's ongoing creation in the world. Churches are less vital than they could be if they are missing opportunities to help people live and serve in God's kingdom.

People learn better to live a new way of life from the spiritual breakthroughs they experience by finding and serving others. When Jesus is present in our lives and we act as disciples, we can begin to help bring others to Jesus (Matthew 28:19–20, Mark 16:15, Acts 1:8) by making invitations to "come and see" and sharing love. We also need to serve others through outreach, compassion, advocacy, and peacemaking ministries, as social minister Jack Jezreel explains: "The critical Christian insight, drawn from Matthew 25, is that this sending is a necessary part, a constitutive part of what it means to be in relationship to God. Whenever we tend to the poor, hungry and naked, we tend to Jesus. To know compassion for God's poor is to know God. If we do not have compassion for those in need, we do not know God."[2] Through involvement in our unique mission and ministries, we see the signs and wonders of lives—including our own—being turned toward God.

Shepherding and missionary communities

A church might consider whether it is both a "shepherding" and a "missionary" community. The traits are compared in the following table.

Shepherding (Peter) (John 21)	Missionary (Paul) (Matthew 10)
"Whenever we have an opportunity, let us work for the good of all, and especially for those of the family of faith." (Galatians 6:9–10)	"Jesus said to them again, 'Peace be with you. As the Father has sent me, so I send you.'" (John 20:21, Matthew 28:19–20, Mark 16:15, Acts 1:8)
Serves others in the church (through fellowship, community, pastoral care, etc.)	Serves others in the world
Brings new people to church	Meets people where they are in a way that causes them to ask why people care about them
Invites people to membership in our patterns of life (worship, fellowship, formation, church work)	Proclaims the gospel: "I am a disciple of Jesus. I am serving him by serving you, because that's what he came to do."
Helps people get the foundations for membership and full participation	Helps people share life in Jesus (through God talk, personal faith sharing, life-experience-based discussion, serving others)

Has ministries primarily at church, targeted to church members or visitors	Has ministries primarily outside church, targeted to people in need; runs church as minimally and efficiently as possible
Grows church members and leaders through church work	Has ministries in church to help in preparation and blessing for mission
Grows in church budget, staff, facilities, and membership	Has a growing presence in the world
Expects people to participate in church; is pastoral or paternal	Expects people to participate in the kingdom; is service-oriented or brotherly

Either a "shepherding" church or a "missionary" church may be living into the Great Commission and the Great Commandment. But shepherding and missions are both ways to participate in the kingdom of God, and they need to go hand in hand. A church community is limited if it describes itself as either a "shepherding" church or a "missionary" church. Without the activities of shepherding, the foundation of the missionary church will be much weaker. And without the actions of sending, the reach of the shepherding church will be much smaller.[3] Although shepherding activities help us prepare for mission, "churches that emphasize gathering and not sending no longer even do gathering well, for we lose a sense of what we are gathering for, what we're preparing for, what we're praying for, what we're learning for, what we're being formed for."[4] And the converse is also true. The church finds purpose and unity in mission if people are centered in God and community and prepared for that mission. We need to meet Jesus, to get ready, and to go serve.

Maintenance churches

The least vital and healthy church communities are neither doing much to form people in relationship with God and one another nor doing much to involve them in caring for others. These churches tend to operate in a maintenance mode, focusing inward. In these communities, it is hard for church members not to see ministry as something that happens primarily at church, especially when clergy are accepted as the primary ministers of the church. Focusing on the need to financially and administratively "maintain" or "preserve" the facilities and operations, they ask, "Can we afford to do this?" even before they have asked, "Are we called by God to do this?" A shortage of money or people may become an excuse for not doing things a church needs to do. Denominational aid or use of endowments may become ongoing necessities rather than a way to new life and growth. As a church scrambles for resources, people may be tempted to think in terms of "us and them" and start to act parochial and fragmented. Life drains out of a community when keeping people in or attracting people to worship or church activities becomes more about surviving than about transforming lives with love:

> [Any time] we hear congregations wishing that the people in the community would become active in their church ... "to keep our programs running and our doors open," we know that the congregation is in trouble. It has moved to the point at which people beyond its doors are valued primarily for what they can bring to the church. People in the community are seen as the congregation's salvation, rather than the other way around. ... The real and deeper issue is that the congregation has lost connection with a Christian church's basic mission: helping people experience God and connect with the gospel message of life and hope. ... Without this sense of mission to keep the congregation focused beyond the doors of the church, the congregation turns inward and loses connection with its community. Before others will turn to a congregation as a life-giving resource in their lives, the congregation has to be a place that offers life.[5]

Churches focusing on maintenance have lost their way. Certainly, we need organization, facilities, and administration to accomplish our purposes, but these are tools, not ends. Following Jesus is the source of joy and fulfillment in our lives (John 10:10). Our church community needs to change if we aren't experiencing a joy and vitality so overpowering that we feel compelled to share it.

When we follow Jesus by pursuing his mission in the world, we become healthy and grow, not just struggle to maintain where we are. We lessen the situations in which we need to be reactive. We are better stewards and more accountable for the gifts we receive, because we use them for decided purposes and prioritize our activities to best accomplish those purposes.

Traditional Programs

With these lessons in mind—and striving for greater growth and vitality—churches often develop specific plans for evangelism, formation, and service. For evangelism, some churches focus on becoming more welcoming through newcomer ministries and encouraging individuals and small groups to develop relationships with people outside of church and bring them to church. For formation, some churches develop more small groups in which individuals may discover the love of a supportive community, become rooted in the gospel and Scriptures, center their lives in prayer, experience the power of God's presence in their lives, discern and follow their unique vocations, and, eventually, gain experience in witness and ministry. Many churches become involved in helping others with pastoral care ministries or community outreach ministries. Some churches develop specific ministries on their own to meet identified local needs, such as shelters or food pantries. Other churches partner with other agencies to meet the needs of the larger community. These agencies become part of the outreach ministries of the church by involving church volunteers, financial contributors, and individuals who lift up their work in prayer.

Traditional churches are structured to do these things through programs. They have learned and implemented processes to bring people to church, form them in the faith, involve them in social activities and ministry, and send them out for mission or outreach.

Not long ago, traditional churches might have expected people to give two hours each week at church for each of these five basic activities (worship, faith formation, social events, ministry, and outreach). Today fewer people are making that kind of commitment to church membership.

An individual may also consider how to participate in each aspect of connection, growth, and service as a path of personal spiritual growth.[6]

A Traditional Process of Discipleship in Church Community

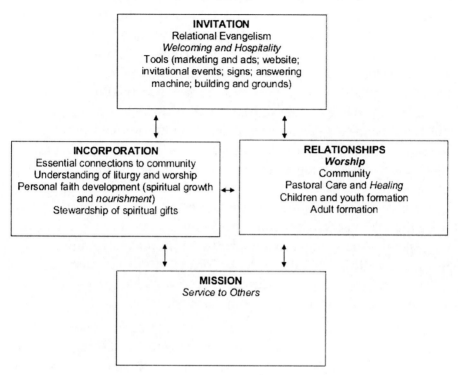

I may need to come and see Jesus day by day through worship, prayer, and other disciplines. I may need to come to know Jesus better through Christian formation. And I may need to serve Jesus in particular ministries. It's often tempting to focus on a particular aspect of this journey, but I need to stretch to grow along this spiritual path toward a more balanced or integrated life.[7]

Moving to integrated lives

Jesus said, "You shall love the Lord your God with all your heart, and with all your soul, and with all your mind, and with all your strength" (Mark 12:30, quoting Deuteronomy 6:5). We must engage our whole beings—to see God, know God, and act with God—to experience and share God's love.

Can we do it all? There is an important distinction between balance and integration. Balance is finding equilibrium among contrasting, opposing, or interacting elements of our life together; it's trying to reconcile competing claims for our time and resources. Churches try to balance their activities with prioritization and allocation in budgets, mission statements, project choices, communications, and staff (positions or time). In contrast, integration is combining and coordinating separate parts or elements of the Christian life into a unified whole; integration makes the sum greater than its parts. Integration occurs when doing fewer activities actually promotes shepherding—stronger connections, inclusion, confidence, competence, unity, and collaboration—at the same time people are actively involved in mission—serving others. Integration may provide a simpler and more holistic experience than balancing too many competing interests. When people recognize that less is more, they can simplify activities by avoiding or removing anything that is unnecessarily complicated, confusing, excessive, exhausting or wasteful—and come up with a better result for the community and the mission.[8] This is what a "rule" or "order" of life of a religious community tries to accomplish. Nearly everyone would like to replace hectic and unbalanced lives with greater integration.

A church community can support and help people grow in closer and more dynamic and holistic relationships with God through integrating experiences involving their hearts, heads, and hands. For example, evangelism engages people more fully if it stresses caring for people and ministering to their needs, sharing the gospel, and relying on prayer and the supernatural power of the Spirit. A small group engages people more fully if it operates as a small faith community by praying together, studying together, supporting one another, *and* reaching out together in social ministries to serve brothers and sisters who are struggling or suffering, to advocate for justice, or to seek peace. Jack Jezreel, founder of Just-Faith, helps identify Christian communities that take more integrated approaches to Christian life:

- The Catholic Worker movement, the Missionaries of Charity, and Benedictine, Franciscan, Jesuit, and other religious communities where people are formed with a purpose to serve others for Christ. "You see, the logic of most religious communities is that they had work to do, that they were called to serve the poor and vulnerable. There were schools to build for poor immigrant children; there were hospitals to build to serve the poor; there were people on the streets of Calcutta who needed love."

- The Church of the Savior in Washington, D.C., where "membership entails an explicit commitment to mission involvement as well as to the community": "In small mission groups, members gather around a shared vision for embodying healing and hope—the outward journey—and the group then becomes accountable to one another for the inward journey, including ordered practices in the areas of prayer, study, money, health, work life and so on. In this way the mission group members, and all with whom they are in relationship on the outward journey, help each other find fullness of life."

- A 3,000-member evangelical church in a Denver suburb which "gathers for worship on the first and third Sundays of the month. On the second and fourth Sundays of the month, however, they go—all 3,000—to a poor neighborhood park and rebuild the playground; two weeks later they rehab a block of houses owned by retired and low income elderly; two weeks later they serve a dinner for an entire neighborhood in distress and become friends."

- A Catholic church in Portland, Oregon, that is purposely located in an area with a large homeless population. This is "a place where all are welcome: where homeless men and women are welcome—welcome to take baths *and* welcome to pray; where addicts are welcome to get something to eat and get access to rehab options *and* are welcome to liturgy; where the mentally ill can get counsel, practical *and* spiritual. . . . Every year dozens of young people commit themselves to working full-time as volunteers at this church precisely because it . . . feeds their faith . . . and . . . forms their lives . . . and . . . gives them a glimpse of Jesus' life and mission." [9]

Often, small groups and ministry teams are created not just to accomplish defined tasks but also to offer holistic experiences of connection, growth, and service. Through these relationships, we engage in a more integrated and holistic Christian way that all at once invites us into loving community, serves the world, and transforms our lives.

Engaging Jesus

To continue engaging Jesus, read and reflect on Luke 10:1–24.

Questions for Personal Reflection:

1. Do you need a Christian community to support your spiritual journey?

2. How could a Christian community better support you in your journey?

3. Do you have a calling to help "build up" the church? Is that the same as or different from "building up" God's kingdom?

4. How healthy and vital is your path with Jesus? Where does your vitality come from? Where does your vitality show? How could you become more vital?

5. At this point in your life, are you focused more on connection, growth, or service?

6. Is your life balanced? Integrated? How could you get better balance? Better integration?

7. How does your church community help you find balance? Integration?

Questions for Group Discussion:

1. What are the purposes of a church community? What is a church for?

2. How can Christian communities change the world?

3. How are Christian communities following where Jesus leads? How are they not?

4. What is ministry? How is a community centered in God different from human communities?

5. Is your church or ministry area

   a. *incarnational* by showing forth God's love for people and creation?

   b. *discipling* by helping people live into the loving relationships of God's kingdom?

   c. *apostolic* by sending people to love and serve God and other people in the world?

6. Is your church more of a "shepherding" church or a "missionary" church? Why does a church community need characteristics of both?

7. How much vitality does your church community have? Where does its vitality show? Where does its vitality come from? How could your church become more vital?

8. Does your church have ministries of evangelism, formation, and service? Where is the emphasis? How effective is your church community at balancing its ministries?

9. Which projects or activities in your community integrate elements of connection, growth, and service? What do people experience there?

10. An executive search consultant made this wish for one of his close friends in a job search: "I hope you find a position

that is accepting, engaging, and exciting." Consider these wishes as criteria for judging how well we will connect people with our church community and think of the experiences we can offer in different terms:

Accepting	Engaging	Exciting
Connecting	Growing	Serving
Seeing Jesus	Knowing Jesus	Serving Jesus
Incarnational	Discipling	Apostolic
Welcoming	Forming	Sending
Relationship	Significance	Meaning
Belonging	Purpose	Passion

These are examples of human terms describing essential and integral kingdom needs. Which activities of your Christian community do people find accepting, engaging, and exciting? Or in which activities are they seeing, knowing, and serving Jesus? And so on?

11. How could your church community be more effective at integrating its ministries?

12. How can we celebrate, grow, and strengthen church communities?

PART 4:

Leading with Jesus

Leading from Relationship with Jesus

A s Christian leaders, we strive first to follow Jesus. This means we strive to stay in close relationship with Jesus so that with Jesus we can proclaim the Good News of God's love, share compassion and love with others, make ourselves vulnerable to serve others, and consistently do the right things and confront wrongs. A Christian life is a life of choosing to be aware of God's presence and, from that awareness, of beginning to manifest God's presence in the world.

Jesus told his followers, "I am the vine, you are the branches. Those who abide in me and I in them bear much fruit, because apart from me you can do nothing" (John 15:5). Jesus' first disciples had an opportunity to live with Jesus and come to know him. Their lives became centered in and around him, and therefore centered in God. "If you know me, you will know my Father also. From now on you do know him and have seen him" (John 14:7). Following his death and resurrection, Jesus told his disciples, "remember, I am with you always, to the end of the age" (Matthew 28:20). Jesus also told his disciples that God the Father "will give you another Advocate, to be with you forever" (John 14:16) and "the Advocate, the Holy Spirit, whom the Father will send in my name, will teach you everything, and remind you of all that I have said to you" (John 14:26).

Centering in prayer

Jesus modeled for his disciples how to live in a close, continuous relationship with God. Jesus was the human being with the ultimate attitude of openness and attentiveness to God, and he is the perfect example of the fact that human beings can live with God all the time and that everything we do can be part of our relationship with God. All of Jesus' human life was made up of prayer and action. He would go and draw renewed strength from his Father, and then he would return to work among people. Jesus remained centered in God and his mission through solitude and prayer.

In many instances, Jesus spent time alone with God to seek God's will and prepare to follow. Mark recorded one instance when, very early in the morning, while it was still dark, Jesus got up, left the house and went off to a solitary place, where he prayed (Mark 1:32–38). Before beginning his public ministry, Jesus spent forty days alone in the desert (Matthew 4:1–11). Before calling his disciples, "he went out to the mountain to pray; and he spent the night in prayer to God" (Luke 6:12–13). When Jesus received the news of the death of John the Baptist, he withdrew in a boat to a lonely place (Matthew 14:13). After feeding the five thousand and "after he had dismissed the crowds, he went up the mountain by himself to pray" (Matthew 14:23). Similarly, Jesus, knowing that the people intended to come and make him king by force, withdrew again to a mountain by himself (John 6:14–15). Jesus was transfigured when he "went up on the mountain to pray" (Luke 9:28–36). And Jesus withdrew to pray in the Garden of Gethsemane (Matthew 26:36–39). Each time, Jesus withdrew and closed off the noise of the world to pay attention to God.

Jesus modeled a life of listening and obedience:

> Obedience, as it is embodied in Jesus Christ, is a total listening, a giving attention with no hesitation or limitation, a being "all ear.". . . When used by Jesus, the word obedience has no association with fear, but rather is the expression of his most intimate, loving relationship. Jesus' actions and words are the obedient response to this love of his Father.[1]

After witnessing the power of prayer and obedience in Jesus' life, his disciples asked Jesus to teach them to pray (Luke 11:1–4). Jesus teaches them the Lord's Prayer (Matthew 6:9–13). In prayer, we offer God time to work in our lives, to make God's presence felt, to help us feel God's love, and to strengthen our faith and our love for others. We need to pray often, because only God can reveal God's presence, God's love for us, and the purposes God has for our lives. Our lives, lived authentically, are prayer. Prayer does not cease when we rise from our knees. We need to continue praying by maintaining as much focus as possible on God and our dependence on God. Prayer is listening for God's guidance. We need to let the experience of prayer set our priorities, center our lives in God, and thereby show forth God's purposes (meaning) for us. Then we must live and accomplish our prayer: "Your kingdom come. Your will be done, on earth as it is in heaven." Prayer transforms us so that we can transform the world.

Serving with humility

When John and James asked to be seated with Jesus in heaven, Jesus explained to his disciples, "whoever wishes to become great among you must be your servant, and whoever wishes to be first among you must be slave of all. For the Son of Man came not to be served but to serve, and to give his life a ransom for many" (Mark 10:43–45). The language used in these verses is shocking. The Greek word used for "servant" is the word for deacon (*diakonos*).[2] The word translated "slave" is *doulos*, the lowest of servants: a slave in bondage. While they could understand becoming servants of their Lord, becoming slaves would be difficult for the disciples to comprehend. Becoming a slave contradicted their Jewish heritage of being freed from slavery by the Exodus:

> In the first century, [a *doulos* slave] was the lowest rung
> of the social ladder. These people were bought and sold
> as property. A *doulos* slave had no rights or privileges, no
> wants or desires, only the commands of the master. . . .
> Being a slave involves several things: the loss of property,
> separation from roots, abuse by unkind owners, loss of
> individuality, and, of course, no freedom to choose . . . This
> is the first step to being first among God's people. Why?
> You cannot be a servant until you give up your personal
> rights to be served. Greatness in service to others can
> never occur as long as you insist that it is your right that
> others serve you. . . . Giving up our right to be served
> frees us to serve others. Choosing the place and work of
> a slave removes every barrier that keeps people apart.[3]

Servant leadership is being committed to meeting the needs of others. Whoever wants to be first must be a slave, willing to serve everyone in any way; greatness in God's kingdom is demonstrated by being a servant to all. Jesus has come to be just this type of slave. In Mark 10:45 and Matthew 20:28, the word "ransom" (*lytron*) refers to the price of buying back someone out of bondage (the price of release or redemption). Jesus will do this with his own service and life. This includes dying for others, but also includes living for others and freeing them by loving and serving them. Jesus challenged his disciples to a radical and paradoxical form of discipleship and leadership and showed that he would be the ultimate example through his life and through his suffering and death.[4]

On the night of the Last Supper, Jesus showed his disciples how important it was for him to serve them as a slave. Jesus got up from the table, removed his outer robe, and tied a towel around himself. Then he poured water into a basin and began to wash the disciples' feet and to wipe them with the towel that was tied around him. When Peter objected, refusing to let Jesus act as a slave to him, Jesus responded, "Unless I wash you, you have no share with me." After he had washed their feet and returned to the table, he asked them, "Do you know what I have done to you? You call me Teacher and Lord—and you are right, for that is what I am. So if I, your Lord and Teacher, have washed your feet, you also ought to wash one another's feet. For I have set you an example, that you also should do as I have done to you. Very truly, I tell you, servants are not greater than their master, nor are messengers greater than the one who sent them. If you know these things, you are blessed if you do them" (John 13:3–17).

Later he said, "This is my commandment, that you love one another as I have loved you. No one has greater love than this, to lay down one's life for one's friends" (John 15:12–13). In Philippians 2:3–13, Paul describes Jesus as the ultimate humble servant, whose followers are called to be the same: "Do nothing from selfish ambition or conceit, but in humility regard others as better than yourselves. Let each of you look not to your own interests, but to the interests of others. Let the same mind be in you that was in Christ Jesus, who, though he was in the form of God, did not regard equality with God as something to be exploited, but emptied himself, taking the form of a slave, being born in human likeness. And being found in human form, he humbled himself and became obedient to the point of death—even death on a cross. Therefore God also highly exalted him."

This humility comes from understanding God's love. Jesus got up to wash his disciples' feet "knowing that the Father had given all things into his hands, and that he had come from God and was going to God" (John 13:3). He knew God's love deeply and fully because he knew he had come from God, he was returning to God, and God had given him an important purpose in the world. Because he was fully grounded in his relationship with his Father, Jesus was able to live out of a consistent, centered integrity and to maintain his compassion and perform his mission whether people accepted, sought, and followed him, or rejected him and tortured him to death. His humility came from understanding who he was and who he was called to be. Now, he wants his followers to understand that they also can risk serving others because God is also in control of their lives in the same three ways.

First, we need to trust that we have come from God—that God has created our lives and uniquely gifted each of us for service among his people. In an earlier chapter, we saw that knowing God's personal love for each of us is an essential part of participating in his kingdom. Our relationship with God, and our entire perspective and approach to life, changes completely if we truly accept ourselves as God's beloved daughters and sons. Jesus fully expects his followers to know this unconditional love deeply and with our whole being—emotionally and spiritually, not just intellectually. Knowing God's love is knowing where we have come from.

Second, we need to trust that we are returning to God both by participating in God's kingdom right now and in the promise of everlasting life. In the story of the Good Samaritan, Jesus ties together loving God, loving one another, and inheriting everlasting life—all by showing mercy to our neighbors. Jesus is saying that we can participate in God's kingdom of love right now by loving and blessing other people.

And third, we need to trust that in our personal relationship with God, we have the power we need to carry out God's call for our lives. We may not believe that we can perform the healing miracles of Jesus, but he sends his disciples to love and serve God and other people with the same compassion he showed to those who are suffering or outcast. Jesus sends his disciples into the world to proclaim the Good News of God's love and cure every disease and every sickness, and he empowers us to participate in God's healing, forgiveness, and reconciliation.[5]

Knowing that the Father has given all things into our hands and that we have come from God and are going to God is all about knowing God's love for us and responding with love. To become like Jesus and serve like Jesus, we need to know whose we are and who we are called to be.[6] While we are often more like one of the sons in the parable of the Prodigal Son, Henri Nouwen reminds us that we want to become more like their father. People who experience God's love act differently and treat others differently. We can also become more courageous, encouraged, emboldened, grateful, accepting, compassionate, and loving. The world is bigger and brighter, and there is a greater sense of abundance. Our relationships with people change. People who lead from love are focused on serving others. We are able to serve with honesty, unselfishness, purity, and love, which all point to humility. Care and compassion for others leads to their trust and engagement as followers.

Today, there are many opportunities to follow Jesus knowing that the Father has given all things into our hands and that we have come from God and are going to God. Any service to others may lead to spiritual growth (in ourselves and in the kingdom of God)—whether it is preaching the gospel, forming others, or serving on a particular ministry team; or it is binding up the brokenhearted and comforting those who mourn (Isaiah 61:1–2); or it is sharing food with the hungry or providing the poor wanderer with shelter (Isaiah 58:7); or it is being "merciful as your Father is merciful" (Luke 6:36). The keys for God's love to transform us are personal involvement and actually serving other people. The particular ministry that we are passionate about will depend on God's particular call to us based on where we are on our own spiritual journey. Mother Theresa reminded us that "there are no great deeds, only small deeds done with great love." We each need to ask ourselves how we are intended to be instruments of God's love in the world.

Mastering fear and anxiety

Jesus asks us to have strength and confidence to accomplish the work we are given to do. Jesus continuously reminds his disciples to have faith in God's love (e.g., Luke 12:32; Matthew 6:25–34; John 14:1, 14:27, 16:33). And Jesus lived this way. In Mark 6:7–12, as he sent out his disciples, he instructed them to take with them no money or food, staff, or spare clothes, and to make no arrangements or plans, but to look for and accept hospitality where they could find it. Apparently Jesus followed these same practices, as he said the Son of Man had nowhere to lay his head (Luke 9:58). Jesus went from place to place speaking and healing and finding food and shelter where he might. He went without baggage or security, trusting in God's love and the hospitality of others.

In many situations, primarily by his calm presence, Jesus revealed who he is and saved and transformed those around him for kingdom living. We speak metaphorically of "calming the storm," but Jesus literally does this (Mark 4:35–41, Matthew 8:23–27). When Jesus and his disciples were out to sea in a boat, suddenly there was a great storm, and "the boat was being swamped by the waves; but Jesus was asleep." The disciples "went and woke Jesus up, saying, 'Lord, save us! We are perishing!' And he said to them, 'Why are you afraid, you of little faith?' Then he got up and rebuked the winds and the sea; and there was a dead calm." Here the disciples' desperate call to Jesus, "Teacher, do you not care that we are perishing?" is not only a cry for help. They want Jesus to be as anxious as they are, to also share in their suffering, because they think he will not help them unless he shares their anxiety.[7] But Jesus refuses to panic and remains serene and centered. He solves the problem by throwing his own calm onto the storm, saying "Peace! Be still." The disciples are amazed and ask: "What sort of man is this, that even the winds and the sea obey him?"

Jesus is fully human and undoubtedly experienced fears, but he did not let them become debilitating. On the night before his crucifixion, Jesus was deeply "distressed," "grieved," and "agitated" (Matthew 26:37–38, Mark 14:33–34), and he went into the Garden of Gethsemane to pray, throwing himself on the ground and asking, "Abba, Father, for you all things are possible; remove this cup from me." And yet, in the same instant, he placed his relationship with God above his own fears and anxiety, saying, "yet not what I want but what you want" (Mark 14:36, Matthew 26:39).

From experience, we know that groups and organizations do not function well when there is a high level of anxiety. People in stressful situations involving crises or change will often make things worse by panicking or acting out rather than calmly dealing with the threats they face. In uncertain and difficult situations, leaders like Jesus who manage their own anxiety are better able to influence others and contribute to the community's health, and even to solve or prevent problems by still-ing anxiety.

Most of us recognize that this type of character is highly desirable, but when we are acting on our own, we struggle at times with fear or a lack of confidence and at other times with overconfidence, personal con-ceit, or ambition. Either reaction takes us off track in life and relation-ships. Family systems theory describes a tendency for leaders of groups in difficult situations to respond to tensions either by becoming overly controlling ("I'm in charge here!") or by seeking acceptance from others and following the crowd:

> The less developed a person's "self," the more impact
> others have on his functioning and the more he tries to
> control, actively or passively, the functioning of others.
> ... People with a poorly differentiated "self" depend so
> heavily on the acceptance and approval of others that
> either they quickly adjust what they think, say, and do
> to please others or they dogmatically proclaim what
> others should be like and pressure them to conform.[8]

According to family systems theory, both responses may further contribute to the stress of the group. Leaders who are able to manage their own personal anxiety and to maintain a healthy balance—between the strong and contradictory personal needs of relating with others and maintaining a unique self—contribute stability and reduce the stress level of the group. This healthy balance is referred to as "self-differenti-ation":

> A person with a well-differentiated "self" recognizes
> his realistic dependence on others, but he can stay
> calm and clear headed enough in the face of conflict,
> criticism, and rejection to distinguish thinking rooted in
> a careful assessment of the facts from thinking clouded
> by emotionality. Thoughtfully acquired principles help
> guide decision-making about important family and social
> issues, making him less at the mercy of the feelings of
> the moment. What he decides and what he says matches
> what he does. He can act selflessly, but his acting in the

best interests of the group is a thoughtful choice, not a response to relationship pressures. Confident in his thinking, he can either support another's view without being a disciple or reject another view without polarizing the differences. He defines himself without being pushy and deals with pressure to yield without being wishy-washy.

Every human society has its well-differentiated people, poorly differentiated people, and people at many gradations between these extremes. Consequently, the families and other groups that make up a society differ in the intensity of their emotional interdependence depending on the differentiation levels of their members. The more intense the interdependence, the less the group's capacity to adapt to potentially stressful events without a marked escalation of chronic anxiety. Everyone is subject to problems in his work and personal life, but less differentiated people and families are vulnerable to periods of heightened chronic anxiety which contributes to their having a disproportionate share of society's most serious problems.[9]

The "self-differentiated" person of family systems theory is a person who is mature and balanced enough not to be driven too heavily by their own needs either for personal control or for acceptance by others. A mature, well-differentiated leader is one "with the courage to define self, who is as invested in the welfare of the family as in self, who is neither angry nor dogmatic, whose energy goes to changing self rather than telling others what they should do, who can know and respect the multiple opinions of others, who can modify self in response to the strengths of the group and who is not influenced by the irresponsible opinions of others."[10]

Based on these definitions, leaders like Abraham Lincoln, Mahatma Gandhi, and Martin Luther King Jr. have been described as excellent examples of well-differentiated leaders. A well-differentiated leader will focus on developing his or her self rather than on everyone else in the group, will make up his or her own mind even if it is different from the group's, and will work to be responsible himself or herself instead of trying to change others. At the same time, the well-differentiated leader will stay connected with the group and influence its members through non-anxious, responsible, and exemplary actions. Accordingly, a non-anxious leader is able to help a community respond to anxiety, remain in the community despite differences, and directly respond to the challenges they face.[11]

For these reasons, many would readily identify Jesus as the most well-differentiated person who ever lived—neither pulled toward the desires of his own ego (selfishness) or trying to please others (the crowd). And this is certainly true, but with a difference. Jesus was not "self-differentiated" but "God-differentiated."[12] For self-differentiation, we recognize a need to personally develop and hold onto a reasonable level of confidence somewhere between too little self-esteem and conceit. But Jesus shows us a different way, and that mature identity is not a proper balance of self-esteem, but rather confidence in a relationship beyond us. Paul writes: "just as we have been approved by God to be entrusted with the message of the gospel, even so we speak, not to please mortals, but to please God who tests our hearts. As you know and as God is our witness, we never came with words of flattery or with a pretext for greed; nor did we seek praise from mortals" (2 Thessalonians 2:4–6). Our personal insecurities (lack of faith) and our overreliance on ourselves (also lack of faith) both come from the same lack of being rooted in God's love. A well-differentiated Christian leader feels God's love and acceptance, and that confidence helps avoid first seeking either an ego-driven sense of control or the acceptance of others. The Christian leader trusts that God is in charge and that he or she neither has to take control nor to make others happy; the focus is on following God's calling. Then the direction of the leader's life can become the direction God leads, rather than being tossed about by our own fears or the anxieties of others.[13]

In family systems theory, a person becomes self-differentiated by defining himself or herself rather than reacting to crises around him or her. A Christian leader does not need to define himself or herself but to discover his or her unique identity in relationship to God. And this begins in prayer: "Do not worry about anything, but in everything by prayer and supplication with thanksgiving let your requests be made known to God. And the peace of God, which surpasses all understanding, will guard your hearts and your minds in Christ Jesus" (Philippians 4:6–7). "That inner voice for Christian leaders is found in a Christ-centered life that is guided by the Spirit in prayer."[14]

Without this centering source in God's love, we become anxious or afraid in difficult situations. Deeply experiencing God's love enables us to approach life and leadership in a non-anxious way. We are able to leave our physical and emotional baggage behind (as Jesus tells his disciples to do in Matthew 10, Luke 10, and Mark 6) and go and serve others. Jesus was God-differentiated not by being focused on his own identity and level of confidence but by being primarily focused on his relationship with God and pleasing God.

This does not mean that Christian leaders don't have fear. Instead, they're able to master their fear and keep it from overpowering them. "Be not afraid" does not mean "that we should not have fears" but "that we do not need to be our fears, quite a different proposition."[15]

The leaders that God uses are required to step out in courage, despite enormous uncertainty and risk. Think of Abraham, Moses, Nehemiah, Esther, Paul, and many others. Not only did these leaders take huge, Spirit-led risks, but they also walked away from comfortable lives to do so. This does not mean that risk-taking leaders are fearless. Abraham wouldn't admit that Sarah was his wife when his life was on the line, and Moses hesitated when Pharaoh balked at his demand to release the Hebrew people. Joshua needed God's frequent urging to "be strong and courageous." Some level of anxiety is natural for any risk-taking leader, but there is a huge difference between feeling fear and leading from fear.[16]

There is certainly plenty to be afraid of, but we can live in a relationship that enables us to live and act with faith, hope, and love without being crippled by fear. We learn this from the experience of Job in probably the oldest book of the Bible. Throughout the book, Job experiences suffering and rages against it. And then God appears. In their conversation, God never explains the reason for suffering. But Job discovers that God's presence is enough to comfort him. Job's experience mirrors the psalmist's: "Even though I walk through the valley of the shadow of death, I fear no evil; for you are with me." Job finds peace of mind and spirit simply in God's presence. Job's problems become meaningless in relation to God's love. Job has faith in God's purpose just because God is there, and any experience of God is enough to reveal God's trustworthiness and our security in God.

The experience of God's presence is the ultimate assurance that God loves us and that we have security independent from the physical world we know we can't control, where we find evil, and from which we feel alienated (Romans 8:31–39). The universe is not uncaring or arbitrary. We have hope, notwithstanding our inability to control the world around us. And this hope, and our faith, spring from God's love for us. The answer God gives to each person is "You are loved." To the extent people are attuned to that love, as through prayer, they can find peace even in a chaotic world. The experience of Job is that active relationship with God provides meaning and security without the necessity of a complete knowledge of, or power over, our personal circumstances. We can be secure in, and only in, personal relationship with God.

Engaging Jesus

To continue engaging Jesus, read and reflect on Mark 4:35–41.

Questions for Personal Reflection:

1. How would your style and habits need to change for you to lead with more humility?

2. John 13:3 says Jesus was able to serve God and other people because he trusted in God in three ways. He knew "that the Father had given all things into his hands, and that he had come from God and was going to God." Can you have this same trust in God so that you can imitate Jesus?

   - First, can you trust that you have come from God, that he has created your life and uniquely gifted you for service among his people?

   - Second, can you trust that you are returning to God both by participating in God's kingdom right now and in the promise of everlasting life?

   - And third, can you trust that, in your personal relationship with God, you have the power you need to carry out God's call on your life?

3. Do you worry about what you will eat, drink, wear, etc.?
   (See Mark 6:25–29, 34; Luke 12:26.)

4. How much do you worry about past failures or what may happen in the future? Why is this wasted energy? How does Jesus direct us to focus on the present?

5. Do you feel more of a need to take charge yourself or to obtain affirmation from others?

6. How clear is your compass, both personally and in terms of organizational direction?

7. How easily are you knocked off your path?

8. What enables you to become the calm at the center of the storm?

Questions for Group Discussion:

1. How are Christian leaders different from other leaders in the world?

2. Why is it difficult for leaders to act like slaves? Why does it require three levels of trust?

3. How is humble service "incarnational"?

4. Why is it difficult for followers to accept leaders who act like slaves?

5. What are the style and habits of a humble leader?

6. Who are humble leaders today? What can we learn from them?

7. Desmond Tutu writes, "Being courageous does not mean never being scared; it means acting as you know you must even though you are undeniably afraid." What is the basis for Christian courage?

8. Describe a time when Jesus spoke to the storm in your life, and the winds calmed and the waves stilled.

9. Why do leaders need to understand their personal motives, especially in times of change, stress, or conflict? How do you get in touch with those motives?

10. How is a "God-differentiated" leader like a well-differentiated leader? How is he or she different? How do we recognize each?

11. How does Jesus teach us to react to fear or anxiety? What are ways to have some success with this?

12. How can church communities prepare and support people for service?

Sharing Leadership

J esus came into the world proclaiming God's kingdom under God's reign. As the king's son, Jesus could claim hereditary authority handed down from a father to a son within a family. Instead of claiming authority based on his title and position, however, Jesus used a rabbinical model to develop other leaders, and then he also turned the rabbinical model upside down—by calling his disciples sons and daughters, brothers and sisters, friends and partners, and serving them himself.

The leader of the Christian community or body is Jesus the Christ himself (Ephesians 4:15). And Jesus is always acting from and through his relationship with his Father and the Holy Spirit (John 14, Ephesians 4:5, 1 Corinthians 12).[1] The persons of God live in familial love of Father and Son and Spirit. As leadership is shared among the persons of the Trinity in love, unity, intimacy, and equality, it can also be shared among people in loving community with God and one another (Ephesians 4:2–3).

The Trinitarian God is an image for interdependent Christian leadership

Andrei Rublev's familiar icon of the Trinity from the early fifteenth century visually articulates many of the understandings we have about the three persons of God and their relationship. As symbols of oneness, the persons in the icon are inclined to one another with the shapes of their bodies creating a circle, each has the same face, each wears a blue garment to symbolize the heavens, and none is shown as greater than the others. Each person also has his own identity. The Father wears a shimmering robe, clasps a staff—symbolizing authority over heaven and earth—in both hands, and sits before a house, perhaps a mansion with many rooms. The Son wears a brown garment, symbolizing the earth and his humanity, balanced in size with his blue, heavenly garment and with a gold stripe symbolizing his kingship. Jesus has two fingers on the table, perhaps also showing his dual human and divine nature, and behind him is a tree, perhaps symbolizing both the cross and new life. The Spirit wears both a blue robe representing divinity and a green robe representing new life and sits before a mountain, perhaps symbolizing coming closer to God and transfiguration. Rublev's icon is most revered, however, for the ways it draws observers into the relationship with the persons of God. There is an open place at the table, and Jesus' fingers point to the chalice at the center of the table. Then, as we come to the table, we find whichever one of the persons of God we encounter drawing us into closer relationship with the others.

Christians can come to the table with God and participate in God's love and action. Each of us is called by Jesus to be his disciple. Jesus calls all people to take up their cross and follow him (Luke 9:23–25) by putting Jesus first (Luke 14:25–35), loving others (John 13:34–36), making disciples (Matthew 28:19–20), and abiding in him (John 15:1–9). Christians are adopted into the family of God (Matthew 12:50, John 17, Galatians 3:26, Ephesians 1:5, Romans 8:15). Jesus commissions people in the power of the Holy Spirit to love and serve with him (Matthew 28:16–20, Mark 16:15, Acts 1:8, John 20:21). The nature of communion, the nature of discipleship, the nature of God's kingdom is that all are invited to participate and contribute.

Notice that many of the gifts of the Spirit are essential gifts for leadership—wisdom, knowledge, faith, healing, prophecy—and these are given to different people (1 Corinthians 12:8–10, 28–30). Each person's gift is important to the body of Christ, and no gift is more important than the others (12:14–23).[2] The statement about the priesthood of all believers in 1 Peter 2:9 is made collectively: "You are a chosen race, a royal priesthood, a holy nation, God's own people, in order that you may proclaim the mighty acts of him who called you out of darkness into his marvelous light."[3] The Christian Way does not accept that there are a few born leaders who will rise to the top and "lord it over" others.[4]

The Christian Way proclaims the primacy of God's loving leadership, but it also proclaims that many people have unique and interdependent roles in leadership. In Christianity, leaders are "born anew" and "equipped" with gifts for ministry and mission. If we are to live into the kingdom of God with all of these leaders, leadership must be lovingly shared. Shared leadership brings about greater cohesion, collective vision, and energy. We may reach better decisions and outcomes from encouraging a greater number of perspectives. But shared leadership also requires greater preparation and guidance—perhaps including tools such as a shared mission statement, agreed core values, and guiding principles, and certainly including leaders committed to following Jesus.

The early church modeled shared leadership

In developing the New Testament churches, the apostles acted in concert with others in mutual relationship with God and one another. The apostles shared leadership among themselves (Acts 6) and with elders in Ephesus (Acts 20:28), Jerusalem (Acts 15:2–25, 16:4; James 5:14), and churches around the world (Acts 14:23; 1 Peter 1:1, 5:1–2). New Testament leadership was mutual, interdependent, collaborative, communal, and consensual.

In Acts 6:1–7, the twelve apostles "called together the whole community of the disciples" to choose "seven men of good standing, full of the Spirit and of wisdom, whom [they] may appoint to this task" of distributing food to widows. The apostles asked the disciples to discern and raise up gifted individuals from the community to effectively act as deacons in serving the needy. Being given this involvement and responsibility "pleased" the community. The community identified seven faithful servants, and the apostles commissioned them by praying and laying hands on them. The result was that "The word of God continued to spread; the number of the disciples increased greatly in Jerusalem, and a great many of the priests became obedient to the faith." The word of God spreads as discernment, calling, and ministry are shared more broadly.

In Acts 13:1–4, there is another example of corporate discernment. While the community is worshiping and fasting, the Holy Spirit reveals that Barnabas and Paul are to be sent out as missionaries: "Then after fasting and praying they laid their hands on them and sent them off." But not only are Barnabas and Paul sent by the community, they are "sent out by the Holy Spirit." God's will is accomplished through the discernment of the community. This is consistent with Matthew 18:19–20:

"Again, truly I tell you, if two of you agree on earth about anything you ask, it will be done for you by my Father in heaven. For where two or three are gathered in my name, I am there among them."

In Acts 15, Paul and Barnabas and others were appointed and "sent on their way by the church" to Jerusalem to discuss the requirements for gentile Christians with the apostles and the elders. In Jerusalem, "they were welcomed by the church and the apostles and the elders," and "the apostles and the elders met together to consider" the issues. Peter, Barnabas, and Paul spoke and were listened to with respect, and James summarized their decisions. "Then the apostles and the elders, with the consent of the whole church, decided to choose men from among their members and to send them to Antioch with Paul and Barnabas" to help them. And they sent a letter with them confirming that "since we have heard that certain persons who have gone out from us, though with no instructions from us, have said things to disturb you and have unsettled your minds, we have decided unanimously to choose representatives and send them to you, along with our beloved Barnabas and Paul. . . . For it has seemed good to the Holy Spirit and to us to impose on you no further burden than these essentials." Again, the apostles used an inter-dependent, supportive, and consensual process of discernment.

In Christian communities, even conflict resolution is not autocrat-ic, authoritarian, or hierarchical. Jesus says, "If another member of the church sins against you, go and point out the fault when the two of you are alone" (Matthew 18:15a). Direct, individual confrontation may lead to reconciliation. "If the member listens to you, you have regained that one" (Matthew 18:15b), and there will be rejoicing like the shepherd who has gone in search of a lost sheep and found it (Matthew 18:12–13). "But if you are not listened to," Jesus says then as a second effort, "take one or two others along with you, so that every word may be confirmed by the evidence of two or three witnesses." Notice that Jesus never refers the conflict to a leader of the community to resolve, but always to members who are interested in restoring community. The third effort of reconcili-ation is this: "If the member refuses to listen to them, tell it to the church; and if the offender refuses to listen even to the church, let such a one be to you as a Gentile and a tax collector" (Matthew 18:17).[5] If there is no reconciliation, then there is no community, and the sinner remains lost. The conflict can only be resolved consensually and in community.

Jesus authorizes the community to shape its own life and to manage its own affairs rather than placing a higher authority above it, because this is the only way reconciliation may occur and the kingdom may come. It's the Way for a shepherd to seek and find a "lost sheep." It's also the only way to develop responsibility and accountability to the community.

Shared leadership makes growth possible

Shared leadership lays the foundation for mutual ministry. For the church to become more of the body of Christ, each person needs to bring and use their special gifts in the community (1 Corinthians 12) and "grow up in every way into" Christ (Ephesians 4). Because all of the members of the body are interconnected, the work of the body is "mutual ministry," and we share responsibility to our ministries within our commitment to follow Christ and be God's people. Mutual ministry enables the community to grow.

For any living organism to grow (whether a tree, a human body, or a church community), structures must grow and change. We need to change form to change size. The best way to do this is by growing through gifted individuals in dedicated ministry teams. This also brings spiritual growth as we strengthen our relationships with God and help others do the same.

If we see a clergy person as *the* church leader, we naturally have a ministry primarily revolving around relationships with that leader. This limits the growth of the church because a limited number of people can relate with a single leader. Sociological research demonstrates growth barriers beyond 150 active participants. Malcolm Gladwell's rule of 150 as presented in *The Tipping Point*[6] shows that a relationship-oriented organization becomes unstable once it approaches 150 active participants. A "rule of 12" suggests why this occurs. The rule of 12 provides that an individual can maintain up to twelve close personal relationships. Each of those twelve can themselves be close to twelve, so a total of 144 individuals can feel close because they have less than one degree of separation. Both theories suggest comfort with 150 active participants around a single leader. The challenges of church growth beyond a pastoral size of about 150 regular participants are well known.[7]

Many churches attempt to cross this barrier by adding clergy. If the first leader or the church community appoints associated leaders, we may see mathematical growth. But because each of the two clergy leaders share certain overlapping relationships, the church does not grow to 288 (12 × 12 × 2) as one might expect, but instead grows in a range from 192 to 240 active participants. With three leaders, the church tends to grow to about 300 active participants and continues to grow at slightly less than 100 with each addition of an associate leader.

This type of clergy-centered growth presents challenges. Each of the seeming strengths of the church community also limits its growth. The closeness of family-type relationships is comfortable to insiders and a barrier to outsiders. Clergy centeredness in pastoral care, worship, Bible studies, and leadership limits development of everyone's gifts in the body of Christ. The church governing board generally focuses as an ad hoc committee on concrete, immediate problems—rather than having active, structural decision making and a big-picture focus. A church with clergy conflict or departures may see a rapid loss of active participants whose relationships are centered in the clergy.

The heart of the answer to growth is not to add clergy or structures—though this will inevitably become necessary—but to become a multiple-cell church. A multiple-cell church is not focused on a single leader or group of leaders but on growing through ministry teams and small groups. When leadership is driven by ministry teams rather than a few individuals, discipleship is active. There is active discernment of call, for it is understood that all are gifted and all are called to use those gifts in ministry. A church begins a cultural shift from maintenance-oriented hierarchical thinking to mission-oriented team driven thinking. Clergy may depart, but the work of the church will go on, and the church will continue to grow. The corollary to the rule of 150 and the rule of 12 is that a relationship-building organization can grow almost limitlessly as long as all subrelational groupings themselves include less than 150 people.

In a multiple-cell church, gifted and passionate ministry teams take care of functions such as evangelism, Christian formation, pastoral care, stewardship, outreach ministries, finance, and buildings and grounds. People understand their roles in terms of their ministry teams and small groups rather than in terms of their relationships to particular leaders.[8]

Overall, a larger community will need a more representative form of leadership where a governing board takes responsibility for discerning and implementing the overall vision and purpose of the community.[9] This is more like a republic than a democracy because leaders must take charge of hard decisions. Frequently, a board of a growing church may not fully accept and grow into this responsibility and will fall back upon pastoral or patriarchal authority for leadership decisions. Larger communities often carry forward the vestiges of leadership styles that work well for smaller groups. Groups tend to gravitate back to family meeting styles that work well with groups of up to about 100 people, or pastoral leadership styles that work well with up to about 150 people. These often feel consensual because of the style of the leader, but they generally rely on a patriarch or matriarch (or council of them) or priest to ultimately make decisions. It will be a challenge to move into mutual ministry (e.g., 1 Corinthians 12, John 21, Matthew 10, Luke 10).

At the same time as leadership structures change to support the growth of a community, communication practices also need to change. In smaller communities, people are used to getting their communication directly from the pastor or from their friends. This may not work for people who are not connected to small groups or ministry teams in communities larger than 144 people (when communication is no longer clergy-centered or patriarchal-centered). The community needs to intentionally develop formal rules, structures, and processes for good communication, and there need to be new and clear guidelines for decision making and for how people interact with one another.

In Christian communities, there are few situations when shared leadership is not more productive and effective than authoritarian direction. Empowering and collaborative leaders share leadership to develop greater involvement, accountability, satisfaction, loyalty and commitment of followers to the mission and community. Shared leadership provides for greater leadership development and, with reasonable boundaries and working relationships, also provides order, consistency, quick decision making, and conflict resolution. Authoritarian or autocratic leaders may make practical arguments for why they're needed to govern our communities. Exercising authority or rank has been shown to be very effective, for example, in emergency or military situations when leaders exercise control to provide order, consistency, quick and accurate decision making, and conflict resolution. However, shared leadership creates working partnerships and a transformative culture that can react quickly, flexibly, and more collectively and broadly to the opportunities and challenges of a community, as the community engages more of its people's gifts for ministry.

Leading in Mutual Ministry

Mutual ministry requires involvement and empowerment at all levels. A community is much stronger and more innovative when individuals and teams are given permission to be creative and to explore and address opportunities and challenges. Leaders gain greater influence, capacity, and success by giving up control and empowering others to take on new responsibilities.

The most critical part of involving all people in the body of Christ is empowering leadership. Early church members took this seriously: "Because these people knew they had been called and commissioned by their Lord to carry on his loving service in the world, they had big, pressing questions. They were driven to ask 'Who are we in relationship to those around us? To whom are we sent?'"[10] Too often, we leave these questions—and even more so, the mission work itself—to the ordained.

To help support "doing ministry together," a "mutual ministry review" process is helpful in understanding what is going on, learning about ministries, supporting communication among ministries and the congregation, celebrating gifts and ministries, and providing a foundation for leadership discernment, planning, oversight, and decision making. Examples of mutual ministry review processes are included in the "Tools for Christian Leadership" section of this book.

Joanne Skidmore and I developed the Organic Mutual Ministry Review model as an alternative for church and nonprofit communities to common business strategic planning tools such as strength, weakness, opportunity, and threat (SWOT) analysis or appreciative inquiry (AI). This organic model is based on considering our church community as a fruit tree or grapevine or food crop. The Bible often uses metaphors of fruit and vineyards to describe the people of God and the work to which we are called. Caring for a church, like caring for a vineyard, requires hard work. We labor in the vineyard with God, and we plant and water, but God gives the growth (1 Corinthians 3:6). To bear good fruit, a vineyard needs to be tended over the course of many years. The farming cycle must be repeated: season after season, crops are planted and tended, and fruit is gathered and stored. Similarly, year after year, we make plans for our church community, act upon them, and review our activities. The work is never ultimately perfected nor completely finished, and the fruit is not always sweet. Sometimes pruning is needed or the land needs to lie fallow.

The Organic Mutual Ministry Review applies an agricultural model to explore our activities according to where each activity is in the growth process and ask in a positive and nonthreatening way what needs digging and fertilizing (reworking); what needs planting; what needs watering or pruning (tending); what needs to lie fallow; what we are overtending; and what is ready for harvest and celebration festival. Discussions are shaped by a natural framework for growth and development and, at the same time, occur in a positive and healthy context that encourages us to be faithful, gentle, patient, and kind and to reveal our passions, peace, joy, and love (Galatians 5:22).

Whenever ministries of a community are being identified and evaluated, the effectiveness of shared leadership also needs to be evaluated by asking critical questions about how we are doing with ministry together: Have we identified leaders for each ministry? Have we created teams where they are needed? How do we invite new people into key ministries? How are we doing on leading these ministries? How do we move the leadership to higher levels of responsibility? Are there areas that could be delegated to others to free up leaders? And a key question: What level of oversight do we need for each ministry area?

Levels of Oversight[11]

Direct inexperienced workers by

- giving explicit instructions,

- closely tracking performance, and

- providing frequent feedback.

Coach moderately competent workers by

- explaining why,

- soliciting suggestions,

- praising nearly right performance, and

- continuing to direct tasks.

Support nearly competent workers by

- sharing decision making,

- encouraging independent problem solving, and

- supporting development of an independent style.

Delegate to fully competent workers by

- empowering the worker to act independently,

- providing appropriate resources, and

- leaving them alone!

Successful delegation happens when a ministry team has (i) a responsible leader or group of leaders, (ii) experienced and enthusiastic workers, (iii) intentional preparation (training, coaching, apprenticing) of new leaders and workers, (iv) a clear role that is appropriately monitored by the leaders, (v) helpful process guides or manuals, and (vi) appropriate communication with and reporting to the governing board.

Another organic model, the "Decision Tree,"[12] is a helpful tool both for delegation and for developing leaders. With a Decision Tree, we think of a ministry area as a growing tree that bears fruit. For the tree or ministry area to grow, leaders need to make decisions. Those decisions can be made at or delegated to different levels in four different ways.

> *Leaf decisions*: At the leaf level, ministry teams make a decision, act on it, and don't need to report back to the board.

Branch decisions: At the branch level, ministry teams make a decision, act on it, and report back to the board.

Trunk decisions: At the trunk level, ministry teams make a decision and report to the board before acting on it.

Root decisions: At the root level, ministry teams and the board make the decision jointly.

Empowering leaders "identify clearly which categories decisions and actions fall into, so that [a ministry area leader] knows exactly where he or she has the authority to make decisions and take action."[13] This creates workable boundaries regarding who will make the decision and how. Most decisions are important, but some are more critical to the overall community and need to be moved to a higher level. In the analogy, decisions that could harm the roots of the community are more critical to its overall health than those that strip away a leaf, prune a branch, or gash its trunk. And people responsible for the roots often have a greater delegated authority from the community, more experience, and a broader perspective on the problem or challenge.

At the same time, the Decision Tree model encourages leadership development by pushing more and more decisions from the root level to the trunk, branch, and leaf levels. As a ministry team or team leader gains experience, the team or individual is able to take on more challenging responsibilities—growing their skills and making the community stronger at the same time:

> Ask each of the people who reports to you to pay attention over the next thirty days to all of the decisions that fall within their responsibilities and to categorize them as leaf, branch, trunk, or root. Review their conclusions and reach consensus about where each kind of decision falls on the Decision Tree. Remind everyone that the goal is to move more and more decisions out to the leaf level. This is the leadership-development path. Following this agreement, adhere to the boundaries and agreements required. For example, if someone comes to you for help in making a decision that falls

within the trunk category, say, "Come back to me when you've made your decision. Then we'll talk."[14]

Empowering ministry teams and leaders

The Organic Mutual Ministry Review and Decision Tree models can be applied as a basis to change structures to increase and strengthen leadership, define leadership roles, recognize boundaries, and expect more from more people so ministries expand. The governing board then has a broader role of discerning the vision toward which God calls the community, articulating and communicating the vision, holding the community accountable for its realization of the vision, and keeping the mission of the church clearly before the church community. The governing board needs to focus on its oversight and leadership of the spiritual development of the community—in evangelism, Christian formation, and pastoral care—acknowledging its role as apostolic leaders (in the nature of Ephesians 4:11–12), its responsibility for equipping all members of the church for the work of the church. Part of this is looking for opportunities to share and delegate and to avoid overfunctioning.

The activities of setting goals and delegating leadership for any ministry area go hand in hand, and generally in this order:

1. Identify specific ministry or project objectives. We need a clearly defined and well-communicated statement of purpose for the team.

2. Identify the leader(s) and ministry team members. The team needs to have enough members and the right members for the project or task the church wants to accomplish. Team leaders need good leadership and communication skills, and other team members need appropriate gifts, skills, experiences, and passions for the particular ministry area or project. Individual roles, relationships, and accountabilities need to be defined and clear to everyone on the team. Team members need to have or receive the technical experience to perform their jobs.

3. Have the ministry team create its job description based on the project objectives and review its roles with the

governing board. The team needs to be part of defining the goals and objectives of the ministry area in order to understand, support, and creatively and enthusiastically lead them.

4. The ministry team develops project strategies and procedures. Senior leaders must call forth and support the vision of the church community without micromanaging strategies. The team itself develops just enough policies and procedures to coordinate and accomplish its tasks. The team, not the board, holds its members accountable for performance and provides individual recognition, encouragement, and supervision as needed.

5. Both the governing board and the ministry team monitor and develop the knowledge, energy, and support of the congregation, especially through communications and involvement. Both the board and the ministry team celebrate the accomplishments of the team and the community. There is open and effective communication among the board, the ministry team, the church community, and other ministry teams. All appropriate stakeholders are involved together in planning and decision making.

6. The governing board and the ministry team agree when steps will be accomplished and evaluated. There is agreement between the board and the team when priorities are revised; team members understand the need for change and what will be involved.

Mutual ministry is not just letting every individual or ministry team do its own thing; leadership aligns activities with real purpose and vision. Decisions made by ministry teams are reviewed by the church governing board in terms of the community's overall vision. However, once a team has its mission to accomplish, the governing board must give up control and let them work without trying to coordinate the team's activities. Pastors and staff do not need to go to team meetings unless they have something to contribute. The individuals gifted in the particular area will determine what is best. If they get in trouble or need help, they should let the governing board know and seek additional help or information. Ministry teams are harmed by having to spend too much time reporting. Committees report; teams do ministry.

God can do amazing things through trusted ministry teams. The biggest challenge for the clergy and governing board is to empower—rather than control—ministry teams. Leaders who take care of the big things and delegate everything else avoid burnout, bottlenecks, or a "single point of failure." Consider how many of the activities above need to take place at the ministry team level, not at the board or senior pastor level. These practices also provide more security and help the community involve others and grow. Some reasons this may not happen are

- the leader's personal sense of responsibility,

- the leader's lack of confidence that another person will do it right (perhaps because others have less skill, different values, different approaches or styles; or perhaps based on a previous bad experience),

- the leader's lack of time or skill for training or supervision,

- the leader's assessment that it is easier or faster to do it himself or herself, or

- the leader's personal insecurity.

All of these behaviors are worsened and prevent the development of other ministers whenever a leader believes he or she should be the one with control, power, or authority. The leader may think he or she should control information, decisions, or permissions; be the expert for the community; come up with the vision or ideas on his or her own; and make all of the plans for the community, and even execute the plans or, worse, give the plans to others and instruct them to execute.[15]

The church community has a unique way of looking at roles and responsibilities of leaders because we focus on the body of Christ and each person's unique contribution to it. Christian leaders do not come to "lord it over" anyone or to be served, but to serve. Serving others primarily means helping them to live in God's kingdom and to be the people God has created them and is calling them to be. This depends much more on discerning God's will and applying the gifts, passions, and abilities of others than it does on any particular leader. The real evaluative question is whether each person is performing his or her particular function within the body of Christ. A key is recognizing and applying individual strengths and finding other people to cover other areas. Each leader has a role in identifying gifts and calling people into ministry. In a church community, rather than asking leaders "How much have you done?" the primary question is "How many others have you involved?" A single individual can't effectively discern for or lead the community. All Christian leaders must be able to accept this and be open to learning and dialogue to fully involve people in the body of Christ and to grow beyond their own personal limitations and perspectives.

Engaging Jesus

To continue engaging Jesus, read and reflect on Exodus 18:13–26.

Questions for Personal Reflection:

1. Imagine how Moses' wife Zipporah described Moses to her father before this passage and after. Would it be easy for you to follow Jethro's advice?

2. What prevents you from delegating tasks to others?

Questions for Group Discussion:

1. Who are the leaders of your church?

2. What are the duties and responsibilities of clergy? Of the church governing board? Of committees or ministry teams?

3. Where are these roles defined? (E.g., denominational rules, church bylaws, job or ministry descriptions.)

4. Consider the "Leadership Responsibilities of Church Governing Boards" listed in the "Tools for Christian Leadership" section in this book. How is your governing board like a corporate board? How is it different?

5. What are the criteria for selecting members of the governing board?

6. Who is responsible for the various roles of the community needing leadership, and are each of these roles effectively cared for? Some examples of leadership areas:

   • Worship, including music, liturgy, and sacraments

   • Pastoral care and outreach to others in need

   • Evangelism (inviting and welcoming people)

   • Christian formation (spiritual development)

   • Christian stewardship, including identifying and deploying spiritual gifts

   • Financial management

   • Buildings and grounds

   • Vision and oversight, including the responsibilities described under "Leadership Responsibilities for Church Governing Boards" in "Tools for Christian Leaders"

7. Can you identify specific ministries that are unduly burdensome because they fall on just one or a few people? What can you let go of? How can you get new leaders involved?

8. In its approach to ministry, is this congregation predominantly staff driven, or is it largely driven by lay initiatives? If it is largely lay initiatives, does the level of trust and the openness to influential lay initiatives reflect the leadership style of a long-tenured pastor? If yes, what will happen when the current pastor leaves?

9. Do we have the people needed to lead and support our key ministries and mission? Where do we need to strengthen critical ministries?

10. Can we develop effective ministry teams to support the work of the church? What would they look like?

11. How does your church community do with each of the following?

- Help people develop their gifts and talents and use them in ministry through encouragement, training, spiritual direction, and practical supervision

- Proclaim a mission that is inspiring and worth achieving

- Set goals that stretch people's abilities

- Create expectations that the goals can be met

- Build a spirit of collaboration and teamwork

- Create a sense of urgency for the mission of the church

- Build a sense of accountability for the mission

- Involve others in deciding on and setting goals and targets

- Show enthusiasm and belief in others

- Acknowledge people's successes

- Avoid micromanaging strategies

Questions for Group Discussion for a particular church ministry area:

1. Who participates in this ministry area?

2. Is there a ministry team? What is it responsible for, directly or indirectly? Is there a job description?

3. What are the goals, if any, for this ministry area?

4. What are the dreams for this ministry area?

5. What has already been accomplished, and what is in process?

6. How have new people come to this ministry in the past? Are they church members, or are some new to church?

7. What might be done to invite new people into the ministry?

8. In this ministry area, how are people having a terrific experience that they want to come back or continue?

9. How could other groups in the church help support this ministry area in its work?

10. How will this area help more people be involved in this and other ministries?

11. What can we let go of, if anything?

12. What are the challenges and opportunities facing this ministry area?

13. What should be celebrated in this ministry area?

4.3

Guiding and Serving

P eople are attracted to Jesus and follow him because of his character and his love, compassion, and concern for them. Jesus leads by
developing personal relationships with his followers, encouraging and
raising them up, and making each of them part of his community and
mission. As the Son of God, a king, Jesus could clearly command authority. But people did not follow Jesus because he ordered or compelled
them to. They followed him because he was a person they marveled at
and chose to follow. And people still choose to follow because of his
personal integrity and love more than his position, charisma, miracles,
or message.

Christian leaders lead through persuasion and influence developed
in trusting relationships rather than coercively based on power or authority:

> The only real power a leader may possess is the power
> to persuade—largely because the majority of people
> simply will not support a dictator. ... When leaders
> begin to coerce or tell people what to do, they are
> essentially abandoning true leadership and embracing
> dictatorship. Moreover, on a practical level, human
> nature is such that people will not follow a new leader
> unless they trust that individual and are persuaded
> that the course advocated is the right one to take.[1]

Christian leaders are given respect and authority because of their
love for others and their work (1 Thessalonians 5:12–13). Christian leaders need to create the conditions for growth, interdependence, and col-

laboration in mission and ministry. This requires a trusting and supportive environment based upon authentic, forward-looking, open, and guiding leadership.

Authentic and loving leaders

Trusting their leaders gives people a security to act—to follow and to take their own risks.[2] In Christianity, leaders help others along the Way. If leaders don't model the journey authentically (this does not mean perfectly), then how can leaders have credibility with followers? Leadership experts Barry Z. Posner and James M. Kouzes point out that credibility is the foundation of effective leadership:

> Before anyone is going to willingly follow you—or any
> other leader—he or she wants to know that you are
> honest, forward-looking, inspiring, and competent. . . .
> Being honest means telling the truth and having ethical
> principles and clear standards by which you live. People
> need to believe that your character and integrity are solid.
> . . . Being competent refers to your track record and your
> ability to get things done. People have to believe that you
> know what you are talking about and that you know what
> you are doing. They want to be confident that you have
> the skills and abilities to follow through on the promises
> that you make, but also that you have the self-confidence
> to admit that you don't know something but are capable of
> learning. Competence inspires confidence that you will be
> able to guide the enterprise, large or small, in the direction
> in which it needs to go. . . . Above all else, people must be
> able to believe in their leaders. They must believe that your
> word can be trusted, that you are personally passionate
> and enthusiastic about the work that you're doing, and
> that you have the necessary knowledge and skill to lead.[3]

Leadership studies invariably identify the most important characteristic of leaders as credibility, integrity, or trustworthiness. A typical definition of these terms is that they "do what they say they will do." But leaders do more than keep promises; they walk the talk. They lead by example and model personal accountability by following through on personal commitments in all areas: work ethic, role performance, and consistency in expectations. Leading by example requires a leader to be clear about his or her beliefs and put them into practice every day: "Becoming a leader begins when you come to understand who you are, what you care about, and why you do what you do."[4] Leaders go first and only ask others to do things they are willing to do themselves. Leaders' statements and actions show people what is or is not important, how to follow, and what following will mean for them. Because these leaders are personally accountable to their mission and followers, they are able to hold each of their followers accountable to similar standards.

Jesus knew where he had come from, where he was going, and the power that had been given to him (John 13:3). Throughout his ministry, Jesus explained and fully demonstrated what living in his kingdom of love is like. He demonstrates his way of life in the kingdom of love he proclaims. Jesus calls his followers "friends" and "brothers" and teaches them to serve others and put others first. He more than models the Way, saying, "*I am* the way and the truth and the life" (John 14:6). Jesus teaches people that they can live in the same relationships with God and one another that he does. He taught in sayings and parables and served in every way possible, even giving up his life for others. His disciples often did not fully understand his Good News, but they saw enough to trust in him and commit themselves to his Way.

People trust and follow because of a leader's integrity, but even more because of a leader's love—because a leader truly and deeply cares personally about followers and where they are going. Jesus loves God and his followers, and those who don't follow him (Mark 10:21), and even his enemies. Jesus is a wholly loving person, so his integrity flows from his deep, constant, and unending love. No leader is more trustworthy than Jesus, and, with his help, Christian leaders may also be loving and trustworthy. In Christian communities, people are appointed to leadership because they are perceived to have a character to love and care for one another in the way Jesus did. Leaders are selected as overseers because of their character and how they will tend God's flock or family as God's steward (John 21:15–22, 1 Timothy 3:1–15, Titus 1:5–9). The qualifying questions Jesus asks Christian leaders over and over again are "Do you love me?" (John 21:15–17) and "Do you love one another as I have loved you?" (John 13:34–35, 15:12).

A leader who acts with integrity shows character and consistency: "The believability of the leader determines whether people will willingly give more of their time, talent, energy, experience, intelligence, creativity, and support. Only credible leaders earn commitment, and only commitment builds and regenerates great organizations and communities."[5] This means that leaders may first need to focus on their own behaviors before they focus on changing the behaviors of others: "One of the primary mistakes that leaders today make, when called to lead, is spending most of their time and energy trying to improve things at the organizational level before ensuring that they have adequately addressed their own credibility at individual, one-on-one, or team leadership levels."[6]

We know that the Christian way of acting lovingly and with character and consistency requires continuous learning and improvement. Christian leaders model the Way for others. Modeling is living a Christ-centered life of faithfulness, humility, prayer, study, reflection, love, service, forgiving, sharing, celebrating, vulnerability, and authenticity. The leader is not "already there," and he or she is helping himself or herself and others to get "there." The journey is as important as the destination. Even more than other people, leaders themselves need to be able to step back, look in the mirror, and make an honest self-assessment of their strengths and weaknesses. This requires leaders to keep open minds, accept feedback, make new evaluations and decisions, admit mistakes, and continue to learn and grow personally. Honest leaders need to admit their mistakes and disclose their vulnerabilities. Showing your vulnerability and desire to improve is part of showing your love and integrity and, paradoxically, becomes part of developing respect and trust.[7]

Forward-looking leaders

Leadership studies also emphasize the importance of a well-articulated and shared vision to effective leadership. Posner and Kouzes include being forward-looking and inspiring in their explanation of credible leadership:

> Being forward-looking means having a sense of direction
> and a concern for the future of the organization. Whether
> it's called a vision, a mission, or a personal agenda, the
> message is clear: You must know where you're going if you
> expect others to willingly join you on the journey. But it's

not just your vision that others care to know. They also expect that you'll be able to connect your image of the future to their hopes, dreams, and aspirations. People won't willingly follow you until they can see how they share in the future you envision ... Being inspiring means sharing the genuine enthusiasm, excitement, and energy you have about the exciting possibilities ahead. People expect you to be positive, upbeat, and optimistic. Your energy signals your personal commitment, and your optimism signals your hope. Others need you to encourage them to reach higher, engage more fully, and put forth greater effort.[8]

Leaders are forward-looking and able to see the directions the community needs to go. Leaders also translate this vision of the future into more specific goals or steps that help make the vision more tangible and specific for members who are not as visionary or forward-thinking. The goals need to be connected to the vision, and both need to be continuously modeled, communicated, and reinforced in ways which are motivating and persuasive:

One of the most powerful internal motivators on the planet is a sense of meaning and purpose. Throughout human history people have risked life, security, and wealth for something that is greater than themselves. People want a chance to take part in something meaningful and important. There is a deep human yearning to make a difference. People want to know that there is a purpose to their existence. They want to know that their lives mean something. A significant part of the leader's job is uncovering and reflecting back the meaning that others seek.[9]

Notice that Posner and Kouzes emphasize, however, that the vision needs to be connected to the hopes, dreams, and aspirations of the followers, not just those of the leaders: "Truly inspirational leadership is not about selling a vision; it's about showing people how the vision can directly benefit them and how their specific needs can be satisfied." They explain:

Leading others is definitely not about getting others to conform to your point of view. Conformity produces compliance, not commitment. Unity is essential, and unity is forged, not forced. . . . What you espouse . . . must resonate with the aspirations of others. People won't fully commit to the group and organization if they don't sense a good fit with who they are and what they believe. . . . Leadership is more often about listening than telling. Your task is to gain consensus on a common cause and a common set of principles. You need to build and affirm a community of shared values.[10]

An effective vision is a practical roadmap and a powerful motivator:

Vision casting is an integral part of leading. Fuzzy communication leads to unclear direction, which produces sloppy execution. Productive leaders create a clear link between the vision of the organization and everyday production of the team. They show how the short term impacts the long term. They are clear in their communication and continually point the way for their team. A compelling vision is clear and well-defined, expansive and challenging. It is aligned with the shared values of the team. It is focused primarily on the end, not means. It fits the giftedness of the team. And when it is communicated and understood, it fills the room with energy![11]

Jesus shares the most inspiring vision ever for our participation in a kingdom of faith, love, hope, and joy. And he casts this vision with his whole life. As Christian leaders, we are responsible for sharing that vision within our unique context and community.

Often we do this by weaving our stories with God's story. Stories are expressions of meaning we share about who we are, where we're going, who we're going with, and why. When Diana Butler Bass studied fifty vital mainline Protestant congregations to identify common practices that strengthen communal life, she discovered an emerging style of "narrative leadership" for congregational renewal. In vital mainline churches, leaders know their stories and live them; narratives are a source of and resource for change.[12] One of the centers of congregational life is our narrative of who we are as people of faith in our community. People join together with a sense of belonging when they see themselves as part of this larger story.

For Christian leaders, sharing stories is essential. When leaders look ahead and see the directions the community needs to go, they need to share their vision. They need to make the vision understandable and motivating for members of the community who are not as visionary or forward thinking. Sometimes they will do this by translating the vision into more specific goals or steps. But a story is often a better and more inspiring blueprint. People connect better to an unfolding story about their relationships with God and one another. In "Telling the Better Story,"[13] Gil Rendle emphasizes the importance of leading a faith community by "shaping and claiming the story of identity and purpose" that is faithful to God's call. He writes:

> Leadership is not telling people what they want to hear. It is not creating the story with enough "spin" to manipulate people for personal or congregational advantage. Leadership happens when the leader tells a story sufficiently healthy, authentic, and purposeful for others to feel connection, respond with resonance, and find greater meaning. Connection happens when people are able to say to themselves, "I see myself in that story." Connection seems not to rely upon full agreement or a need for compliance from others. To feel like a part of the larger whole seems to be enough. Resonance suggests that the historicity or accuracy of the story is not as important as the question of whether or not it rings true. When the story rings true it enables the listeners to generate a new way of thinking and acting that embraces—and even advances—the truth the story represents. ... The life-giving story has to point beyond ourselves and our congregation to some greater purpose. As such, the empowering story of the congregation must be connected to the much larger story of our faith.

Rendle identifies three steps to learn and use the power of the congregation's story to shape the community and guide ministry. The first step is learning how the community describes itself in terms of its context of history, culture, and environment by "listening to how people talk about themselves: the metaphors they use, the way in which behavior and attitude do or do not match their words, the memories captured and retold, and also the memories forgotten or denied." Leaders consider how the story connects to God's story, including biblical texts and spiritual practices. In the second step, leaders "re-tell" the story and confront the identity of the congregation, challenging "whether there can be more or less to the story—more health, more depth, more meaning, or less fear, less caution, less control." This confrontation produces uncertainty, anxiety, and possibly even a feeling of wilderness or chaos, and leaders "must provide support and safety" in these conversations "to help people stay with and live into their new story." In the third step of leadership by story, leaders and people "together use what they have learned to collaborate on the new telling of the story or the writing of its next chapter," asking "Who are we? What has God called us to do? Who is our neighbor?"

There are many opportunities to share our stories in community. We often hear them in sermons or during annual stewardship campaigns as people witness about their faith experiences. Sometimes, they are shared along with our prayers for ministry teams or with announcements encouraging participation in activities or ministries. Remembering, sharing, and celebrating our stories are inherent in and important to team and small group meetings. We need to intentionally encourage sharing stories throughout our life together.

Proclaiming Good News is important. Sharing your individual and communal faith stories and hearing the stories of others can build a stronger sense of relationship with God and others. When you share your story and hear the stories of others, you can begin to draw a connection between how God has acted in Scripture, liturgy, and history and how God draws you into relationship. We need to share that our lives are being transformed not in our own power but through the power of God's love. We need to gently and wisely and appropriately share our stories about what God is doing in our lives. And then we can invite others to join us on the Way.

Open leaders

Another key to building trust for effective leadership is being "forthright, candid, and clear in your communication" because "leaders are far better served when they're forthcoming with information. There's nothing more destructive to trust than deceit, and nothing more constructive than candor."[14] Leaders may try to hide information for various reasons. A leader may feel others do not "need to know," that information may be misunderstood, that not providing information may actually protect others or help them feel more secure, or that keeping information to oneself gives the leader greater power over a situation or other people. In each of these situations, when people learn that the leader has withheld information—regardless of their actual "need to know" it or not—they lose trust in the leader.

Being open includes communicating how decisions are made. Cisco executives Ron Ricci and Carl Wiese explain the importance of this practice:

> Relentlessly pursue transparent decision making. Decisions are always about making choices; it's critical that you are clear about how you make them. Tell people your style and thought process for navigating tricky, or even everyday, decisions. In our experience, and this is backed up by research, there's a direct relationship between the agility and resilience of a team and the transparency of its decision-making processes. When you're open and transparent about the answers to three questions—who made the decision, who is accountable for the outcomes of the decision, and is that accountability real—people in organizations spend far less time questioning how or why a decision was made. Think of how much time is wasted ferreting out details when a decision is made and communicated because the people who are affected don't know who made the decision or who is accountable for its consequences. ... As a leader, your responsibility is to document the key decision paths of your organization and communicate them to your team as often as you can. There was a time in business when hoarding information was a source of organizational power.

Today, the inverse is true if you want to motivate a team
that is increasingly mobile, global and socially driven.[15]

Along the Way, there are rarely times for a leader not to openly share information. Followers are told where Jesus is going and where they are going (e.g., Mark 8:31, 9:31; John 11:16, 14:5, 21:18–19), even when the news is challenging or something they may not want to hear. Disciples are given information even when they do not understand all of the information they are being given and it is being modeled and learned along the Way. For people to learn, they need to understand what is expected, choose to follow, and find opportunities to grow and to serve together. In addition to building trust, there is a bigger reason for openly sharing information. Eventually, disciples will also be trusted to learn and lead others along the Way. Christian leaders need to empower and delegate more to prepare their followers for sharing ministry, and that means their followers need to learn how things work to achieve better results, help others, and build teams.

Guiding leaders

The model for trusted leaders in the Bible is the good shepherd. Jesus says, "I came that they may have life, and have it abundantly. I am the good shepherd. The good shepherd lays down his life for the sheep" (John 10:10–11). The good shepherd is a trusted leader who secures and cares for his or her flock (Psalm 23, 2 Samuel 7:7, Zechariah 11:4–17, Ezekiel 34, John 10:1–16). Jesus commissions Christian leaders as shepherds in John 21. All Christian leaders are encouraged to be good shepherds. Paul tells the elders of Ephesus in Acts: "Keep watch over yourselves and over all the flock, of which the Holy Spirit has made you overseers, to shepherd the church of God that he obtained with the blood of his own Son" (20:28). And 1 Peter 5:1–5 says,

> Now as an elder myself and a witness of the sufferings of
> Christ, as well as one who shares in the glory to be revealed,
> I exhort the elders among you to tend the flock of God
> that is in your charge, exercising the oversight, not under
> compulsion but willingly, as God would have you do it—not
> for sordid gain but eagerly. Do not lord it over those in your
> charge, but be examples to the flock. And when the chief

shepherd appears, you will win the crown of glory that never fades away. In the same way, you who are younger must accept the authority of the elders. And all of you must clothe yourselves with humility in your dealings with one another, for "God opposes the proud, but gives grace to the humble."

Good shepherds

- are with their flocks,
- nurture the little lambs,
- tend the sheep,
- strengthen the weak,
- heal the sick,
- bind up the injured,
- bring back the strayed and seek the lost,
- protect and rescue them from dangers,
- save and restore their flocks,
- feed the sheep,
- guide them to green pasture and rich vegetation,
- bring them to clear water to drink,
- provide them with safety and peace and rest,
- lead with staffs of favor and unity,
- lead beside still waters and with comfort,
- take away their fears, and
- anoint and bless them.

As their shepherd, Jesus loves and prays for all of his followers (John 17:6–19). He has taught his disciples to love God and love one another so that they are prepared to live and lead in God's family. Jesus offers his disciples to God and asks God to consecrate them, to set them apart (v. 17), to make them one with God and one another (v. 11), to guard and protect them (v. 15) and to give them joy (v. 13). He asks God to care for them physically, emotionally, and spiritually, as he has cared for them as the Good Shepherd. Jesus asks these things "not only on behalf of these, but also on behalf of those who will believe in me through their word, that they may all be one. As you, Father, are in me and I am in you, may they also be in us, so that the world may believe that you have sent me."

A Christian leader's role is to guide or shepherd followers to grow in Christian unity and maturity. With the least mature members, this may require exercising authority as parents do when setting boundaries to guard and protect their children. Paul encourages leaders and other members of Christian community to "admonish" people who are not doing what they are supposed to (Colossians 3:16, 1 Thessalonians 5:12–14). This is not just chastising, but warning or giving friendly, earnest advice in an encouraging manner (1 Corinthians 4:14). This guidance is gentle, loving, and nurturing—not forceful or violent. Its purpose is to serve the other person rather than to exercise, maintain, or increase the leader's own position or power. With a good shepherd, the lost will be found, the injured will be bound up, the weak will be strengthened, life will be restored, and followers will be welcomed home (Isaiah 40:1–11).

As people grow to maturity, leaders will rely less on admonishment. And they will be respected and followed for their compassion, experience, and wisdom. People will see them as imitators and representatives of Jesus and will willingly obey by listening and being guided:

> *The sheep hear [the shepherd's] voice. He calls his own*
> *sheep by name and leads them out. When he has brought*
> *out all his own, he goes ahead of them, and the sheep*
> *follow him because they know his voice. They will not*
> *follow a stranger, but they will run from him because*
> *they do not know the voice of strangers. (John 10:3–5)*

Christian leadership is based not in righteousness, authority, or power—for all these belong only to God—but in compassion for God and God's family. This means that Christian leadership that wants to reach the world needs to rely primarily on developing and leading from trusting personal relationships.

Engaging Jesus

To continue engaging Jesus, read and reflect on Ezekiel 34, Psalm 23, and John 10.

Questions for Personal Reflection:

1. Answer the following questions as if the Good Shepherd is asking them before sending you into ministry:

    a. Do you believe that I always love you whatever you do?

    b. Do you love me?

    c. Do you trust me to be with you?

    d. Will you serve me by serving others?

2. Name three ways you nurture trust in relationships at work and at home.

3. Reflect on a time when you lost trust in a leader and how it impacted your relationship. What about a time when someone lost trust in you?

4. Ask yourself the Good Shepherd's questions again.

Questions for Group Discussion:

1. Reflect on Psalm 23, Ezekiel 34, and John 10. What are the leadership characteristics of a shepherd?

2. How are you doing as leaders of a community with these characteristics?

3. As leaders, do you have a compelling vision to lead your community? What is it? How do you share it?

4. What is your strategy to serve and help your people live according to that vision?

4.4

Developing Followers and Leaders

A significant focus of Jesus' ministry is making disciples who will bring other people to Jesus to be reconciled with God and one another (Matthew 28:19–20). Jesus' plan for expanding and deepening kingdom love is to provide for the growth and development of people into his disciples. As people discover that Jesus and his disciples offer an opportunity for personal growth and relationship with God and one another, they also come to Jesus. Jesus chose to have disciples to continue his mission, and he made disciples indispensable to his ministry. While the disciples' confused questions might have seemed annoying and slowed down other aspects of his ministry, Jesus took the time to help the disciples understand and grow. Jesus helped his closest followers grow into leaders who could help others become disciples, who in turn would serve others and help others become disciples, too. Helping to develop people brings in even more people. Although the disciples did not seem very successful at first, ultimately disciples will reach "all nations" by also helping others to grow and use their gifts as disciples.

Few activities are more rewarding or loving than helping another person with opportunities to grow as a Christian follower and leader. Along the Way, as Christian leaders develop and empower followers, these followers become stronger disciples. They develop loving relationships with God and other people. They become more Christlike. They become apostles. More disciples are able to reach and help more people. They help share the mission. They share God's love with more people and help those people to do the same. They help lead. And the cycle repeats and love grows. "Every time you develop a leader, you make a difference in the world. And if you develop leaders who take what they've learned and use it to develop other leaders, there's no telling what kind of an impact you'll have or how long that impact will last."[1]

Help followers work in God's kingdom

Making new and stronger disciples is a central activity of Christian leaders. Disciples are people who "do everything I have commanded you." We are people who do the work of God's kingdom of loving God and loving one another. As we follow Jesus on the Way, we need to learn enough from him to do this work of God's kingdom. As followers we need to ask if we are becoming better disciples. As leaders, we also need to help to develop each person for effective ministry and for producing good fruit for God's kingdom. We need to regularly evaluate our effectiveness in helping all people, not just new Christians, become better disciples.

Helping people feel they belong to the kingdom and are growing and producing good fruit is much more than just adding members to a church. Saint Paul explains that this happens through equipping, uniting, and empowering people and helping them grow together to become the body of Christ (Ephesians 4:11–16). This means that we must focus—as Jesus did during his earthly ministry and still does—on being "people developers." Most people (and communities) are not natural people developers. Judging by historical results, there is no better people developer than Jesus. So we need to pray and encourage others to pray for help in becoming leaders who help Jesus make new and stronger disciples. As he says, Jesus is with us always in this process.

In helping people to connect with a community and do the work of the kingdom, we can actually learn a lot from a secular Gallup research study. This survey asked more than a million talented employees about all aspects of their working life and clearly identified what they need from a workplace to be successful. The study found that the strength of a workplace can be evaluated by asking twelve questions to measure effectiveness in attracting, retaining, and developing the "most talented" workers. These same questions can be asked "to attract, focus, and keep" people who are joining a community and becoming disciples of Jesus:

1. Do I know what is expected of me?

2. Do I have the materials and equipment I need to do my

work right?

3. When working, do I have the opportunity to do what I do best every day?

4. In the last seven days, have I received recognition or praise for doing good work?

5. Does my manager or someone at work seem to care for me as a person?

6. Is there someone at work who encourages my development?

7. At work, do my opinions seem to count?

8. Does the mission or purpose of my organization make me feel my work is important?

9. Are my coworkers committed to doing quality work?

10. Do I have a best friend at work?

11. In the last six months, has someone at work talked to me about my progress?

12. This last year, have I had opportunities at work to learn and grow?[2]

Imagine the experience of a church member who can answer "yes" to each question with respect to his or her church activities. The study elaborates:

> If you can answer positively to all of these twelve questions, then you have reached the summit. Your focus is clear. You feel a recurring sense of achievement, as though the best of you is being called upon and the best of you responds every single day. You look around and see others who also seem to thrill to the challenge of their work. Buoyed by your mutual understanding and your shared purpose, you . . . look out and forward to the challenges marching over the horizon . . . it is quite a feeling.[3]

This seems to describe the joyful experience church members are looking for. Next, imagine the person who cannot answer each question positively. They will often feel lost and unhappy with their church community. Most people probably expect their church communities to be able to provide greater satisfaction to these questions than other organizations. And that is why churches can be so disappointing.

The Gallup study shows that the twelve questions need to be satisfied in order. For example, it's not enough to obtain a positive answer to question 8 before questions 1 and 2 are satisfied. And the first six questions are more critical for a strong, vibrant, and effective community than the last six. Focusing on later questions to the exclusion of the earlier may diminish the experiences of members and harm a church community.

The Gallup study finds that for a mentor or leader to be successful in satisfying the first six questions, he or she must act as a catalyst and "be able to do four activities extremely well" to unlock the potential of each worker:

- When selecting someone, select for talent not simply experience, intelligence, or determination.

- When setting expectations, define the right outcomes not the right steps.

- When motivating someone, focus on strengths not on weaknesses.

- When developing someone, help find the right fit not simply the next rung on the ladder.[4]

These four leadership activities place the right people in the right roles with the right mentors, where they are much more likely to be fully engaged, effective in their work, and contributing to a strong and vibrant community. Rather than feeling miscast, individuals will work in roles for which they have the right talents, skills, and experience. Rather than lacking direction, individuals and teams will focus on the steps they need to take to reach common goals and will feel that they are respected and recognized for their work and growth.

Notice, however, that these activities are largely accomplished not through programs or processes but through individual and team relationships, through understanding the unique place of an individual member and helping that individual take the next step along his or her spiritual path.[5] Like Jesus, we must engage people by helping them to take the next steps on their spiritual journeys as they become incarnational disciples and apostles. This is mentoring more than preaching, teaching, or training; it requires both our support and the other person's active involvement. Much of the work of the church must happen not through preaching or worship or programs but in personal relationships. Helping people develop their gifts and talents and use them in ministry is primarily a one-to-one or team function. "The behavior of leaders explains more about why people feel engaged and positive about their workplaces than any particular individual or organizational characteristic."[6]

Select for individual talent

In a Christian community, we may select clergy and staff by hiring them, but most members come in response to invitations. In either case, the church tries to match an individual with the work of ministry according to his or her gifts, passions, abilities, personality, and experience. This requires mutual discernment, asking "What is this person's unique contribution?" and then helping equip the individual according to his or her gifts and desires, not just according to what the church seems to need at the time. Followers of Jesus find joy and satisfaction in using their unique talents to make contributions to common purposes as part of a community. To fully become the body of Christ, we need to discern the calling and capabilities of each person and give them as much authority and responsibility as they can handle. The challenge is that this requires leaders to know their people, particularly their gifts and aspirations, and to make assignments with personal development in mind.

A church community supports diversity and inclusiveness by helping all members appreciate and encourage the great variety of gifts that people bring to the community. Each of us needs to support the gifts of others, to be careful not to protect our own turf in the church community. We will all thrive if we broaden the opportunities for people to get involved in the church according to their gifts and desires. We need leaders like Jesus and Moses who bless us for ministry and encourage us to share and participate in God's kingdom. And we each need to bless others in this way as well.

Set expectations for outcomes

According to the Gallup study, the first question a worker asks is "Do I know what is expected of me?" Someone new to a church might ask initially, "How do I participate in worship?" and later, "How do I become a member?" The Ethiopian eunuch asked Philip, "How can I, unless someone guides me?" and "What is to prevent me from being baptized?" (Acts 8). Those who follow need to know where they are going and what is expected of them. We may better connect with people and support their spiritual journey in community by making expectations clear.

Setting expectations is more than just stating a vision for the organization. Leaders need to share a vision that will help individuals feel their work is important (question 8 of the Gallup study). But, more important to discipling, leaders also need to make each person responsible for helping meet that vision and for his or her own spiritual development. We need to share the challenges, explain the boundaries and desired outcomes, help equip each person, and encourage them to minister to others. It is not enough for the community to have a significant purpose and to help people belong to the community.

"Expectations" (from the Latin word *expectare* or "to look forward to") are things that we hope people will experience because they are important to deepening their spiritual journeys and transforming their lives. Expectations help describe what the church is looking forward to for members of the body of Christ. These are not ethical or moral rules, but more often are statements of spiritual reality such as, "If you love one another, you will participate in God's kingdom (right now)." Expectations help people identify the commitments they want to make and learn to take personal responsibility for their spiritual development.[7] Studies show that any kind of real expectation increases commitment, raises levels of participation, and enables a group to offer more benefits to current and potential members. A church that fails to set expectations—often from fear that members want freedom and will reject accountability—will have less commitment, participation, member satisfaction, and mission focus.[8]

Jesus had expectations for his disciples. Jesus asked more of his followers than anyone ever has. Contrast "My yoke is easy" with other expectations he's given: *Take up your cross and follow him. Do good to those who harm us. Pray for those who persecute us. Turn the other cheek. Give not just our coat but our cloak. Go the extra mile. Give to whoever asks. Refrain not just from killing but from anger or calling someone a fool. Refrain not just from adultery but from wrongful desire.* Each of these expectations will help a follower to find a better way of life. That is what Jesus is looking forward to for his followers, and that is what his followers look forward to for themselves. Christians have big expectations.

A Christian community might set expectations for participation in worship, small groups, ministries or missions, and financial stewardship.[9] Less often, we set expectations to encourage individual members to discern what God wants to create through them, to strengthen Christlike character through intimate relationship with God, or to show compassion for others. Questions to answer include, "What are the benefits of being a member?" "What are the requirements for membership in this community?" "What are the responsibilities of membership?" "How can I get involved in ministry?" and "What do I do now that I am a member?" More than an ethical pronouncement of what a person "should" do, expectations need to be a statement of the reality of how we may strengthen our spiritual growth and development, and we need to affirm each person wherever they are in their spiritual journey. We may better structure the discipleship process by making expectations clear.

Motivate positively and personally

One of the important qualities that healthy, growing Christian churches have in common is empowering leadership: "Leaders of growing churches concentrate on empowering other Christians for ministry. They do not use ... workers as helpers in attaining their own goals and fulfilling their own visions. Rather, they invert the pyramid of authority so that the leader[s assist] Christians to attain the spiritual potential God has for them. These [leaders] equip, support, motivate and mentor individuals, enabling them to become all that God wants them to be."[10] Empowering leaders "take actions that make people strong and capable. They make people feel that they can do more than they thought they could. One of the reasons people want to follow a leader is because they know that they will be better off as a result of being in that relationship than they would be otherwise."[11]

Empowering leaders are good at preparing others for ministry through encouragement, training, spiritual direction, and practical supervision. This takes time and energy because it requires empowering leaders to build close, open relationships; actively listen; provide the necessary resources; involve the person in setting goals and targets; show enthusiasm and belief in the person; acknowledge the person's successes; reflect back on the skills and talents the person has already demonstrated; and be honest about the person's worries and concerns, openly discussing fears and considering challenges and possible outcomes. "When we ask people to describe their relationships with the leader they most admire and look up to ... they tell us that when they are with this leader they feel empowered, listened to, understood, capable, important, like they mattered, challenged to do more, and other similar descriptors."[12] All of these leadership activities require time for, presence with, and attention to followers.

The Gallup study reminds us to focus our efforts on the other person's needs. As a mentor or leader, do I care for each individual I lead as a person? (question 5). Am I daily or weekly offering recognition or praise for doing good work? (question 4). Am I encouraging his or her development? (question 6). Have I talked with the individual about his or her progress? (question 11). Positively answering any of these questions requires me to be in close and regular contact with the person I am working with, to know how and what he or she is doing, and to make engaging and encouraging responses. "Leaders are obsessed with what is best for others, not what is best for themselves."[13]

Consider how Jesus prepared his disciples: calling them into ministry (Mark 1:16–20), encouraging them (John 15:11), supporting Peter when he was about to sink into the sea (Matthew 14:28–31), sharing vision and expectations (Matthew 5), teaching them how to do ministry (Matthew 10), directly explaining why they sometimes failed (Matthew 17:15–16), being honest about when they were likely to be challenged (Mark 8:31–35, Matthew 10, John 21) or fail (Matthew 26:75, Mark 14:72, Luke 22:61, John 13:38), teaching them to pray (Matthew 6:8–13, 21:21), praying for them (John 17:6–19) and for their followers (John 17:20), and reconciling with them and restoring them to ministry when they fell away (John 20:19–31, John 21). Jesus brought his disciples with him and was with them (Matthew 28:20), knew and understood them, loved them (Mark 10:21), and was actively involved in their lives and ministries. Jesus demonstrates an amazing model of mentoring and coaching and actually bringing people into loving kingdom relationships so they can bring others.

Many leaders today would see this as an impossible or inappropriate commitment to people:

> Very few people are both able and willing to develop others
> to become leaders. That is why most leaders only ever
> lead followers. Anyone who can relate well with people,
> produce personally, and communicate a vision is capable
> of attracting following. However, attracting, developing,
> and leading other leaders is much more difficult. And most
> leaders are not willing to put forth the tremendous effort
> it takes and to make the sacrifices necessary to do it.[14]

Some leaders neither value nor serve other people in this way; instead, they treat them as replaceable, unnecessary, or unworthy. But Jesus says, "Love one another as I have loved you" (John 13:34–35). Similarly, Paul writes, "in humility regard others as better than yourselves. Let each of you look not to your own interests, but to the interests of others. Let the same mind be in you that was in Christ Jesus" (Philippians 2:3–5). And "the aim of such instruction is love that comes from a pure heart, a good conscience, and sincere faith" (1 Timothy 1:5).

Christian love means helping one another grow without placing our own limits on another person's growth. It means taking more time to train someone than it would take to complete the task yourself. It means giving people time to learn new things and allowing them to make mistakes. It means raising others up as our peers or leaders to the full extent they are called and capable—even when you are more senior or more experienced. Some followers will even take over positions or responsibilities you have held. Some will become your critics. These are not good reasons for holding on to responsibilities or holding others back.

Empowering others means letting go of our own fears and giving others room to grow. Leaders who maintain tight control over everything and everyone don't understand the paradox of empowering others: the more power you give away, the more you have. This is kingdom, not selfish, thinking: "Give, and it will be given to you ... for the measure you give will be the measure you get back" (Luke 6:38). The challenge is to risk ourselves to others: "to be abandoned to the talents and skills of others, and therefore to be vulnerable. The same risks as one has when falling in love."[15] We must do what it takes to love and empower the people we lead.

Help people grow

Jesus' generosity and stewardship of people is the foundation of Kingdom relationships now and for the future. If we can't do this as fully or as well as Jesus by ourselves, we can do this better in Christian community. The activities of the church community may serve as a crucible for growth. And people at different levels of leadership can provide different kinds of support for one another. Places this occurs in church communities are small groups and ministry teams. If we are to help support and develop disciples with these teams, we need to be developing leaders and mentors for them: "High-quality relationships don't happen spontaneously. They require leadership. It's your job to interact with others in ways that promote connection, collaboration, confidence, and competence. When you do, you'll see learning, innovation, and performance soar."[16]

Personal and team growth can happen in various ways. Some things can be learned through reading, study, observation, or reflection on one's own experiences. Other personal growth requires participation in activities and working through challenges together. Although teaching or training is important, people development is much more than classes, lectures, seminars, or workshops. People need to share in special tasks and projects, share their experiences, and learn with and from one another. For example, a person can't truly discover spiritual gifts without using them or become effective in pastoral care without practicing. Because the Way is a journey together, people need to grow together. Discipling largely happens through learning and involvement in ministry together. And when people are involved in ministry together, coaching is one of the most effective tools for personal and team development.

It may seem surprising that a worker's question about personal growth—"have I had opportunities at work to learn and grow?"—is all the way down the Gallup list at question 12. In this hierarchy, however, all of the other components—good mentors, friends, purposes, expectations, tools, and opportunities—need to come together to support personal growth. Just as disciples need Jesus, all followers need leaders and teams to help them grow and develop.

The Gallup study reminds us not to simply move people to "the next rung on the ladder." In this regard, it is important to recognize that the Holy Spirit provides the gifts for ministry (1 Corinthians 12, Romans 12, Colossians 1) and gifted leaders help equip others for ministry (Ephesians 4:11). The purpose is not to move up a ladder of success but for "all of us" together to "come to the unity of the faith and of the knowledge of the Son of God, to maturity, to the measure of the full stature of Christ" (Ephesians 4:13). There is no organizational chart except Jesus as Leader and Savior (Acts 5:31), and no single direction on that chart to help people grow in. Personal development as a Christian is a journey, not a position or an achievement.

On this journey, however, people do need to move on and find new challenges and fulfilling ministries. Leaders and other team members can help identify the next step, which might be in any direction along a spiritual path, not just the next rung on a ladder or organizational chart. Some organizations have mechanisms to encourage people to keep moving, such as term limits or apprenticeships. To some extent these may create artificial deadlines, but most organizations can give examples of people who stayed in positions "too long." It is healthy from the very beginning of a new ministry to estimate a time to move on, assuming this fits the individual's development plan and aspirations. This helps both the community and the individual to plan and prepare for the journey ahead.

As we journey and practice and learn together, many disciples will become leaders. In this sense, Christian theology agrees with leadership studies that find that leadership skills are far more broadly distributed among people than was expected by traits-based leadership theories. Some people may have certain gifts that help them with leadership, but that does not mean either that they are natural born leaders or that they are the only ones with gifts for leadership. People can develop leadership skills and abilities through practice, experience, and learning. And any Christian involved in serving others will ultimately discover that the Holy Spirit provides gifts and helps him or her do far more than he or she could ever do on his or her own.

Notice that empowering leadership requires leaders to spend additional time at the level of leadership development (versus incorporating new church members). Leaders who are developing other leaders and multiplying growth need to continue to ask and build upon the following questions: (i) Are we developing leaders to whom we can *delegate* leadership of our ministry teams? (ii) Are we developing *empowering* leaders who help team members feel connected and effective? (iii) Are we developing leaders of our ministry teams to *integrate* aspects of spiritual development—prayer, Bible study, and formation—with the ministry activities to help transform individuals and teams? and (iv) Are we continually identifying and preparing leaders who accept delegation of ministry responsibilities and are *accountable* for empowering and transforming their teams and serving their ministries?

The objectives of Jesus and all other Christian leaders are to love their followers and to transform their followers into leaders. Christian followers never become wholly independent (i.e., "I am the vine, you are the branches" and "I am with you always"). But they do grow into responsibility for leading others to live into and serve in God's kingdom. Jesus focused significant time on training followers who would become leaders, and those leaders became responsible for significant kingdom growth: "But as for what was sown on good soil, this is the one who hears the word and understands it, who indeed bears fruit and yields, in one case a hundredfold, in another sixty, and in another thirty" (Matthew 13:23). Jesus showed confidence that his disciples loved him (John 21:15) and were ready to lead by sending them to take care of his flock (John 21) and to go and make disciples of all nations (Matthew 28). All Christian leaders want the same for their followers.

Engaging Jesus

To continue engaging Jesus, read and reflect on Acts 8:26–40.

Questions for Personal Reflection:

1. What expectations do you have for your Christian journey?

2. What expectations does your church community have for your Christian journey?

3. How well do you encourage and involve others in ministry?

4. Ask yourself the following questions suggested by Ken Blanchard to gauge your progress in leading like Jesus:

   - How well am I doing in preparing others to take my place when the time comes?

   - Do I consider them a threat or an investment in the future?

   - Am I willing to share what I know and provide opportunities to learn and grow for those who will come after me? If not, why not?

   - Do you view training your successor or the next generation as a threat, a burden, or an opportunity to extend your leadership impact beyond your season of influence?

   - How does your succession planning impact your daily, weekly, quarterly, or yearly priorities?

Questions for Group Discussion:

1. As a community, how do you empower others to ministry and mission? How is this working?

2. How would members of your community respond to each of the 12 questions from the Gallup study?

3. What are your expectations for members of your community? What are the requirements for becoming a full "member" or for qualifying for various volunteer ministries?

4. How would your congregation react to clearer expectations?

5. Can you have expectations and still accept people wherever they are on their spiritual journey (recognizing God's love for them)?

6. What kind of expectations does your community need?

7. How is your church community doing with each of the four ways to unlock the potential of each Christian worker?

8. How are you developing new and apprentice small group and ministry team leaders and board members?

4.5

Discerning God's Call to the Community

J esus asks us to participate in and share the Good News of God's kingdom, and we are responsible for doing this *with him* in our own place and time. Jesus has not directly told our church community how to produce fruits of the kingdom in our specific context. We need to focus on translating his mission, vision, and values into our own context. Primarily, then, this means seeing our unique context and what God is trying to do with and through us.

Unique vocations

Each church has a unique mission to respond to God's calling in the world. The Great Commission and the Great Commandment provide a broad framework for the mission of the Church and require individual definition by each congregation. And even though we're following Jesus, there isn't a single path. Part of God's call is to find what we are gifted at or enjoy doing. God's call always allows the freedom of choosing among unique opportunities that God has placed before the community.

As leaders of a Christian community, we are primarily listening for God's answer to the key question: Who is God calling this church to be? And then we can begin to answer a second question: How is this congregation going to respond to that call? Many people are surprised to learn that communities have a vocation—something God is calling them to do—just as individuals do. Who we are as a community depends on who God calls us to be. And by discovering this identity, we can become who we are called to be. Answering these questions about vocation is important because a community can only know its identity by knowing what it's called by God to be and to do.

Discernment is a process of identification, of connecting to a spiritual path or journey, not simply a means of solving problems or creating new church programs or tasks. If we know our true *purpose* from God, we can more easily decide which paths we are called to take on our spiritual journey. We can clearly say who this congregation is, who this congregation is becoming, and who might find a wonderful church home in this congregation.

There is no single way for a church to serve God, and discernment is not measuring the church against some third-party, objective standard of what a church should be. Each community needs to be aware of its unique context and personality and hear God's particular call. Because God's plan is unique and individual (based on our own settings and gifts), it is our responsibility to discern our response to that plan. We can look at other church plans as models, but not as formulas or rules.

To respond to God's calling in the world, we need to identify and *evaluate* our circumstances: Where are we? Who are we? What is our current reality? Who are the people, communities, or areas this congregation is called to serve? From this, we may understand a more specific vision of *where God is calling us*.

Discernment is the opportunity to recognize and celebrate God's blessings and presence in our community. The fundamental church health and growth principle is that authentic ministries flow out of a genuine *relationship* with Jesus Christ. We can grow within from the vine and be fruitful and be creative and "ask for whatever we wish" if we recognize and abide in God's love. A church striving to be the body of Christ needs to become Christ centered and, like Jesus, continually strive to discern God's will for the community. Discernment is listening to and distinguishing God's voice and action from other voices and activities in the world. An effective discernment process helps us to recognize the presence of God and respond accordingly: "Do not be conformed to this world, but be transformed by the renewing of your minds, so that you may discern what is the will of God—what is good and acceptable and perfect" (Romans 12:2).

Processes of discernment

God is always with us, but we often miss God. We get caught up in our own concerns. We need to turn our focus from our own concerns to God, and we need to listen carefully (Mark 9:7). Because the focus of discernment is on God's presence with us and our response to that presence, the heart of the process is prayer and following other spiritual disciplines to help open our hearts and pay better attention. Prayer begins in gratitude for the gifts and opportunities the church has received and continues with a careful listening for God's will for the church. We need to consider past and present as well as future. We need to listen to what has happened and is happening to understand where and who we are. And we especially need to spend time with God in the present to begin to understand our special relationship with God and God's plan for us.

As we go through discernment for a church community, we need to ask the same kinds of questions about the church that we might ask ourselves in our own personal discernment processes:

What are the gifts and abilities that God has given us? What can we do well (and in a way that pleases God)? How will we make our talents and abilities available to God and use them for his glory? To discern God's unique and individual call to our spiritual community, we need to recognize our unique context, personality, gifts, aspirations, and callings.

What is our unique situation, and what are the opportunities that we have? Where are we in the world? Where can we go from here? God will grant us a sense of who we are in response to the particularities of our time and place. An authentic Christian community is never simply church for ourselves; we must help introduce others to Jesus. Our activities need to bring people to Jesus or serve people for Jesus.

Where is our organization developmentally? Intentional evaluation also helps us to be direct and realistic about the challenges facing the congregation in its particular context and development stage. What are the problems and possibilities we have? What are the choices we have made? What are our responsibilities? In a sense, what are our limits because of where we are right now? But also, what are our possibilities? We tend to think (or accept without thinking) that we are more limited than we are. So in these questions, we need to be realistic (not negative) about our limits and imaginative of our possibilities.

What brings us joy? Identify what are the desires of our hearts. What are we most passionate about? What energizes us? What do we long for? Jesus said, "I have said these things to you so that my joy may be in you, and that your joy may be complete" (John 15:11). Another way to ask this: Is there something we'd grieve if we didn't do?

It helps to ask these questions all of the time because they point us to the ultimate question: Where is God present with us in this journey?

In "Discernment as Worshipful Work,"[1] Stephen Bryant describes ten important actions in corporate discernment.

1. Framing: "Let's tell stories that celebrate how God has been at work in and through our church, as the church in the village serving ... and as a means of grace in our families and personal journeys." Questions to respond to are *What is God's will for us and for our next steps as a community of Christ-followers?* and *What has been and continues to be the gift of God at the heart of this community of faith?*

2. Grounding: "Let's test the adequacy of our mission statement as a guiding principle—to live and serve as a community of Christ-followers growing in the love of God and neighbor." A question to respond to is *What principles guide our discernment of how Christ may be calling us to live out God's mission here today?*

3. Shedding: "Let's be honest with God and with each other to name any attitudes, assumptions, prejudgments, influences, or fears that limit our openness to God." A question to respond to is *What stands in the way of an unreserved openness to hearing and doing God's will for our church, to being attentive and available to God and God's direction?*

4. Rooting: "Let's recall the sacred stories from Bible and tradition that come to mind as we tell our stories, that inform our sense of the mission, that we associate with the dilemmas we face. ... Listen for what God is saying to us." A question for response is *What does God want us to hear through Scripture and tradition?*

5. Listening: Let's listen carefully to "others in the church, God, the cry of the needy, our neighbors, data, church development specialists, denominational leaders or staff

persons." A question for response is *Are we listening for what God is saying to us through others and giving thanks?*

6. Exploring: "Let's name and explore each of the paths presenting themselves thus far." A question for response: *What are the paths before us?*

7. Improving: Let's improve each path to make it "as viable and workable as it can be." A question for response: *What does each path offer at its very best?*

8. Selecting: "Let's offer the options to God [in prayer] and listen in our hearts to God's response along with [our] sense of consolation or desolation, assurance or anxiousness with each. . . . Let's then share out of the silence what we heard, saw or felt." Questions for response: *Where do we have peace, and where do we lack peace about each option? Do we have a clear selection emerging within us as a community?*

9. Offering: "Let's name the path that we sense is the most faithful and viable option (is 'right with us and right with the Spirit'–Acts 15)." A question for response: *Have we circled "back to earlier steps as needed and unearthed insights, cautions, or concerns that are rising to the surface until we have a sense of peace with God and one another on a common path"?*

10. Action: "Let's go forward in the peace and power of the Spirit to step forward with faith into the future that Christ is calling us to inhabit."

We cannot know in advance where our discernment will lead. If we take this time together, we will all come to a clearer conception of where God is trying to lead us. But it will take some patience, and it will depend on everyone's participation because we don't know how the Spirit will work. In the process, we also particularly benefit by listening to one another and building relationships.

Discernment in church communities is far different from secular strategic planning, since it emphasizes listening to God and one another more than assessing the situation and making choices. This listening is a dialogue between who we are and whom God is calling us to be. Better discernment comes from developing an ever-closer relationship with God:

> Come now, you who say, "Today or tomorrow we will
> go to such and such a town and spend a year there,
> doing business and making money." Yet you do not even
> know what tomorrow will bring. What is your life? For
> you are a mist that appears for a little while and then
> vanishes. Instead you ought to say, "If the Lord wishes,
> we will live and do this or that." (James 4:13–15)

The primary goal of discernment is not deciding where to go. It's listening to God and to one another. Discernment can lead to planning and often does, but it is critical not to abandon ongoing discernment purely to execute a plan. The most important thing is keeping the community in close, conscious relationship with God and one another. By no means does this mean a church community should not have a plan. It means only that planning must follow effective and ongoing discernment. God calls each church to new realizations and activities, and the process of learning and growth will continue as long as the church community is alive.

We need to give discernment the time it needs. It is often harder to discern our identity in community than individually. We have responsibility for more people. We have a broad spectrum of gifts to open and use in the body of Christ. We need time to reflect on and pray about what we talk about. We need more time to listen to each other and share. If we talk too early about strategy, we may rule out possibilities for ourselves too early. We may also keep ourselves from doing things we would like to do by assuming they'd be too hard.

A number of tools are available to help in assessments of a congregation's current reality—who and where we are—including surveys, gifts inventories, demographic studies, and mutual ministry reviews. However, discernment and planning cannot be a mechanical process; it must involve listening, study, prayer, imagination, and reflection on God's Word. From our listening to God and one another, we need to be as clear as possible about God's calling to us and then plan to follow that calling.

A key focus of discernment is identifying your "mission fields"

When church communities are weak in discernment, it's often because they focus more inward than outward. We need to focus on seeing our "mission fields." Our mission or purpose (what the church community is primarily here for) and our vision (what the church community will look like when it is achieving its mission) depend primarily on *whom* the community is to serve and *how* the community can love and serve the needs of these people. We need to be able to answer the question "Who is my neighbor?"

Remember that in answering this question Jesus tells the story of the Good Samaritan. From this story, we learn that neighbors are people in need who may or may not be members of our community. A question to ask is *What needs would Jesus see in your mission field?* Jesus directly identifies needs of people on the margins: the sick, poor, widowed, orphaned, disabled, immigrants, or prisoners (Matthew 25:35).

Identifying a mission field means seeing the people around us and identifying their needs. A first step might be to look at demographic factors of the people within reach of our community. From a census, we might learn socioeconomic characteristics of the nearby population, such as age, sex, education level, income level, marital status, occupation, religion, birth rate, death rate, average size of a family, average age at marriage, ethnicity, rate of movement (locals or transplants) and so on. From this information, we might project types of physical, educational, relational, or spiritual needs our neighbors may have. Our guesses may be limited, and possibly wrong because demographic generalizations may not apply to specific individuals and speculations about their needs may be limited by our preconceptions. Moreover, challenges people face may be local (crime or unemployment), cultural (ethnic or racial conflict) or systemic (schools or politics), not just personal. Better information about people's needs may come from social service agencies, schools, and other institutions, or from walking through neighborhoods and talking with people.

When Jesus responded to individual needs, he always first asked the individuals what they needed. In addition to looking for ways to solve problems by trying to change the system, we must not ignore or forget the individuals who are falling through the cracks. Jesus calls his disciples to help people one by one, two by two, and through our flock. We cannot distance ourselves from personal relationships because this is where people can also encounter and accept the kingdom of God. People come to Jesus one person at a time and most often through someone else. We are not just solving problems; we are sharing God's love with people who especially need it.

Global problems are rising.[2] Identifying our neighbors isn't easy, because Jesus did not place any boundaries on sharing love. If we look, we will see many needs both within our community and in widening circles around us, as illustrated in the accompanying figure.

Reaching Out to Share God's Love

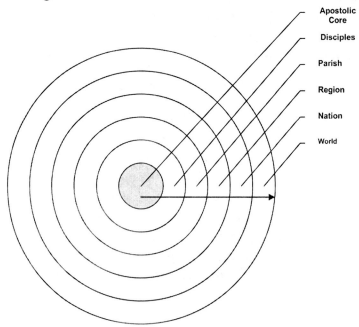

The *apostolic core* is made up of committed disciples who lead disciplined spiritual lives, participate in building up the community, and help the community respond to the needs of the world. *Disciples* are people who are also preparing to live this way. The *parish,* in a traditional sense, is the neighboring geographical area or the larger community from which the congregation draws its members.

Individually, and even more as a community of followers, we can share the love of God to the world within these ever-widening circles:

We share God's love with our family, friends, and neighbors in our everyday lives.

We share God's love with people who come to join in worship and fellowship. Here we serve by helping shape people's everyday lives with an awareness of God's love and the love of community.

We share God's love with people who are made one with Christ in baptism and are being formed as disciples. Baptism initiates us both into Christian community and into Christian ministry. For ministry, we help people discern their vocations and become equipped for the work of their lives (inward and outward journey and growth), work within the church community (religious life, ministry teams, sometimes ordained ministry), and work in the world (ministry to those around us in need).

We share God's love with people when we offer hospitality and community by sharing our facilities and services for programs, meetings, or events, or as a haven. Some churches have created havens for quiet peace and reflection with midday or midweek reflective or meditative times, guided contemplative meditation or prayer offerings, or forms of embodied prayer such as yoga. Some offer a reflection garden, an outdoor prayer space where people can record and leave their prayers, a community rain garden, a labyrinth, a columbarium, or a pet cemetery. Some bring in artists, musicians, and poets for shows or concerts, or coffee houses featuring visual and performing arts. Others host events such as bike rides, fun runs, hikes, tai chi, aerobics, or softball tournaments to help build community (with or without a non-profit fundraising component). Some offer facilities and facilitators for support groups for grief, alcoholics and their loved ones, sexual assault survivors, military veterans and families, and others. Some offer food pantries, supply closets, backpack programs, or clothing drives or sheds.

We share God's love with the people in the larger community and region around us as we reach out to help with their needs for food, shelter, clothing, comfort, and concern. Some churches help in nearby schools as tutors or helpers, in food kitchens or meals on wheels, in homeless shelters, in domestic violence shelters and support services, in mentoring programs for youth or immigrants, in job networks, in visiting prisoners and helping prisoners' families, or in support for released prisoners.

We share God's love with people in our nation, such as those we help who are suffering from poverty, homelessness, or natural or human catastrophes. For example, our communities often mobilize and send people and supplies to help following tornadoes, hurricanes, flooding, or explosions.

And, as Jesus says, we share God's love "even to the ends of the earth." For some churches, this includes foreign mission projects such as packing food, resettling refugees, building wells or schools or churches, or helping to fight malaria with Nets for Life. Stewardship of creation and the environment may extend from recycling and sustainability in our homes and churches, to community gardens and urban farming projects, to dealing with air and water quality and global climate issues.

We will have a tendency to feel that there are not enough resources to fully serve the needs of any mission field. This may constrain us to staying closer to home. At the same time, we need to learn that there is an unlimited abundance of faith, hope, and love and not let our own fears prevent us from answering God's call.

Serving any mission field will require real collaboration with diverse groups of people around us. This may require engagement with city officials and other civic and church leaders to determine the best ways to meet community needs together. It may require working at state and federal levels to assess the systemic causes of poverty and hunger and address the government's role in their alleviation. It may require establishing or strengthening networks dedicated to ecumenical, interfaith, and cross-cultural understanding, healing, and love. This would include ecumenical and interfaith dialogue and dialogue around issues of race, culture, and other forms of diversity, as well as shared activities bringing people to work together to serve others and solve these problems.

Challenges to keep in mind in identifying our mission field are that there may be more needs than we can deal with and that different people may be passionate about wanting to deal with particular needs in particular ways. Together we represent Christ to our world, so it's imperative that we spend some time identifying our particular passions and gifts. We can't ask "How should I respond to the brokenness of the world?" without asking "How do I?" In other words, we ask not only what needs we're serving but also what gifts and passions we're bringing to serve them. This recognizes that God's calling on our lives is congruent with where we see and feel the brokenness of the world and the gifts God has given us to respond. We need to connect our processes of discernment and planning with our mission fields.

Trying to understand our mission fields will give us a new understanding of who we are in relationship with others, and who God is calling us to be. We will discover our identity as a community in relationship to the people whose needs we serve. This identity will reach beyond the culture, nationality, language, racial heritage, or other defining characteristics of our members. It is likely to reflect, at least in part, the area in which we are located because we, at least in part, are called to serve those in proximity to us—where we often have greater connections and resources and opportunities to develop loving relationships. And as we reach into these relationships, we'll discover that our identity as a community has little to do with being a chosen remnant (for example by our denominational affiliation, the prominence and influence of our pastor, or our particular worship style, beliefs, or traditions) and everything to do with our ways of following Jesus and loving and serving others. In discernment, we enter into our community, hear from each other what dream or vision we have for the place in which we find ourselves (neighborhood, city, county, state, nation, world), listen for what God would like to do through us, then consider and name together what strengths or assets we have to get there (perhaps with an asset based community development analysis).

Discernment may lead to planning

From listening to God and one another, we will often have an idea of where to go. Churches with well-discerned plans are undoubtedly more effective. With plans, we can begin with the end in mind, know where we want to go, act more decisively and effectively, and make ourselves ready to accomplish more. A plan provides a basic map for the spiritual path we will travel.[3] As we act on our plans, our actions bring us closer to our intention and even more opportunities become evident. This may happen because as we move nearer to something, we can see it better, and we can also better see the means for achieving it. Or this may happen because our planning enables us to determine which activities are important and to focus on them more successfully, with fewer distractions. Certainly this happens when God responds personally to, and supports, our actions in accordance with God's plan (Proverbs 14:22; Isaiah 14:24, 32:8; Ephesians 1:8–10). Planning is an important part of developing consciousness of God's plan and acting upon it. We become more aware of God's love by moving toward it in our choices, in our creative acts. Our plans help us to journey spiritually, by working to become more conscious of God and God's plan and accept the challenge and reality of acting upon that consciousness into a better future.

Even though our discernment may not provide as much clarity and direction as we would hope, having a plan enables us to learn from the journey and continue discerning. Planning enables us to look at our objectives and evaluate potential challenges and contingencies. This gets us ready to understand the road we'll travel. We won't know everything about the route we are taking, but planning helps us prepare to meet opportunities or challenges as we encounter them. Planning is learning, and learning involves designing capabilities in advance to embrace opportunities and challenges as they occur, and then later adjusting based on new understandings.

Planning is more tangible than determining values, vision, and mission. It flows out of these activities and includes specific goal setting, action planning, and assignment of duties, as well as eventual follow-up to evaluate results. Planning describes and initiates the disciplined actions that will accomplish our vision. Even a shared vision will fail if we don't create an objective measuring stick of our performance against that vision.[4] Once goals are defined, we need to create action plans and follow up on them. The easiest way is to create a table with columns for the goal, the particular action step, who is responsible for the action step, the time for achieving the action step, and the current status of the project. The governing board needs to review project status and priorities regularly. Leaders need to regularly communicate about progress toward the goals or the reprioritization or addition of goals.

Whenever visions are discerned and goals and action plans are defined, they must be shared with and affirmed by the broader church community who will implement them. In most cases, there will need to be ministry teams to support and carry out the goals. Most new visions and new goals require new initiatives and new changes. Leaders will need to bring followers along to make these changes. The opportunities and challenges of leading change are discussed in the next chapter.

Engaging Jesus

To continue engaging Jesus, read and reflect on 1 Kings 19:9–18.

Questions for Personal Reflection:

1. Have you tried to listen for God's voice in your life? What happened?

2. What are ways God communicates to you?

3. What does silence have to do with hearing God?

4. What other voices in our lives drown out God's voice?

5. Have events in your life led you to hear or experience God?

6. Do you regularly reflect on the opportunities and choices you have in your life and listen for God's calling in them?

7. What do you need to do to set effective goals? Do you have effective goals for your spiritual life?

8. Have you ever been a member of a church or organization with a strong mission or purpose? What was that like?

Questions for Group Discussion:

1. Elijah knew that he was the Lord's servant, but he feared for his life and hid in a cave in despair. Israel had forsaken God's covenant, demolished the Lord's altars, and killed the prophets. Now they were after Elijah to kill him. When God told Elijah to prepare to listen, what does Elijah expect to hear?

2. As Elijah stands and pays careful attention, where is God present?

3. Why is God's message startling to Elijah?

4. When has God spoken to people in the Bible?

5. How does God call us? Do we recognize and listen to the voice of God?

6. Are we celebrating what God is doing in our community? How might we better focus our attention on God and one another?

7. Why is it important for a church to have a mission, a vision, and goals?

8. Where does a church's mission come from? Does every church have the same mission? What does Jesus say about church missions?

9. How can a church identify a mission, rooted in Scripture and the congregation's identity, which is simple and understandable and continues to challenge the church to answer God's call?

10. Where are we called to share God's love? (Where are our mission fields?) To whom are we sent?

11. What are the needs of people in our mission fields?

12. How are we being effective missionaries of God's love to those around us? What would be missing in our community if our church ceased to exist?

13. How does our community know that our church loves them?

14. What do we, as a congregation, do best in ministry?

15. How is this community called to serve God's people? Who is our neighbor? How will we show forth God's healing love like Jesus?

16. Has our church overlooked its mission fields?

17. What does God seem to be calling our congregation to do

at this time? What are the unique needs that we can meet? What is our particular focus as a congregation?

18. What is the distinctive identity or role of this congregation in this community? Who will this church be for the larger community (in very specific terms)?

19. How is our true identity different from the way we often define ourselves (by the characteristics of our members or our leaders, our denominational affiliation, or our beliefs and traditions)?

20. Do we have mission and vision statements? Do they adequately describe who we are (and whose we are)? What will this church look like in five, ten, or twenty years? Who will this church be for the larger community (in very specific, not general or abstract terms)? What community needs will this church satisfy?

21. Do we have a plan for our community? Does the plan clearly outline how we'll fulfill our dreams for the community? What are the essential priorities for our community?

22. How much will we have to grow? How will we support this growth?

23. Have we planned answers to the questions of who, what, where, when, why, and how for each of these priorities?

24. Have we shed all goals that are not essential to the plan? Do we have contingencies for if we do not meet certain benchmarks?

25. Why are we here as the leaders of this church? What are our roles in helping the church fulfill its purposes? What resources do we bring to the mission of the church in the area of planning and visioning, and what resources do we need to bring?

26. What outside resources do we need?

4.6

Working for Transformation

Leaders are change agents:

> In essence, change is what leadership is all about.
> Leaders are change-makers, they are masters of
> change. By helping followers achieve goals, they lead
> people to where they've never been before. Leaders
> blaze new trails. They plow new ground. They sail
> uncharted waters. Leaders are out in front.[1]

Jesus is the greatest leader of all time. He transforms individual lives to transform the world. He declares a whole new way of life. He creates a revolution of new ideas by describing a new world framework and vision. The Christian Way is a journey that needs leadership, and those who follow Jesus must also be transformational:

> The study of leadership is the study of how men and
> women guide people through uncertainty, hardship,
> disruption, transformation, transition, recovery, new
> beginnings, and other significant challenges. It's also the
> study of how men and women, in times of constancy
> and complacency, actively seek to disturb the status quo,
> awaken new possibilities, and pursue opportunities. . . .
> Just take a look around today's neighborhoods, homes,
> and workplaces, and you'll see lots of things that aren't
> going as well as they could. There are no shortages
> of opportunities to change the way things are.[2]

Jesus came to change the world. His purpose is to bring about people's transformation so that they can live in loving relationships with God and one another. This is both comforting and disturbing. We'd like to know that God loves us and to live in a more loving world. But we know that we need to change ourselves and change the world for this to happen. We are anxious about taking up our crosses to follow Jesus.

Imagine if we all realized that inherent in Christianity is transforming (changing) ourselves and the world! Our response to the kingdom of God would be more energetic, active, and growing. The kingdom of God has come near, but it is not fulfilled. We are called to make changes to participate in and realize more of its potential.

Change can certainly make things better

Only through change can we achieve a new and better situation. There is creativity and innovation in being a Christian because we are not simply living according to cultural expectations but instead seeking to be different ourselves and to shape new experiences of life. On the Christian journey, we need to expect and enthusiastically embrace change as a constant part of life. Christianity is never safe or comfortable; its end is never achieved in our lifetime. There is no complete and permanent prescription for worshiping God, developing character for loving relationships with God and other people, and living into God's kingdom. We have a collective and individual responsibility for doing these things within our own context and then adapting when the context changes (including possibly developing new frameworks and new organizations for action). In this way, the Christian journey is constantly being remade. The challenge for Christians is that we must constantly rediscover that repentance is not just a one-time event.[3]

The world is changing whether we like it or not. Think, for example, about how the norms about attending church have changed in just four decades. Mainline Protestant denominations declined significantly because they haven't adapted to cultural changes. Churches now need to reach people in new ways rather than simply expect them to come to church and Christian faith on their own. Most churches can't expect growth from doing things the same old way. Adapting does not necessarily mean abandoning all traditions, as some seem to fear, but it does require some new approaches.

To carry out its mission, a church community needs to adapt. It needs to identify and respond to the needs of the world for God's love, and to do so it needs to adopt new approaches and methods to meet needy people where they are. Otherwise, it becomes blind to the needs of the world in the same way the Pharisees were. Because loving relationships are involved, there is no single way for the church to help individuals follow and find transforming union with God or for the church to serve the poor, sick, hungry, suffering, or oppressed.

If we embrace change rather than avoid it, we have an opportunity to significantly improve our response to the changing world. We need to think and act past "the way something was always done" to improve on the old way or find a new and better one. We will not get a different result by doing the same things we have always done. Our people and communities must become more flexible, more willing to adapt to the new conditions where we find ourselves. People who initiate change are more successful than those who merely react or adjust to it. Effective flexibility means anticipating, monitoring, and quickly adapting to change, changing ourselves, enjoying the change, and being ready to quickly change again and enjoy it.[4]

As the visions for our church communities become clear, our challenge as leaders is to successfully put our new insights into practice. A new focus calls for a new way of doing things. We need to add new activities to support our vision and eliminate old practices that don't support it. Innovation does not mean having to try harder or do more difficult things. To achieve more, we have to adopt new attitudes and behaviors. We need to try new things, to simplify and eliminate unnecessary or ineffective processes. Each of us needs to put some adventure into our approach and to constantly look for new ways to do everything better.

People often resist change

Often, the accepted way of seeing things and doing things gets in the way of transitions from the old to the new. Change always brings resistance. The change Jesus brought was resisted by both religious and secular authorities. When we lead in church or in society, we will also encounter resistance:

> Leadership is a perilous business because most people
> will resist change—and sometimes they will take their

opposition to the most extreme ends. Initially, when a
new idea is proposed, many members of an organization
will respond by saying things like "Leave things the way
they are"; "Hey, we don't want you stirring things up";
"If it ain't broke, don't fix it"; or the old standby, "We've
been doing it this way for thirty years and I don't see
any need to change now.". . . Those who do not want to
change will fight those who do—for no rational reason
whatsoever. . . . It is a fundamental human tendency for
people to resist nearly any form of change if they have
not been prepared in advance for the transformation.
Effective leadership, in part, requires understanding this
fact among other important aspects of human nature.[5]

Not everyone enjoys change. When faced with a challenge, we tend
to go back to the basics and do what we do best. We rely on behaviors
that have enabled us to perform well and succeed. We depend on old
habits and resist new ones because they make us feel clumsy, awkward,
and more at risk. For these reasons, a basic and initial human response
to change is resistance.

Different people have different approaches to change. Statistics show
that 3 percent of people will be innovators, 13 percent early adopters, 34
percent middle adopters, 34 percent late adopters, and 16 percent laggards.[6] A person may fall into a different category of adoption for each
new change or opportunity, depending on his or her familiarity with the
particular change and his or her passions and energy for it. Each group
of adopters needs different information and time to adopt a practice and
is only influenced by seeing the successful results of the group before
them. So everyone cannot be convinced at once! Groups adopt changes
dynamically, systemically, and over a period of time.

This is why leadership is needed in any situation involving innovation
or change. First, leaders need to identify and advance visions and behaviors early in a process and help others adopt and follow them within a
reasonable time. Second, leaders must lead before there is full consensus
about the direction to go—because initially most people will not be on
the same page even if the direction is the correct one. Shared leadership
is mutual but not democratic. Third, leaders need to constantly measure

the pulse of the community to determine where different people are in the process of acceptance and encourage positive and growing energy, adoption, and support. And fourth, and most importantly, leaders need to maintain trusted relationships and communications with people at all stages of adoption, because people will only follow people they trust.

People under greater stress may resist change more. Different people have different stress tolerances and respond to stress differently. But a natural response to stress is to slow down to get our bearings (to resist change rather than responding to it). Stress comes from a sense of loss of control, and anxious people feeling stress tend to resist change at the level where they feel they have the most control. For example, a person going through a divorce may feel helpless to reconcile that relationship but may feel better able to resist a smaller change in a church community. Such a stressed person may be feeling a need to try to return to "the good old days" rather than dealing with the real stressors of his or her present situation. So, when leaders encounter an individual who is "acting out" (or bringing their anxiety to the system), they need to pastorally consider whether the individual's reaction stems not so much from the desired change as from either a lower stress tolerance or other significant stressors in his or her life.

As leaders, we need to recognize stress levels in the community as we seek to bring about change. The changes we are creating will bring about additional stress, but there may already be significant stress from other sources. We must be aware of the whole range of life events that may be causing stress: (i) events in the church community (such as new leaders and leadership styles, perceived changes to worship style, the arrival of new members, or beginning new projects); (ii) events outside the community on a macro level (such as war, natural disasters, or economic distress); and (iii) events on a personal level (such as illness, concerns about children, loss of a job, divorce, or life transitions). People feel helpless in the face these types of chaotic changes. Change causes stress. Cumulative change causes greater stress for the people involved.

Some people are distracted from our common mission by focusing on other things. One distraction is individual goals. It is not uncommon for people to focus on their own needs and enhancing their own positions to the detriment of the community and mission. Churches can exacerbate these problems when they emphasize personal development or personal salvation over the ultimate purposes of loving and serving God and other people. Remember, Jesus says, "For those who want to save their life will lose it, and those who lose their life for my sake will find it" (Matthew 16:25). Another distraction is member status. For some church members, just being part of the church is enough to satisfy them, and they may avoid inconveniences or sacrifices necessary to achieve mission goals. Members may be mistaken that their status and success in being associated with a special community or a worthy cause is enough. In this way, they may begin to act more like Pharisees. A third distraction is an emphasis on maintenance: Both individual goals and member status may contribute to churches focusing on institutional survival more than mission.

Most resistance to change is rooted in fear. When things are changing, it's easy to become anxious about the future or to focus too heavily on what has not worked. Generally our fear of what change will require (our cross) feels worse than the change itself. Being flexible and willing to change means overcoming our fears of changing or of what the change will bring. A person cannot change unless he or she is willing to let go of the past and trust what lies ahead. This should be easier for us who believe in God. But life is a risk. God's call requires us to stop holding on to our false sense of understanding and control and to look forward to the surprises (and costs) of discipleship. Nothing improves until we change ourselves. We need to change who we are and what we believe so we can change what we do. Our lives and our community need to be centered in God, and God will transform them. In prayer, we realize that God is with us. We won't help people to experience God's kingdom until we have experienced God's love and felt responsible for sharing it with others. Making changes is not easy, but often there will be joy in the process of bringing about change.

Ways to bring people along

The Way of Jesus is a process of change and transformation. It is a path or journey we lead others on even though they may wish to stay home or sit comfortably in their pews or chairs. For them to experience the Way, we need to bring them along as Jesus brought his disciples along even when they were afraid. The process we lead our people in can help overcome their resistance and fear and increase their skills and confidence as disciples.[7] Leadership needs to continue to steer in the right direction and help others develop confidence in that direction. A challenge of leadership is taking the energy surrounding a response to change and making it positive.

Each of the processes or techniques discussed earlier for building trusting relationships between leaders and followers particularly applies in leading change. Trust reduces fear and stress. A process for leading change based on these principles follows several important steps, expanded on in the sections below.

1. Begin with a clear, shared, and compelling vision.

We continually draw and inspire people with a significant mission to be accomplished together in a supportive community. If we understand where God is calling us, we need to change to answer that call. We can lead proactively because we have an agreed goal or direction. We are more focused outward to what we are called to do, which is to share God's love. With a common vision, we can become a larger supportive community and act more like the body of Christ.

We need to focus on the desired result itself, more than the process or the means necessary to achieve the result. We do not have to know how we're going to get there, but we need to know where we want to go. Having a clear picture of what we want to accomplish is crucial. We need to start by defining our goals, not by worrying about everything that will be involved in getting from here to there. By visualizing our arrival, we begin to "magnetize" ourselves to the ways and means for getting there. We can never get everything neatly organized and eliminate all risks. But if we are open minded, goal-focused, and willing to experiment, we may shape our specific techniques as we go.

2. Develop a trusted leadership group.

The pace and tone of the leaders often becomes the pace and tone of the community. Enthusiasm and commitment are highly contagious and inspire others to action. At the same time, the non-anxious presence of leaders reduces stress. Leaders avoid trouble by acting confidently, purposefully, and concertedly during times of change.

People need a "guiding coalition." Middle adopters, late adopters, and laggards are influenced by the results of the group before them. In addition to proclaiming a mission that is inspiring and worth achieving, leaders need to set goals that stretch people's abilities, create expectations that the goals can be met, build a spirit of teamwork, and help create a sense of urgency for the mission of the church.

3. Involve other people effectively.

Each of us needs help and support from the people around us. Jesus was careful to make formation of a team a priority of his ministry, even though at times his followers must have seemed a nuisance. When a single leader is resisted or persecuted, a dozen others will carry on the mission. The mission of the church is the work of all of us:

> Involving people in the planning process tends to alleviate the anxiety associated with massive change—thereby giving people a higher level of security. Personal involvement [provides individuals with a better understanding] of the changes involved, which, in turn, essentially eliminates fear. [Learning through involvement] is often the best change agent available to a leader because it binds people together and instills a sense of pride and responsibility. In general, effective leaders first make the case for change by persuading people to become committed to the new endeavor. Then, through teamwork, members of the organization become immersed in formulating specific goals and recommendations. The leader next works with others to achieve those objectives.[8]

Effective teams generally achieve more than individuals. Because a team has more gifts, skills, resources, and perspectives than a single individual, a team is often able to reach better decisions and respond more quickly and productively to tasks. Teamwork around a shared team mission motivates people and produces enthusiasm and energy. And belonging to a team offers individuals personal support and reduces fear and increases confidence and hope.

4. Over communicate.

Communicating helps individuals to understand their spiritual journeys and also strengthens the bonds between people in the congregation. Use all possible forms of communication, and have a variety of leaders share information to build broader trust.

> The first step in the change process centers around raising awareness. The earlier people are forewarned of the proposed change, the better. ... Furthermore, leaders continually reassure members of the organization that the changes made were necessary and will pay off in the long run. Lastly, when things go well, strong leaders will give other people credit for making it all happen; conversely, they'll accept full responsibility if things go awry.[9]

As discussed earlier, make sure communication is open and honest to build trust: "When people are in the dark, they start to speculate about what's happening. And their assumptions are often wrong. Inform people so that everyone is on the same page."[10]

Leaders need to share stories and personal experiences. In churches advancing their missions, people talk comfortably and often about the significant role Jesus (rather than the congregation) plays in their everyday lives.

And, equally important, leaders actively listen. Be sure people know they are heard. But also be sure people understand that being heard does not mean they must have their own way.

5. *Create action and build momentum.*

Jesus tells us that we need to be transformed, to be born again. This kind of breakthrough requires a radical departure from old habits. In contrast, most people assume success comes incrementally—one step at a time—and we must move systematically from our present level of understanding to the next. But if we need to do several things to get to the next level of understanding, we may be able to get to the next level faster by learning or doing several new things at once. It may be just as easy to change several of the habits we need to change at the same time. We need to consider whether we are taking *all* of the actions we need to truly bring about the changes we desire.

This approach recognizes the challenges of individuality, complexity, interconnectedness, and interdependence in nearly every change we try to make. The letters of Paul identify these complexities: there are varieties of gifts, services, and activities; the body has many members; and all are unique, necessary, indispensable, respectable, and worthy of care (1 Corinthians 12). We have to be careful not to look at things too simply. We need to carefully consider the Body and the Kingdom and how they interrelate.

But we cannot let complexity and analysis bog us down. Paul's response to complexity is not inaction, but unity in God (1 Corinthians 12:4–13) and love (1 Corinthians 13). Acting requires us to take loving and calculated risks. We can't be sure of what works until we try it; we often will not know where a path leads until we take it.[11] Sometimes, we need to trust and improvise rather than overanalyze and delay. Otherwise, we will not make the journey. And the journey is important.

Learning from mistakes and moving on creates energy and momentum—unless we take ourselves too seriously. Once we take action, building momentum can help the cycle of change:

> Good results create momentum. Having momentum
> gives you greater results. Greater results create even
> more momentum. Production creates a positive cycle
> that can continue to roll on and on. With momentum,
> an organization can overcome problems, negativism,
> past issues, pettiness, and upcoming obstacles.[12]

Momentum increases energy and can make our task seem less overwhelming. By celebrating early achievements, we demonstrate progress and encourage each other to keep pursuing our mission. People begin to enjoy being part of a growing mission-oriented community. Slowing down may give some people a sense of safety, but if our vision is true, we are safer moving toward it as quickly as possible.

Leadership guru Ronald Heifetz illustrates the need to use the right amount of energy to create action and momentum with a metaphor of cooking stew in a pressure cooker. The goal is a rich medley whose carrots, parsnips, lentils, and beets all retain their distinctive flavor while gently contributing to the flavors they mix with. (This tastes and smells like the body of Christ.) The challenge is not to turn it into mush, or worse, to blow the top off the pot by overheating:

> The cook regulates the pressure of the holding
> environment by turning the heat up or down, while the

relief valve lets off steam to keep the pressure within
a safe limit. If the pressure goes beyond the carrying
capacity of the vessel, the pressure cooker can blow up.
On the other hand, with no heat nothing cooks.[13]

6. Respond to resistance.

Monitoring and managing levels of energy and stress in the community is important. In addition to building momentum from positive
energy to advance the community's mission, leaders must be able to help
concerned members avoid becoming overstressed and prevent dependent or recalcitrant members from undercutting the community's vision
and strategies. The best way to reduce people's stress is to listen carefully
to their concerns. Ideally, leaders honestly discuss the changes people in
the community are experiencing, especially their personal feelings about
them.[14] The stress in a system may also be reduced by showing that much
of the stress people are feeling is external to the system or that the changes within the system are relatively small, purposeful, and reasonable.

If the stress of change rises to the level of unproductive conflict, more
drastic steps may be needed. There are three ways to address unproductive resistance: (i) slow or stop the changes (which may be like giving in
to a child's tantrum or may not even be possible if the real stressors are
beyond the community), (ii) allow the stressed person to find a different setting where they feel more safe, or (iii) apply authority and place
boundaries to define how individuals must act—even when they are
stressed—as members of a loving community.

If a community learns to define and support boundaries, it becomes
much stronger and healthier to face challenges and grow going forward.
However, this will be difficult if a community has not already accepted
the leadership style it needs to manage a community of its size, deal with
crisis, and provide vision, and adopted processes that support effective interactions, communications, and decision making. These things
may happen in a stressful situation, however, through effective, adaptive
learning.

Adaptive learning

Some resistance to change is good and needs to be encouraged.
"Negative" energy may also help bring about positive change if it leads to

honest and direct confrontations. There are often real benefits to working through disagreements over values, goals, or methods if they are relevant to the mission of the community or the challenges the community is adapting to. In church communities, productive confrontations help leaders take time for conversation, prayer, reflection, and discernment, and they reveal broader or deeper perspectives. Leaders need to encourage and mediate confrontations that may help the community make better, positive decisions about questions that don't have clear answers and solutions. Avoiding loving confrontations undermines change by harming relationships, preventing reconciliation, and closing off the productive learning that differences in perspective may spur. Our community is healthier when we can talk about these things—even if we might prefer to avoid a disagreeable conversation to keep the peace or some semblance of unity.

It's critical for leaders to bring the community together to wrestle with difficult issues or problems and to determine solutions. The challenge is having the community question its attitudes, actions, behavior, or beliefs. In these situations, the leader does not come up with an answer or solution on his or her own but encourages the confrontation.[15] Leaders may need to begin the conversation by identifying or raising issues that everyone else is avoiding. This, of course, puts the leader in the position of having anger and resentment surrounding the issue directed towards him or her. And, unless the leader strives to act in a "God-differentiated" way, he or she may react negatively and unproductively shift the focus from the issue to his or her reactions (making it personal). Instead, we need to approach confrontations in a manner that will have a positive impact in answering the open questions. This means that we need to control our own reactions and encourage (or admonish) dialogue. If we do so, we also help people learn how to work through loving confrontations and develop stronger, reconciling relationships. This, in itself, is kingdom work.

Effective steps for leading "adaptive" confrontations are identified by Ronald Heifitz:

1. Identify the adaptive challenge. Diagnose the situation in light of the values at stake, and unbundle the issues that come with it.

2. Keep the distress within a tolerable range for doing adaptive work. To use the pressure cooker analogy, keep the heat up without blowing up the vessel.

3. Focus attention on ripening issues and not on stress-reducing distractions. Identify which issues can currently engage attention; and while directing attention to them, counteract work avoidance mechanisms like denial, scapegoating, externalizing the enemy, pretending the problem is technical, or attacking individuals rather than issues.

4. Give the work back to people, but at a rate they can stand. Place and develop responsibility by putting the pressure on the people with the problem.

5. Protect voices of leadership without authority. Give cover to those who raise hard questions and generate distress— people who point to the internal contradictions of the society. These individuals often will have latitude to provoke rethinking that authorities do not have.[16]

Heifetz expands on his pressure cooker analogy in order to explain how leaders can best help people work through their differences:

> A key imperative for a leader trying to achieve significant change is to manage people's passionate differences in a way that diminishes their destructive potential and constructively harnesses their energy. Two techniques can help you achieve this. First, create a secure place where the conflicts can freely bubble up. Second, control the temperature to ensure that the conflict doesn't boil over—and burn you in the process.
>
> The vessel in which a conflict is simmered—in which clashing points of view mix, lose some of their sharpness, and ideally blend into consensus—will look and feel quite different in different contexts. It may be a protected physical space, perhaps an off-site location where an outside facilitator helps a group work through its differences. It

may be a clear set of rules and processes that give minority voices confidence that they will be heard without having to disrupt the proceedings to gain attention. It may be the shared language and history of an organization that binds people together through trying times. Whatever its form, it is a place or a means to contain the roiling forces unleashed by the threat of major change.

But a vessel can withstand only so much strain before it blows. A huge challenge you face as a leader is keeping . . . stress at a productive level. The success of the change effort—as well as your own authority and even survival— requires you to monitor your organization's tolerance for heat and then regulate the temperature accordingly. You first need to raise the heat enough that people sit up, pay attention, and deal with the real threats and challenges facing them. After all, without some distress, there's no incentive to change. You can constructively raise the temperature by focusing people's attention on the hard issues, by forcing them to take responsibility for tackling and solving those issues, and by bringing conflicts occurring behind closed doors out into the open.

But you have to lower the temperature when necessary to reduce what can be counterproductive turmoil. You can turn down the heat by slowing the pace of change or by tackling some relatively straightforward technical aspect of the problem, thereby reducing people's anxiety levels and allowing them to get warmed up for bigger challenges. You can provide structure to the problem-solving process, creating work groups with specific assignments, setting time parameters, establishing rules for decision making, and outlining reporting relationships. You can use humor or find an excuse for a break or a party to temporarily ease tensions. You can speak to people's fears and, more critically, to their hopes for a more promising future. By showing people how the future might look, you come to embody hope rather than fear, and you reduce the likelihood of becoming a lightning rod for the conflict.[17]

Bringing about transformation:
Example 1—Leading a Mission Project

A project to reach into a new mission field "began" with this announcement by a church board member during worship:

> As most of you know by now, our church board was given a proposal several months ago to assist in the building of a school in Monrovia, Liberia, Africa.
>
> After much deliberation, the board was excited by the project, but couldn't go forward without getting more details. For that reason we decided to send a delegation to Good Shepherd Church in Monrovia to investigate the project and meet the congregation.
>
> The delegation of [four respected members of the congregation] traveled to Monrovia and back. They made a presentation at the Annual Meeting to let our congregation know what they experienced while they were in Liberia.
>
> Friday night they made an additional presentation to the board on the specifics of the school project.
>
> The board was impressed by the planning that has taken place—over many years, to plan for this school—and with the determination of Good Shepherd Church to proceed with the project. We then voted that we want to partner with Good Shepherd Church in the endeavor to build THIS SCHOOL (show picture).
>
> We anticipate spending a yet to be determined amount from the Undesignated Gifts Fund. The amount would not exhaust the Fund. There will still be chances for other projects to be proposed and funded by the Undesignated Gifts Fund.

To augment what we give, we also plan to invite other organizations, both local and national, to join with us in helping Good Shepherd Church. It is also thought that we may be able to help in other non-monetary ways, such as acquiring building materials and furniture at lower cost than they could be obtained in Liberia.

Before any further decisions can be made, we need to create a Ministry Team that will work with Good Shepherd Church to coordinate our efforts. It will be made up of at least one person from the delegation, one member of the board, and other church members. Once this Team is functioning, it will work with the board to determine the specific contribution our church will provide. If anyone is interested in being involved, or just wishes to comment on these plans, please see any board member, delegation member, or the Pastor.

We also plan to have more parish conversation on this project, including the chance for everyone to see the detailed presentation that the delegation made to the board.

Please stay tuned for further information on this exciting opportunity. We feel that there is the possibility that our church could be transformed by this relationship as much as Good Shepherd Church, Monrovia.[18]

Beginning this new ministry required leadership. The board considered whether this was even a realistic mission field for this church community and whether they were hearing God's call. The parishioner who made the proposal to the Undesignated Gifts Fund had grown up in the Monrovian church, still had family in that community, and knew the people and their needs, especially for education after devastating civil war. The delegation was a way to develop closer ties to the community, see the needs firsthand, understand the project, and determine how an American church might help. The American church would not be in charge of the project, and there were concerns because the building design and process might not be up to "American standards." For heaven's sake, members of the Monrovian church would themselves be helping make the bricks and build the school! Any questions about whether the African church would be faithful stewards of the resources were put to rest by visiting the area, meeting members of the congregation, and experiencing their mission work and commitment.

The church pursuing this mission was not large or wealthy. The Undesignated Gifts Fund came from bequests, and the board decided to spend them only for new programs or outreach ministries, not for the congregation's operating budget. But this church was also located in a suburb close to Detroit, which had been severely hit by recession and faced its own seemingly insurmountable needs from poverty, hunger, and homelessness. Board members knew church members who felt the church should deal with its operating deficit or further address local problems before reaching across the world.

The board recognized that it needed to lead by making some decisions before there was consensus among church members about the project, because most members were not ready for the project. They recognized that this important decision about the future and direction of the community could be made representatively, but not democratically. When board members decided to go forward, they shared a vision and invited others to become involved in the process. In stating their vision, they wanted to be clear that the project would not use all of the resources of the congregation or detract from other worthy missions. The leaders outlined a process of acceptance and encouraged positive and growing energy, adoption, and support. And they strove to act together, maintain trusted relationships, and open and broaden communications. Members accepted that the board was making decisions prayerfully, collaboratively, consensually and in community and not leading coercively.

Bringing about transformation:
Example 2—Leading Congregational Revitalization

Revitalization is the transformational change needed when congregations are struggling or declining. In these situations, a church community cannot reach new vitality without doing things differently.

In many congregations, financial challenges or crises are strong motivations for congregational revitalization and improving personal discipleship. In these congregations, leaders may begin to recognize that they cannot solve financial problems by focusing just on the financial problems or on the processes or structures of the church. We might encourage better planning by analyzing the church budget, especially for realistic cash flows, but most congregations have already cut expenses about as far as they can before they begin to accept the need for change. Focusing on financially and administratively maintaining or preserving facilities or operations leads to a "maintenance" mentality. Life drains out of a community when keeping people in or attracting people to worship or church activities becomes more about financial survival than about transforming lives with love.

Although this seems like a negative place to begin, we can begin revitalization with positive energy or negative energy, but not without energy and motivation for change. Paradoxically, while a shortage of money or people becomes an excuse for not doing things a church needs to do, the way to attain and sustain new vitality is to grow. Leaders should think about "investments" the congregation needs to make to grow the community and where the investments will come from. Leaders need to identify where there is positive energy in the community and build on it, focusing on mission (purpose) and community building (belonging). In following Jesus, positive energy and vitality comes from experiencing incarnation, discipleship, and apostleship in the community's specific context. Often this happens by involving ministry teams in accomplishing unique and important purposes.

Steps to revitalization include the following:

- Discerning where God is already acting in the life of the community (often with a Mutual Ministry Review or Appreciative Inquiry). This is an opportunity to begin to identify the community's unique identity and call, respond to it, and become more than a worshiping or pastoral care chaplaincy.

- Identifying mission fields the congregation is called to serve (with both shepherding—John 21—and missionary— Matthew 10—activities).

- Helping leaders understand (John 14:12) and accept their

roles with humility and confidence (John 13:3), and begin to share a compelling vision and specific goals for the community.

- Connecting with people, preparing (equipping) people to serve and getting them engaged in service; ministry teams and small groups can help initiate and support each of these activities.

- Focusing on mutual ministry (using all of the gifts of the body of Christ) and involving everyone (not seeing just the clergy or staff as service providers).

- Developing empowering leaders.

- Getting the church community to see themselves as transforming the world and their own lives by sharing God's love.

Individual churches have discovered that any *one* of these activities can help to generate new energy and get more people involved. People connect with the unique identity shared in the mission and culture of the community. They better understand that there are "expectations" ("what we are looking forward to") for the community and individual members. Commitment increases—both to the community and the mission. Engagement and energy increases. Leaders who integrate more of these activities into the process of transformation increase this vitality and progress. And a transformation process may become the foundation for improving various church activities—evangelism, formation, pastoral care, outreach, and so on—as part of building community and pursuing mission.

Returning to our example of financial stewardship, the church community discovers that traditional financial stewardship activities work much more effectively when steps to revitalization are occurring. Stewardship activities become much more than fundraising. In this context, leaders can help church members to

- come together and celebrate in community;

- tell the story through sharing the vision, personal witnesses, and marketing materials;

- be clear about financial plans and needs, perhaps by providing a narrative budget connected to elements of the vision;

- build momentum and ask for renewed commitment with an intentional "campaign";

- rededicate themselves to God, community, and mission, including bringing pledge cards or personal commitments to the altar;

- make the changes necessary to live into new commitments using gifts, passions, abilities, personalities, and experiences as well as financial resources; and

- affirm all givers in a celebration of ministries, including recognizing generous "gifted" financial giving as a spiritual gift.

When a congregation is not experiencing revitalization, each of these stewardship activities is harder to accomplish. Fewer people gather, they have less of a story to share, and little energy. Fewer people make a renewed commitment or make changes in their lives and there is less to celebrate.

Revitalization is a longer-term, cyclical process of adaptive learning, transformation, and renewal, and provides all of the challenges of leading any change process. Revitalization requires guidance through leadership, coaching, and mentoring. The transformational community needs to develop trusted leaders, a shared and compelling vision, effective communications, team involvement and delegation, awareness and management of stress, and new relationships and boundaries. And this needs to happen while the church community is going through various steps to revitalization. The methods and processes for making these changes are only tools. Above all, the motivation and foundation for transformation is striving to follow where Jesus leads.

Engaging Jesus

To continue engaging Jesus, read and reflect on Ephesians 4.

Questions for Personal Reflection:

Consider changes that have happened in your personal life during the past year or two. What were their effects and your responses to them?

Questions for Group Discussion:

1. In Ephesians 4, what does Paul mean when he speaks of the unity of the spirit and of oneness (vv. 1–7, 11–16)? What does maintaining the "unity of the Spirit in the bond of peace" require, and what works against this?

2. Saint Paul describes the constant struggle the church faces to become more mature and Christlike. When does the church get it right?

3. How do we "grow up in every way into him who is the head, into Christ"?

4. If your church were to grow more Christlike, what would it look like?

5. Consider changes that have happened in your personal life or church community during the past year or two. List them and discuss some of their effects and the responses to them.

   Examples of significant changes a church community might experience include:

   - *New clergy and/or leadership styles*

   - *Loss of a long-time pastoral-style leader (especially if this was not alleviated by an interim or grieving period)*

   - *Beginning implementation of growth objectives by new leaders*

- *Natural differences in style, approach, and activities between leaders*

- *Size transition*

- *Recognition of earlier growth when connection with pastor is lost (sense of church being larger, loss of home)*

- *New people*

- *Restated desire for more growth*

- *Broader context*

- *National church issues*

- *Economy*

- *Political events, such as war*

- *Personal and family changes*

6. What is the stress level in our community? How might it affect changes we need to make? How do people feel about growth or change?

7. What changes do we need to lead in our congregation?

8. Is there energy or a sense of urgency for these changes? How do we create or sustain energy for changes?

9. Are we in this together? Do we have healthy interpersonal relationships now? How will we strengthen them? Do we have healthy processes for resolving disagreements?

10. How will we develop a shared vision? Do we see this as a mission from God?

11. How will things look if our vision is accomplished? What will be different? What changes do we need to make? Have we identified the various complexities and stakeholders? How will we minimize unnecessary changes?

12. How will we assemble a guiding team? Who is passionate about this project? Who has the gifts and skills? Are support groups and processes in place to sustain and refresh leaders who are under stress and heavy workloads? Are ministry roles clearly defined and boundaries maintained?

13. How do we communicate our plans and changes? Can we add effective communication processes to stay in touch with members and connect with newcomers as our community network grows larger? What do we need? How can we be more intentional and improve communications?

14. Are we prepared for loving confrontations?

15. How will we celebrate this journey and build momentum?

16. Considering a holistic revitalization process, what steps need to be taken together to bring about transformation in our community more fully and effectively?

17. How (and when) are we going to focus our attention on the changes we need to make and move them along?

CONCLUSION

Follow Where Jesus Leads

I n the gospel stories, we learn about God breaking into our time, appearing to us in the flesh as a rabbi and a miraculous healer. We hear about the calling of the disciples, and we too are invited to follow Jesus. The light of God's revelation in Jesus becomes clearer as the disciples are called and the word is proclaimed. Like Peter, we identify Jesus as the Messiah, the liberating king promised by God, and we begin to follow Jesus. We discover new life given to us through God's generosity in forgiveness and abundant love. We start to learn about discipleship and God's expectations for us. We discover that God wants us to be part of a kingdom of love and to change the world and help bring others into that kingdom. God wants and needs us to participate in a new way of life and to begin to show others this Way too. By our participation, the world is transformed. God has called us to be followers (disciples) and agents of change (leaders).

Effective Christian leaders have many of the characteristics of effective leaders anywhere. All true leaders believe they can personally make a difference in the world.[1] But effective Christian leaders are also different from other effective leaders. The difference for Christian leaders is that our faith, love, hope, perseverance, joy, and journey together begin with Jesus, not with us. Through living with Jesus, God has given us "everything needed for life and godliness" so that we "may become participants of the divine nature. For this very reason, you must make every effort to support your faith [with goodness, knowledge, self-control, endurance, godliness, mutual affection, and love]. For if these things are yours and are increasing among you, they keep you from being ineffective and unfruitful" (2 Peter 1:3–8).

Faith: Jesus asks each of us to change our way of life, experience God's love for us, live out of a close relationship with God, and humbly serve God. A Christian leader trusts that God is in charge and that he or she neither has to take control nor to make others happy. The direction of the leader's life can become the direction God leads, rather than being tossed about by our own fears or the anxieties of others. Jesus says our faith can move mountains (Matthew 21:21–22). If we truly have Jesus in our lives, his presence works to shape us more into his own image (Galatians 4:19), more into God's image as we were created to be (1 John 3:2).

Love: Jesus reveals that God is love and that life in God's kingdom is love. We are asked to share the Good News of God's love for each person and to help each person live in loving relationships with God and other people. In this world, the kingdom of God is revealed by our showing, telling, and offering the hope, listening, forgiveness, reconciliation, healing, and love God has for each person and helping each person live more fully into loving relationships. The kingdom of God happens when the love of God is poured out in us and through us, when we experience God's love and reveal God's love to others.

Hope: Followers of Jesus are not really participating in God's kingdom if they are only waiting for a perfection or realization of that kingdom in the next life through some sort of belief in Jesus. By his death and resurrection, Jesus has destroyed death and made all things new. We need to participate in this new creation. Jesus calls his followers to follow him today in this life and he calls his disciples to live with him and continue his role in this world. As Christian leaders, we must share the hope that we have for this world and hold on to this hope through struggle and suffering, by following Jesus and keeping Jesus in sight.[2]

Perseverance: Disciples are called to represent Jesus in his ministry, and their ministry is virtually identical to that of Jesus. We are not just followers; we are partners with Jesus in the sharing and creation of God's kingdom of love. The kingdom of God is present with us; it is still opening and unfolding before us, and this is also happening through us. There is a tension that the kingdom of God is "already here" and that the kingdom is "not here yet." We are called to follow, to imitate, to share, to reveal so that others will see Jesus in our lives and also be drawn to him. Christian leaders serve others for God's kingdom, take part in transforming the world, and face resistance. We will need to persevere in the face of challenges and even hardships: "As for you, always be sober, endure suffering, do the work of an evangelist, carry out your ministry fully" (2 Timothy 4:5).

Joy: To truly become followers of Jesus, we need to go into the world and serve others and share this Good News we have about God's love. As we proclaim Jesus, Jesus comes to be with us. We experience his presence. In proclaiming and sharing the Good News, we become the body of Christ. We become Christ's arms and legs, hands and feet, eyes and mouth. And because Jesus is with us, our lives and bodies, like our risen Lord's, can become places where God is revealed in this world. Our joy as Christians comes both from experiencing the presence of Jesus in our lives and sharing that presence with the world. In our journey with Jesus and in finding our way home in God's kingdom, we will find joy made complete in us (John 17:13).

Journey: Faith, love, hope, perseverance, and joy are continuing activities of our lives in relationship with God and other people. In this life, they are not a place we reach once and for all, nor a position that we achieve and hold onto, nor a principle we know for all time. They are a journey or a Way of following Jesus. Jesus has saved us and made us part of God's family, but we and our world are being sanctified, and we are participating in that sanctification. The Christian journey is a journey together. Church communities grow out of our efforts to create and support true, transforming relationships with God and other people. These relationships are incarnational (showing forth God's love for people and creation), discipling (helping people live into the loving relationships of God's kingdom), and apostolic (sending people to love and serve God and other people in the world). A church community shows forth God's love to the world when that love is experienced, shared, and manifested within the community itself and taken out into the world—in every way striving to love one another as Jesus has loved us.

On our journey, we need to pay attention to Jesus—to keep Jesus in sight and follow. And along the Way, we will continually love and serve God, become more like Jesus, discover what God wants to create through us, love one another as Jesus has loved us, help reveal more and more of God's kingdom, and bring others along with us. This is where Jesus leads and where we are engaged in the Way as disciples and as leaders.

Engaging Jesus

To continue engaging Jesus, read and reflect on John 15:3.

Questions for Personal and Group Reflection:

1. What will you do to actively live your faith? What practice or rule will you use or is God calling you to?

2. Where do you feel God calling you or your church community?

3. Begin to evaluate your leadership and ministry area with the following questions:

    a. Have we identified in a reasonable way challenges and opportunities facing our church?

    b. What questions do I have about where we are and where we're going?

    c. What am I personally most excited about in church life?

    d. What do I feel is important to the church at this time?

    e. What are my hopes and dreams for the church or my ministry area(s)?

    f. Where do I feel we're on track or off?

    g. What ministry areas need the most attention at this time and place in our history?

TOOLS FOR
CHRISTIAN LEADERSHIP

A

Responsibilities of Church Leadership Teams

Church leadership teams customarily conduct the following activities:

1. **Support unity and love**
    "Love one another as I have loved you." (John 13:34)
    "By this everyone will know that you are my disciples, if you have love for one another." (John 13:35)

2. **Discern the church's mission and purposes**
    This means asking, "What is God calling us to do and to accomplish here in this place?" and "How can we best practice this ministry?" to clearly articulate the unique mission of the congregation to respond to God's calling in the world. This includes identifying the populations, communities, or areas the congregation is called to serve and defining the congregation's goals.

3. **Ensure effective planning**
    The leadership teams develop a depth of knowledge of the communities being served; review and approve staff and ministry team plans to accomplish congregational goals; understand and question the assumptions upon which the plans are based; and help strengthen the plans to realize progress toward the goals.

4. **Determine, monitor, and strengthen the church's programs and services**
    The leadership teams introduce, alter, or eliminate programs

as needed to involve gifted individuals in fulfilling the congregation's mission and regularly monitor results to evaluate whether plans are being achieved and operations are being properly managed.

5. **Select, monitor, evaluate, compensate, support, and—if necessary—replace the ministry leaders, and ensure management succession**

6. **Provide proper financial oversight**
    The leadership teams review and approve the church's financial objectives, plans, and actions, including significant capital allocations and expenditures.

7. **Ensure adequate resources**

8. **Ensure legal and ethical integrity and maintain accountability**
    The leadership teams ensure that the church has in place systems to encourage and enable ethical behavior and compliance with laws and regulations, auditing and accounting principles, and its own governing documents.

9. **Recruit and orient new board members and assess board performance**
    Leadership teams assess their own effectiveness in fulfilling these and other board responsibilities.

10. **Enhance the church's witness and reputation**
    Leadership teams serve as models for Christian community, mutual ministry, and open communication, especially constructive criticism and feedback.

Adapted from Ten Basic Responsibilities Of Nonprofit Boards *(BoardSource, 2003) and* The Report of the NACD Blue Ribbon Commission on Director Professionalism *(National Association of Corporate Directors, 2005).*

Mutual Ministry Reviews

What is a mutual ministry review (MMR)?

A mutual ministry review is a discernment process in which the leaders of the congregation ask who God is calling this congregation to be, how this congregation is presently responding to God's call, and how this congregation is going to respond to God's call. The MMR is an effort to discern God's will for the church and call for all ministers (lay and clergy) to be accountable for it.

Why conduct a mutual ministry review?

A mutual ministry review offers opportunities (i) for the clergy, the vestry, and the parish community to assess how effectively they are fulfilling their responsibilities to each other and their ministries, (ii) to celebrate the ministries of the congregation, (iii) to identify areas for growth and development, and (iv) to identify ways to enhance the various ministries of the church and all its people.

A complete mutual ministry review process will provide

- an effective *evaluation* of what is going well and what needs attention (especially in terms of how well we are living into our baptism and becoming disciples);

- a shared *vision* of where God is calling the congregation; and

- a *strategy* that produces clear priorities and objectives for the congregation, specific goals for achieving them, and an understanding of the shared expectations, formation, leadership, and resources needed to accomplish them.

What is the theological basis for mutual ministry review?

The church can become the body of Christ in the world if we "grow up in every way into him who is the head, into Christ, from whom the whole body, joined and knit together by every ligament with which it is equipped, as each part is working properly, promotes the body's growth in building itself up in love" (Ephesians 4:15–16). For the church to become more of the body of Christ, each person needs to bring and use their special gifts in the community (1 Corinthians 12). Because all of the members of the body are interconnected, the work of the body is "mutual ministry," and we share responsibility to observe and review our ministries within our commitment to follow Christ and be God's people.

A mutual ministry review helps us to be accountable to God for our actions, a stewardship responsibility portrayed in the parable of the talents (Matthew 25). Most importantly, a mutual ministry review enables us to share and witness to the activity of God in our lives and community, as when the seventy disciples returned to proclaim what miracles had happened in God's name (Luke 10).

An organic model for mutual ministry review

1. *Read the following Scriptures together:*

Mark 4:26–32

Jesus said, "The kingdom of God is as if someone would scatter seed on the ground, and would sleep and rise night and day, and the seed would sprout and grow, he does not know how. The earth produces of itself, first the stalk, then the head, then the full grain in the head. But when the grain is ripe, at once he goes in with his sickle, because the harvest has come."

He also said, "With what can we compare the kingdom of God, or what parable will we use for it? It is like a mustard seed, which, when sown upon the ground, is the smallest of all the seeds on earth; yet when it is sown it grows up and becomes the greatest of all shrubs, and puts forth large branches, so that the birds of the air can make nests in its shade."

Luke 13:6–9

Then Jesus told this parable: "A man had a fig tree planted in his vineyard; and he came looking for fruit on it and found none. So he said to the gardener, 'See here! For three years I have come looking for fruit on this fig tree, and still I find none. Cut it down! Why should it be wasting the soil?' He replied, 'Sir, let it alone for one more year, until I dig around it and put manure on it. If it bears fruit next year, well and good; but if not, you can cut it down.'"

Matthew 7:16–20

You will know them by their fruits. Are grapes gathered from thorns, or figs from thistles? In the same way, every good tree bears good fruit, but the bad tree bears bad fruit. A good tree cannot bear bad fruit, nor can a bad tree bear good fruit. Every tree that does not bear good fruit is cut down and thrown into the fire. Thus you will know them by their fruits.

Isaiah 5:1–4, 7a

Let me sing for my beloved my love-song concerning his vineyard: My beloved had a vineyard on a very fertile hill. He dug it and cleared it of stones, and planted it with choice vines; he built a watchtower in the midst of it, and hewed out a wine vat in it; he expected it to yield grapes, but it yielded wild grapes. And now, inhabitants of Jerusalem and people of Judah, judge between me and my vineyard.

What more was there to do for my vineyard that I have not done in it? When I expected it to yield grapes, why did it yield wild grapes? . . . For the vineyard of the LORD of hosts is the house of Israel, and the people of Judah are his pleasant planting.

2. *Discuss the following questions as appropriate*

- What did you hear?
- What do these passages say about where our growth comes from?
- What do we need to do to grow?
- What are the critical functions of this church community?
- Are our actions producing fruit for the kingdom of God?
- Do we want or need to grow as a church community?
- What do we mean by growth?
- How will we grow?
- Can we grow without making changes?
- What kinds of changes would we need to make in order to grow?

3. *Place your ministry activities in appropriate categories.*

The Bible often uses metaphors of fruit and vineyards to describe the people of God and the work to which we are called. Caring for a church, like caring for a vineyard, requires hard work. We labor in the vineyard with God, and we plant and water, but God gives the growth (1 Corinthians 3:6). To bear good fruit, a vineyard needs to be tended over the course of many years. The farming cycle must be repeated: season after season, crops are planted and tended, and fruit is gathered and stored. Similarly, year after year, we make plans for our church community, act upon them, and review our activities. The work is never ultimately perfected nor completely finished, and the fruit is not always sweet. Sometimes pruning is needed or the land needs to lie fallow. Yet when good fruits are gathered, we celebrate and give thanks for the rich harvest. The good fruits of the harvest, as Saint Paul describes, are love, joy, peace, patience, kindness, generosity, faithfulness, gentleness, and self-control (Galatians 5:22).

MUTUAL MINISTRY REVIEW

DIG: What needs digging into (prep work) or digging around and fertilizing (reworking)?	**PLANT**: What needs planting (exploring, starting, leading)?	**WATER**: What needs watering (tending, oversight, encouragement)?
NEW SEEDS: What might we start or add?	**LIE FALLOW**: What needs to be put on hold for a while?	**CELEBRATE**: What needs harvesting and/or a harvestfest (celebration)?
	PRUNE: What needs to be pruned or weeded out (let go of)?	

This is an opportunity to use an agricultural model to explore our activities according to where they are in the growth process to see in a positive and nonthreatening way: what needs digging and fertilizing (re-working); what needs planting; what needs watering or pruning (tending); what needs to lie fallow; what we are overtending; what is ready for harvest and celebration festival. *Consider which category each of your church's mission fields or ministry areas belong to.*

Some ministry areas to consider placing:

Ministry Area	Description
Administration/ oversight	overseeing all aspects of congregational ministries, including programs, finances, etc.
Adult Formation	nurturing and equipping people for growth within the faith community and for mission; developing opportunities for prayer and faith sharing; and sharing expectations for ways to strengthen our spiritual development
Children/Youth	designing and implementing effective programs of Christian formation and education; inspiring and incorporating youth fully into the life and ministry of the church; and encouraging and equipping leaders to work with youth.
Communications	using appropriate tools to communicate the story and mission of the Church for the success of its work
Evangelism	training and leading persons to proclaim the gospel of Jesus Christ and to invite others into Christian fellowship
Facilities	taking care of maintenance, working on new construction, and eliminating debt

Leadership Development	strengthening the capacity of church leaders to engage in mission and ministry; discerning potential leaders; making provisions for ongoing leadership education, formation, and training; and developing functional ministry teams
Outreach	empowering and equipping persons within the congregation to become aware of and participate in ministry to individual and community needs and concerns beyond the faith community
Pastoral Care	providing pastoral response at significant life stages (e.g., death, dying, sickness, birth, crisis, success), including caring through home and hospital calling
Social	supporting fun fellowship events for the church and community
Stewardship	leading the congregation and individuals to identify, develop, and offer their gifts and resources
Worship	offering glorious worship services

4. *Once you have filled in ministries and activities on our Mutual Ministry Review chart above, ask some additional critical questions about how you are doing with mutual ministry:*

    a. Have you identified leaders for each ministry?

    b. Have you created teams?

    c. How do you invite new people into key ministries?

    d. How are you doing on leading these ministries?

5. *Different ministry areas need different levels of oversight. Consider different areas in terms of different categories identified by Ken Blanchard:*

Level of Oversight	Where do your ministries fall?
DIRECT inexperienced workers by • giving explicit instructions; • closely tracking performance; and • providing frequent feedback.	
COACH moderately competent workers by explaining why; • soliciting suggestions; • praising nearly right performance; and • continuing to direct tasks.	
SUPPORT nearly competent workers by • sharing decision making; • encouraging independent problem solving; and • supporting development of an independent style	
DELEGATE to fully competent workers by • empowering the worker to act independently; • providing appropriate resources; and • leaving them alone!	

Place each of the ministry areas in this chart according to the levels of oversight required. Identify areas that presently require clergy or staff involvement by placing an asterisk (*) in front of them.

Successful delegation happens when a ministry team has: (i) a responsible leader or group of leaders, (ii) experienced and enthusiastic workers, (iii) intentional preparation (training, coaching, apprenticing) of new leaders and workers, (iv) a clear role that is appropriately monitored by the leaders, (v) helpful process guides or manuals, and (vi) appropriate communication with and reporting to the governing board.

6. *Begin to set goals for the community or ministry area, asking:*

- Are we sensing a call in certain areas?

- What would you like to build on or do differently, if anything?

- What do you sense God might be calling you to do in the coming year or two?

- What one thing would you like to see enhanced or added in the coming year or two?

- What goals would we like to set? Where (to whom) will our activities be?

- Have specific answers to four questions for each goal:

  - Who (will do this)?

  - What (will they do)?

  - When (will it be done)?

  - How (will it be done)?

A ministry team model for mutual ministry review

Individual ministry teams may also apply the organic mutual ministry review process above to evaluate their progress. Where leadership is effectively delegated, a governing board may also ask individual ministry teams to take the lead by participating in the following process:

1. The governing board sets a schedule for ministry area information requests and discussion times during governing board meetings over a period of months. A twelve- or twenty-four-month proposed schedule of

ministry review times is prepared.

2. The governing board asks ministry area leaders, teams, or committees to (i) share and develop their hopes, dreams, goals, and strategies in their particular ministry areas, (ii) answer the following questions for the ministry area, and (iii) present the answers in a short report to the governing board at least a week before the ministry area will be discussed.

    •   Who is part of this ministry?

    •   What do you believe is the strength of this ministry?

    •   How do you invite people into this ministry? Is it working?

    •   What would you like to build on or do differently, if anything?

    •   What do you sense God might be calling you to do in the coming year or two?

    •   What one thing would you like to see enhanced or added in the coming year or two?

    •   What are your goals for the next year or two, including specific answers to four questions for each goal: Who will do this? What will they do? When will it be done? How will it be done?

3. The governing board (i) reviews ministry team reports and suggests additions or changes, (ii) prioritizes and coordinates ministry team recommendations with overall plans for the church community, and (iii) monitors, adjusts, and follows up with ministry team plans as needed.

Emphases of this process are to help everyone understand what is going on, learn about ministries, support communication among ministries and the congregation, celebrate gifts and ministries, and provide a foundation for governing board discernment, planning, oversight, and decision making.

C

Leading Change in Church Communities: 10 Important Questions

O God,
who has made us creatures of time,
so that every tomorrow is unknown country,
and every decision a venture in faith:
Grant us, frail children of the day,
who are yet blind to the future,
to move toward it in the sure confidence of your love,
from which neither life nor death can ever separate us.
Amen.

—Reinhold Niebuhr

1. *Do we need a change process?*

    • What is the adaptive situation we are facing?

    • Are we responding to symptoms or purpose?

    • How will this change help us to respond to God's call/live more fully into God's Kingdom?

    • How are we making things better?

2. *How much do we need to change, and how quickly?*

    • *Incremental change:* Most people assume success comes one step at a time and are more comfortable changing one habit at a time.

- *Systemic change*: We may need to reach the next level faster by learning or doing several new things at once. Consider whether we are taking all of the actions we need to truly bring about the changes we desire.

3. *Are we prepared for resistance?*

- Different people have different approaches to change: only 3 percent will be innovators, 13 percent early adopters, 34 percent middle adopters, 34 percent late adopters, and 16 percent laggards.[1]

- Different people have different stress tolerances, and different people face different levels of stress.

- Since stress is cumulative, be aware of all stressors:

  - events in the church community, such as new leaders and leadership styles, new projects, perceived changes to worship style, or the arrival of new members

  - events outside the community on a macro level, such as war, natural disasters, or economic distress

  - events on a personal level, such as illness, concerns about children, loss of a job, divorce, or life transitions

- We need to monitor resistance and build critical mass with pastoral and behavioral responses.

4. *What is our level of trust?*

- Most resistance to change is rooted in fear and/or need for control.

- People will follow those they trust: God/Jesus/Spirit, leaders (clergy and lay), ministry teams, themselves.

- It's important to develop a trusted leadership group that is

  - non-anxious;

  - God-differentiated (not self-differentiated);

  - confident;

  - purposeful; and

  - concerted.

- Leaders need to set the pace and tone: enthusiasm and commitment is contagious.

5. *Do we have a vision?*

   - Begin with a clear, shared, and compelling vision.

   - Draw and inspire people with a significant mission (purpose) to be accomplished together in a supportive community (belonging).

6. *Do we have a guiding coalition? This coalition should*

   - be trusted (above);

   - create urgency (momentum below);

   - inspire and set an example for later adopters;

   - set goals;

   - create expectations that goals can be met; and

   - carry as much forward as possible in a ministry team (versus the whole congregation).

7. *Are we fully involving others?*

   - The mission of the church is the work of all of us (1 Corinthians 12).

- Teams achieve more than individuals (due to the variance of gifts, skills, and resources).

- Involvement in planning and execution provides understanding and eliminates fear.

- Teamwork increases energy and enthusiasm.

8. *Are we overcommunicating?*

- Make sure communication is open and honest to

  - build trust;

  - raise awareness;

  - reassure members that the changes are necessary and will pay off in the long run; and

  - give other people credit for making it all happen.

- Good communication includes

  - sharing stories and personal experiences;

  - talking comfortably and often about the significant role Jesus (not us!) is playing; and

  - listening!

- Be sure people know they are heard—but also be sure people understand that being heard does not mean they must have their own way.

9. *Are we building momentum?*

- Is there a growing sense of urgency that changes need to occur?

- Is there a growing confidence that changes will occur?

- Are resistance levels decreasing? Remember to

    - maintain the right amount of energy, as in the pressure cooker analogy (cook but don't blow the top off);

    - help concerned members avoid becoming overstressed; and

    - prevent dependent or recalcitrant members from undercutting the community's vision and strategies.

- How are we encouraging healthy reactions to stress?

    - Reduce people's stress by listening carefully to their concerns.

    - Honestly discuss the changes people are experiencing, especially their personal feelings about them.

    - Point out which stress is external to the system or that changes within the system are relatively small, purposeful, and reasonable.

- How are we reacting to unproductive conflict? Remember to

    - slow or stop the changes (though this can be like giving in to a child's tantrum and may not be possible if real stressors are beyond the community);

    - allow the stressed person to find a different setting where (s)he feels more safe; and

    - apply authority and place boundaries to define how individuals must act—even when they are stressed—as members of a loving community.

10. Are we learning?

- Productive confrontations help leaders take time for conversation, prayer, reflection and discernment, and they reveal broader or deeper perspectives.

- Leaders need to encourage, facilitate, and mediate confrontations that may help the community make better, positive decisions about questions that do not have clear answers and solutions.[2]

- Avoiding loving confrontations undermines change by harming relationships, preventing reconciliation and closing off the productive learning that differences in perspective may spur.[3]

There are real benefits to working through disagreements over values, goals, or methods if they are relevant to the mission of the community or the challenges the community is adapting to.

D

For Further Reading

General Leadership

Heifetz, Ronald A. *Leadership without Easy Answers*. Cambridge, MA.: Belknap Press of Harvard University Press, 1994.

Heifetz, Ronald A., Alexander Grashow, and Martin Linsky. *The Practice of Adaptive Leadership: Tools and Tactics for Changing Your Organization and the World*. Boston: Harvard Business Press, 2009.

Johnson, Spencer. *Who Moved My Cheese? An Amazing Way to Deal with Change in Your Work and in Your Life*. New York: Putnam, 1998.

Kotter, John P. *Leading Change*. Boston: Harvard Business School Press, 1996.

Kotter, John P., and Holger Rathgeber. *Our Iceberg Is Melting: Changing and Succeeding under Any Conditions*. New York: St. Martin's Press, 2006.

Kouzes, James M., and Barry Z. Posner. *The Truth about Leadership: the No-Fads, Heart-of-the-Matter Facts You Need to Know*. San Francisco: Jossey-Bass, 2010.

Maxwell, John C. *The 5 Levels of Leadership: Proven Steps to Maximize Your Potential*. New York: Center Street, 2011.

Scott, Susan. *Fierce Conversations: Achieving Success at Work & in Life, One Conversation at a Time*. New York: Berkley, 2004.

Christian Leadership

Blanchard, Kenneth H., and Phil Hodges. *Lead Like Jesus: Lessons from the Greatest Leadership Role Model of All Times*. Nashville: W Pub. Group, 2005.

Bonem, Mike. *In Pursuit of Great and Godly Leadership: Tapping the Wisdom of the World* for *the Kingdom of God*. San Francisco: Jossey-Bass, 2012.

McFayden, Kenneth J. *Strategic Leadership for a Change: Facing Our Losses, Finding Our Future*. Herndon, VA: Alban Institute, 2009.

McNeal, Reggie. *The Present Future: Six Tough Questions for the Church*. San Francisco, CA: Jossey-Bass, 2003.

Payne, Claude E., and Hamilton Beazley. *Reclaiming the Great Commission: a Practical Model for Transforming Denominations and Congregations*. San Francisco: Jossey-Bass, 2000.

Roxburgh, Alan J., and Fred Romanuk. *The Missional Leader: Equipping Your Church to Reach a Changing World*. San Francisco: Jossey-Bass, 2006.

Steinke, Peter L. *A Door Set Open: Grounding Change in Mission and Hope*. Herndon, VA: Alban Institute, 2010.

Church Mission

Bonhoeffer, Dietrich. *Life Together* and *Prayerbook of the Bible* in *Dietrich Bonhoeffer Works 5*. Minneapolis: Fortress Press, 2004.

Hunter, George G. III. *The Celtic Way of Evangelism: How Christianity Can Reach the West . . . Again*. Abingdon, 2000.

McLaren, Brian D. *Everything Must Change: Jesus, Global Crises, and a Revolution of Hope*. Nashville: Thomas Nelson, 2007.

Pippert, Rebecca Manley. *Out of the Saltshaker & into the World: Evan-*

gelism as a Way of Life, 20th anniversary ed. Downers Grove, IL.: InterVarsity Press, 1999.

Rusaw, Rick, and Eric Swanson. *The Externally Focused Church*. Loveland, CO: Group Pub., 2004.

Warren, Rick. *The Purpose Driven Church: Growing without Compromising Your Message & Mission*. Grand Rapids, MI: Zondervan, 1995.

Spiritual Growth

Bonhoeffer, Dietrich. *Discipleship* in *Dietrich Bonhoeffer Works 4*. Minneapolis: Fortress Press, 2003.

Manning, Brennan. *The Ragamuffin Gospel*. Sisters, OR: Multnomah Publishers, 2000.

Merton, Thomas. *New Seeds of Contemplation*. New York: New Directions, 1972.

Nouwen, Henri J. M. *Home Tonight*. S.l.: Darton, Longman & Todd, 2009.

Nouwen, Henri J. M. *In the Name of Jesus: Reflections on Christian Leadership*. New York: Crossroad, 1989.

Nouwen, Henri J. M. *The Return of the Prodigal Son: a Story of Homecoming*. New York: Doubleday, 1994.

Tutu, Desmond. *God Has a Dream: a Vision of Hope for Our Time*. New York: Doubleday, 2004.

Mutual Ministry

Bugbee, Bruce. *What You Do Best in the Body of Christ: Discover Your Spiritual Gifts, Personal Style, and God-given Passion*. Grand Rapids: Zondervan, 2005.

Bugbee, Bruce. *Discover Your Spiritual Gifts the Network Way: 4 Assessments for Determining Your Spiritual Gifts.* Grand Rapids: Zondervan, 2005.

Bugbee, Bruce L., Don Cousins, and Wendy Seidman. *Network Kit: The Right People, in the Right Places, for the Right Reasons, at the Right Time.* Grand Rapids: Zondervan, 2005

Christian Leaders

Coles, Robert. *Dorothy Day: a Radical Devotion.* Reading, MA: Addison-Wesley Pub. Co., 1987.

Day, Dorothy, and Robert Ellsberg. *Selected Writings: by Little and by Little.* Maryknoll, NY: Orbis Books, 2001.

Metaxas, Eric. *Bonhoeffer: Pastor, Martyr, Prophet, Spy: a Righteous Gentile vs. the Third Reich.* Nashville: Thomas Nelson, 2010.

Phillips, Donald T. *Martin Luther King, Jr., on Leadership: Inspiration & Wisdom for Challenging Times.* New York: Warner Books, 1999.

Emergent Church

Anderson, Leith. *A Church for the 21st Century.* Minneapolis: Bethany House Publishers, 1992.

Bass, Diana Butler. *Christianity after Religion: the End of Church and the Birth of a New Spiritual Awakening.* New York: HarperOne, 2012.

Hirsch, Alan, and Debra Hirsch. *Untamed: Reactivating a Missional Form of Discipleship.* Grand Rapids: Baker Books, 2010.

Jones, Tony. *The New Christians: Dispatches from the Emergent Frontier.* San Francisco: Jossey-Bass, 2008.

Kimball, Dan. *The Emerging Church: Vintage Christianity for New Generations.* Grand Rapids: Zondervan, 2003.

McLaren, Brian D. *A New Kind of Christianity: Ten Questions That are Transforming the Faith*. New York: HarperOne, 2010.

Mead, Loren B.. *The Once and Future Church: Reinventing the Congregation for a New Mission Frontier*. Washington, DC: Alban Institute, 1991.

Pagitt, Doug. *Church Re-imagined: the Spiritual Formation of People in Communities of Faith*. Grand Rapids: Zondervan, 2005.

Regele, Mike, and Mark Schulz. *Death of the Church*. Grand Rapids: Zondervan, 1995.

Tickle, Phyllis. *Emergence Christianity: What It Is, Where It Is Going, and Why It Matters*. Grand Rapids: Baker Books, 2012.

ENDNOTES

Introduction

[1] John 1:47–51. Using an image of Jacob's ladder from Jacob's dream at Bethel (Genesis 27:35–36), Jesus is referring to God's promise to Jacob in Genesis 28:10–15: "you shall spread abroad to the west and to the east and to the north and to the south; and all the families of the earth shall be blessed in you and in your offspring. Know that I am with you and will keep you wherever you go, and will bring you back to this land; for I will not leave you until I have done what I have promised you."

[2] Thinking about who Jesus is and where he is leading us is very important. Gary E. Peluso-Verdend, *Paying Attention: Focusing Your Congregation on What Matters* (Herndon, VA: The Alban Institute, 2005), 52–53, writes:

> We, the church, will always bring a framework to reading the text that will affect what, and who, we find there. We will always bring, implicitly or explicitly, theology. Theology matters. It is an essential discipline for the church. As it is said that war is too important to be left to the generals, so it is that theology is too important to be left to professional theologians in seminaries, in colleges and university religion departments, or even to the clergy. Theology needs to be a congregational discipline and practice. After the practices of worship and prayer … theological reflection is the most essential practice to enable Christian communities to attend well. Theological reflection brings Jesus' teachings and actions regarding the kingdom of God and helps the church attend lovingly to God and to neighbor today.

He adds, "Theology frames what we see and lures us in one direction or another. Choosing a theological frame and living within it is one of the primary means that shapes our attention as Christians. Theology can and should serve as an everyday discipline, a framework and lens for seeing everyday life" (55). He encourages congregational leaders to take the gospel message and try to "apply it to a *community in a context* today" and reminds them that "our question should not be first or primarily what this text means for *me* but what the text means for *us*" (80).

[3] A recent study of Christianity's slipping image among 16–29 year olds is explored in *unChristian: What a New Generation Really Thinks about Christianity... and Why It Matters*, by David Kinnaman and Gabe Lyons (Baker Books, 2007). Half of young churchgoers said they perceive Christians as judgmental, anti-homosexual, hypocritical, overly political, and sheltered. One-third said Christianity was old fashioned and out of touch with reality. The harshest criticism of the church is that it doesn't act much like Jesus. The greatest attraction to Jesus for these younger people is the abundance of love Jesus offers.

[4] Both church members and nonmembers are continually surprised and disappointed when people do not even get along in and among our church communities and church communities can certainly do better. As Eugene Peterson writes, "When Christian believers gather in churches, everything that can go wrong sooner or later does. ... Christian churches are not, as a rule, model communities of good behavior. They are, rather, places where human misbehavior is brought out in the open, faced, and dealt with." ("Introduction to James" in *The Message*). We see in Ephesians 4, and certainly in other Pauline letters, that church communities must always grow beyond dissension into maturity.

[5] Some people may have difficulty with my focus here on Jesus rather than God the Father or God the Holy Spirit, with whom they may feel a closer relationship. On the Christian Way, Jesus brings us into relationship with all of the Persons of the Trinity, but this does not happen only through Jesus. We experience the love of God in the creation of ourselves and our world by the Father (Transcendent, God above us), the redeeming love of Jesus who saves us (Personal, God with us), and the energy available through the power and presence of the Holy Spirit (Immanent, God in us). And we tend to draw closer to these different persons of God through different faculties and experiences, with our heads, our hands, and our hearts.

1.1 Good News of God's Kingdom

[1] Dietrich Bonhoeffer, *Discipleship* in *Dietrich Bonhoeffer Works 4* (Fortress Press), 227–228.

² The Hebrew word is "mashach," often used in the Hebrew Scriptures for the anointing of a king.

³ The New Testament contains 148 references to the "kingdom" of God. The New Testament is a kingdom book. It is about Jesus' presence and God's reign in the world.

⁴ In the Lord's Prayer:

> We proclaim our allegiance to the Lord, which surpasses our allegiance to any other ruler. The Lord's Prayer begins with confessing that God is the Father ... in heaven—the place of ultimate power and governance. This Father is holy. ... Then comes the first and governing petition in the prayer: "Your kingdom come, your will be done, on earth as it is in heaven." Reciting this prayer is the church's pledge of allegiance to the reign of God. Allegiance to every other power is secondary. In this kingdom, we have daily bread—the essentials for our existence. All debts, material and spiritual, are mutually forgiven. The evil one cannot distract us, because no power of any kind can compare with God's reign, God's power, and God's glory. The church needs no "keys to the scriptures" other than this prayer. At the heart of Jesus' teaching, at the core of his mission, as the central object of his evangel, at the focus of his attention is the reign of God: what it is, where we should look for it, how we can access it, when it is, how should we act in response to it and as citizens of it.

Gary E. Peluso-Verdend, *Paying Attention: Focusing Your Congregation on What Matters* (Herndon, VA: The Alban Institute, 2005), 35–36.

⁵ Repentance is not just something we do but something we ask and prepare for and the Holy Spirit effects. Jesus applies an organic metaphor to this rebirth, describing a grain of wheat that was put in the earth and died, in its death germinating and then sprouting; so we die and, in dying, live. He says to Nicodemus the Pharisee, "Very truly, I tell you, no one can see the kingdom of God without being born from above" (John 3:3) and proclaims that he himself answers this need for germination, "For God so loved the world that he gave his only Son, so that everyone who believes in him may not perish but may have eternal life"

(John 3:16). Jesus compares the kingdom of God to a tiny mustard seed: planted in the earth, decomposing, and then sprouting forth in the largest of plants, as we may also. This kingdom is not something we do, but something we receive as a child receives a gift that is not earned. "Truly I tell you, whoever does not receive the kingdom of God as a little child will never enter it. And he took them up in his arms, laid his hands on them, and blessed them." (Mark 10:15–16). But once the gift is received, we can fully participate in this new Way of life.

[6] Footnote *a* to Mark 10:24 NRSV (Oxford University Press) states that other ancient authorities add the bracketed words "for those who trust in riches." Other versions, such as the International Standard Version, the King James 2000 Bible, and the Aramaic Bible in Plain English, include these words in the verse.

1.2 The Way of Jesus

[1] John makes the connection between Jesus, the Passover lamb in Exodus 12 and Isaiah's description of the Messiah as a sacrificial lamb (Isaiah 53:7) who dies for the sins of the world (Isaiah 53:12).

[2] Disciples learned by listening, memorizing, and repeating back what a rabbi said. If they made a mistake, they repeated the process until they knew a teaching by heart. This is how we can have the teachings of Jesus preserved in the Bible.

[3] Consider the total difference here from a theological or philosophical description of God as eternal, omnipotent, and omniscient (also huge concepts that we cannot fully comprehend). God is a person to be lived with, to be loved and transformed by. He isn't a concept or belief system for logical argument. The way of love is a living relationship with God and other people, not a morality, ethic, or belief.

[4] Dietrich Bonhoeffer, *Discipleship: DBW 4*, 304.

[5] These quotes are:

> This is the work of God, that you believe in him whom he has sent. (John 6:29)

This is indeed the will of my Father, that all who see the Son and believe in him may have eternal life; and I will raise them up on the last day. (John 6:40)

I told you that you would die in your sins, for you will die in your sins unless you believe that I am he. (John 8:24)

I am the resurrection and the life. Those who believe in me, even though they die, will live, and everyone who lives and believes in me will never die. Do you believe this? (John 11:25–26)

The one who believes and is baptized will be saved; but the one who does not believe will be condemned (Mark 16:16).

[6] On the day after an attempt on Hitler's life failed, Dietrich Bonhoeffer reflected on his Christian journey in a letter to his friend, Eberhard Bethge (*Letters and Papers From Prison*, in *DBW 8*, 537):

I thought I could acquire faith by trying to live a holy life, or something like it. ... I discovered later, and I'm still discovering right up to this moment, that it is only by living completely in this world that one learns to have faith. One must completely abandon any attempt to make something of oneself, whether it be a saint, or a converted sinner, or a churchman (a so-called priestly type!), a righteous person or an unrighteous one, a sick person or a healthy one. By this-worldliness I mean living unreservedly in life's duties, problems, successes and failures, experiences and perplexities. In so doing we throw ourselves completely into the arms of God, taking seriously, not our own sufferings, but those of God in the world—watching with Christ in Gethsemane. That, I think, is faith; that is metanoia [repentance]; and that is how one becomes a human being, a Christian (cf. Jer. 45!).

In *Discipleship*, he also wrote: "The aim and objective is not to renew human thoughts about God so that they are correct, or that we would subject our individual deeds to the word of God again, but that we, with our whole existence and as living creatures, are the image of God. Body, soul, and spirit, that is, the form of being human in its totality, is to bear the image of God on earth" (299).

[7] "Those following Jesus must ask what is the ultimate standard of measure of who will be accepted by Jesus and who will not. Who remains and who does not? Jesus' answer to those who are rejected at the end says it all: "I never knew you" (Matthew 7:23). That is the final secret, which has been kept from the beginning of the Sermon on the Mount up until its end. That alone is the question, whether we were known by Jesus or not." Dietrich Bonhoeffer, *Discipleship*, 190.

[8] Parker J. Palmer states in *Leading from Within: Reflections on Spirituality and Leadership* (Indianapolis: Indiana Office for Campus Ministries, 1990), 4:

> Spirituality is not primarily about values and ethics, not about exhortations to do right or live well. The spiritual traditions are primarily about *reality*. The spiritual traditions are an effort to penetrate the illusions of the external world and to name its underlying truth—what it is, how it emerges, and how we relate to it. Let's go back and read some of Jesus' sayings which we often take as ethical exhortations, as guides to what we *ought* to do: "The person who seeks life will lose it; but the person who is willing to lose life will find it." That is not an ethical exhortation. It is not an 'ought' statement. It is simply a description of what's real, of what is! Time and again, things Jesus said that we take as statements of ethics are simply his statements of where it's at and what it's like. That's the nature of great spiritual teaching.

[9] Marcus J. Borg writes in *Meeting Jesus Again for the First Time* (San Francisco: HarperSanFransisco, 1994), 75: "As a teacher of wisdom, Jesus was not primarily a teacher of information (what to believe) or morals (how to behave), but a teacher of a way or path of transformation. A way of transformation from … a life in the world of conventional wisdom to a life centered in God."

[10] Examples of popular recent books about personally and communally approaching faith as a way of life (rather than just as a belief system) and about critical questions facing the post-Christendom church include: N.T Wright's *The Challenge of Jesus* and *Simply Christian*; Eugene Peterson's *The Jesus Way*; Brian McLaren's *Finding Our Way Again: The Return of the Ancient Practices*, *A New Kind of Christianity*, and *Everything Must*

Change; Marcus Borg's *The Heart of Christianity* and *Embracing an Adult Faith*; and Reggie McNeal's *The Present Future*.

[11] A prayer attributed to Saint Richard of Chichester is:

Day by day, day by day,

O, dear Lord, three things I pray:

to see thee more clearly, love thee more dearly,

follow thee more nearly, day by day.

The prayer was popularized in the musical *Godspell* by Stephen Schwarz and is also found in more than a dozen hymnals with various tunes, including *Hymnal 1982: according to the use of the Episcopal Church* #654.

1.3 Following Jesus

[1] See also Matthew 4:19–22 and Luke 5:1–11. (In which these disciples recognized Jesus in a marvelous catch of fish "and Jesus said to Simon, 'Do not be afraid; from now on you will be catching people.' When they had brought their boats to shore, they left everything and followed him.")

[2] God forgives human sins. "All wrongdoing is sin, but there is sin that is not mortal" (1 John 5:17). In other words, God forgives some wrongdoing. Exodus 34:7 says that God forgives iniquity, transgression, and sin, but does not clear the guilty. Jeremiah 31:34 says, "I will forgive their iniquity, and remember their sin no more." Without presuming God's judgment, it seems that the sins that are not forgiven are contempt or rebellion against God—refusing to live in relationship with God. (See 1 Samuel 12:17.)

[3] Dietrich Bonhoeffer, *Discipleship*, 50–51. He continues, "If Jesus said: leave everything else behind and follow me, leave your profession, your family, your people, and your father's house, then the biblical hearer knew that the only answer to this call is simple obedience, because the promise of community with Jesus is given to this obedience. . . What [Jesus] really meant was that final inner willingness to invest everything for the kingdom of God" (71).

[4] Dietrich Bonhoeffer, *Discipleship*, 154.

[5] Eugene Peterson, *The Contemplative Pastor: Returning to the Art of Spiritual Direction*, (Grand Rapids, MI: Eerdmans Publishing, 1989) pp. 102–105.

[6] Dietrich Bonhoeffer wrote in *Discipleship: DBW 4* (Dietrich Bonhoeffer Works) (Fortress Press), at 84:

> Bearing the cross does not bring misery and despair. Rather, it provides refreshment and peace for our souls; it is our greatest joy. Here we are no longer laden with self-made laws and burdens, but with the yoke of him who knows us and who himself goes with us under the same yoke. Under his yoke we are assured of his nearness and communion. It is he himself whom disciples find when they take up their cross.

[7] Henri J.M Nouwen, *In the name of Jesus: reflections on Christian Leadership* (New York: Crossroad, 1989), 82–84.

1.4 Accepting God's Love

[1] The parable of the king and the maiden appeared in Søren Kierkegaard's *Philosophical Fragments* in 1844. I have considered this parable more extensively in *God's Love, Human Freedom and Christian Faith* (Chalice Press, 2003).

[2] "God is love" (1 John 4:8), "love is from God" (1 John 4:7), and "we love because he first loved us" (1 John 4:19). God's love always comes before our own, and our love is only a response to God's love. "Beloved, since God loved us so much, we also ought to love one another" (1 John 4:11).

[3] Henri J.M. Nouwen, *Home Tonight: Further Reflections on the Parable of the Prodigal Son and a Guide to Finding Your Spiritual Home* (New York: Doubleday, 2009), 93–97.

[4] Ibid., 61.

[5] Brennan Manning, *The Ragamuffin Gospel* (Sisters, OR: Multnomah Publishers, 2000), 75.

[6] In some ways, the story of the Prodigal Son seems very different from the Old Testament stories, where God expels or exiles people from their home because of their disobedience—stories of Adam and Eve, Cain, Noah, the migration to Egypt, the Babylonian captivity. Archbishop Rowan Williams explains that these stories also reveal God's love:

> [These stories hint] very strongly that life as a human being, even as a human being befriended by God, is a life where growth always means a step beyond what is familiar, a step away from home; that "exile" is a state of being for us. The further back we look at our story, the more clear it becomes that we are, in one sense, never at home. Or rather, being at home is a matter not of settling down for good somewhere, in a place beyond questions or growing; it is something to do with a fundamental trust in the God who accompanies us in our travelling. Because the other great theme . . . is "covenant"—the repeated promises made by God [that . . .] whatever happens, however they have ignored or offended against what God asks of them, God commits to being there alongside them. . . . Home is God's company: something that can only be discovered as the history of disruption and exile unfolds. . . . Where do we come from? . . . We come from the decision of a God who shows endless, even alarming flexibility in arranging to stay near us, even when we show ourselves incapable of any stability in the place given us to occupy.

Joan Chittister and Rowan Williams, *Uncommon Gratitude: Alleluia for All That Is* (Liturgical Press, 2010), 84–87.

[7] Some wonderful books about the journey to accepting God's love are: Henri J.M. Nouwen, *Home Tonight: Further Reflections on the Parable of the Prodigal Son and a Guide to Finding Your Spiritual Home* (New York, Doubleday, 2009); Henri J.M. Nouwen, *The Return of the Prodigal Son: A Story of Homecoming* (New York: Doubleday, 1994); Brennan Manning, *The Ragamuffin Gospel* (Sisters, OR: Multnomah Publishers, 2000); and Desmond Tutu, *God Has a Dream: A Vision of Hope for Our Time* (New York: Doubleday, 2004).

[8] Nouwen, *Home Tonight* (New York: Doubleday, 2009), 26–28.

[9] Ibid., 41.

1.5 The Great Commission

[1] 1 Corinthians 6:11: "You were washed, you were sanctified, you were justified in the name of the Lord Jesus Christ and in the Spirit of our God."

[2] In the Apostles' Creed, one of the most ancient statements of Christian faith, we proclaim, "I believe in the communion of saints." God called the Jewish people out of slavery in Egypt, in order for them to be "a holy nation" (Exodus 19:6). He told them, "You shall be holy, for I am holy" (Leviticus 11:45). Saint Peter quotes the same words to New Testament people (1 Peter 1:16), agreeing with Saint Paul that Christians are "called as saints" (Romans 1:7). In living with Jesus, "the fruit of the Spirit is love, joy, peace, patience, kindness, generosity, faithfulness, gentleness, and self-control" (Galatians 5:22–23). Christians are people who become like Jesus.

[3] Desmond Tutu, *God Has a Dream: A Vision of Hope for Our Time* (New York: Doubleday, 2004), 15.

[4] It is important to recognize their representative status and who they are sent to serve; they are not given exalted status. Matthew does, however, imply that the number 12 and the Twelve represented the creation of new Israel. As the twelve patriarchs founded old Israel, the twelve apostles would begin the new Israel. And their ministry is for the renewal and restoration of Israel. They are to prepare their own people for the coming of the kingdom of God.

[5] "Whoever welcomes you welcomes me, and whoever welcomes me welcomes the one who sent me. Whoever welcomes a prophet in the name of a prophet will receive a prophet's reward; and whoever welcomes a righteous person in the name of a righteous person will receive the reward of the righteous; and whoever gives even a cup of cold water to one of these little ones in the name of a disciple—truly I tell you, none of these will lose their reward."

[6] Rick Warren writes in *The Purpose Driven Church: Growing Without Compromising Your Message & Mission* (Grand Rapids, MI: Zondervan, 1995), 63:

What is fruitfulness? The word *fruit*, or a variation of it, is used fifty-five times in the New Testament and refers to a variety of results. Each one of the following is considered by God to be fruit: repentance (Matt. 3:8; Luke 13:5–9), practicing the truth (Matt. 7:16–21; Col. 1:10), answered prayer (John 15:7–8), an offering of money given by believers (Rom 15:28), Christlike character; and winning unbelievers to Christ (Rom. 15:28). Paul said he wanted to preach in Rome "in order that I might obtain some fruit among you also, even as among the rest of the Gentiles" (Rom. 1:13 NASB). The fruit of a believer is another believer. Considering the Great Commission that Jesus gave to the church, I believe the definition of fruitfulness for a local church must include growth by the conversion of unbelievers. Paul referred to the first converts in Achaia as the "first fruit of Achaia" (1 Cor. 16:15 NASB). The Bible clearly identifies numerical growth of the church as fruit. ... Colossians 1:6 says, "All over the world this gospel is bearing fruit and growing, just as it has been doing since the day you heard it."

2.1 By Listening

[1] Bartimaeus cries out, "Jesus, Son of David, have mercy on me!" This is the same prayer Jesus commends in Luke, in the parable of the Pharisee and the tax collector, when the tax collector beats his breast and prays, "God, be merciful to me, a sinner." This cry is now commonly called the Jesus prayer. As Margaret Guenther points out (in *The Practice of Prayer*), "it is a complete prayer, containing adoration, petition and confession in [seven or eight words]. St. John Carpathos offered the comforting idea that after each petition for mercy God secretly answers, 'Child, your sins are forgiven.'" We can pray this prayer as the breath of our lives, inhaling as we pray "Lord Jesus Christ, Son of God, have mercy on me, a sinner!" and exhaling our sins as we hear God answer "Child, your sins are forgiven." The prayer reminds us of our needs and the power of Jesus to respond.

[2] Saying that our faith makes us well is not saying that we save ourselves. But it is saying that we must accept our dependence on Jesus and the gift of his mercy. We are only saved if we take action consistent with our rec-

ognition of our dependence on God. If we want to grow and become disciples, we need to be aware of our dependence on Jesus and think about how we are approaching Jesus. The type of transformation Bartimaeus experienced does not just happen to us. We need to ask for help in the spiritual life, and we need to take certain actions. We need to approach Jesus for Jesus to respond to us. Jesus says Bartimaeus' faith makes him well. That faith is revealed by his crying out. Even more, it is expressed by his throwing off his cloak, springing up, and going to Jesus. Bartimaeus believes. He sees that Jesus is the Messiah and knows that Jesus can heal him, if he chooses. Jesus listens, sees the need and chooses to heal.

[3] Dietrich Bonhoeffer, *Life Together and Prayerbook of the Bible,* in *Dietrich Bonhoeffer Works 5* (Fortress Press), 82–83. Bonhoeffer continued: "Many people seek a sympathetic ear and do not find it among Christians, because these Christians are talking even when they should be listening. But Christians who can no longer listen to one another will soon no longer be listening to God either; they will always be talking even in the presence of God. ... Those who think their time is too precious to spend listening will never really have time for God and others, but only for themselves and for their own words and plans. ... Christians have forgotten that the ministry of listening has been entrusted to them by the one who is indeed the great listener and in whose work they are to participate. We should listen with the ears of God, so that we can speak the Word of God." 83–84.

[4] Simone Weil, *Waiting for God,* trans. Emma Craufurd (New York: Perennial, 2001), 64. Weil equates the love of our neighbor with the love of God and identifies attention as the substance of both. Commenting on this passage, Gary E. Peluso-Verdend writes, "Attention is the most precious gift any of us has to offer to anyone else. ... To receive undivided, undistracted, compassionate, and truthful attention from another is a healing gift. It is also, clearly, a risk for the attentive one. Giving attention requires that '[t]he soul empties itself of all its own contents in order to receive into itself the being it is looking at, just as he is, in all his truth' [citing Weil at 65]." *Paying Attention: Focusing Your Congregation on What Matters* (Herndon, VA: The Alban Institute, 2005).

[5] Listening is also the primary tool of leaders. "The primary way that you show that you care for someone is by paying attention to them. ...

You have to reach out to others, listen to their words and emotions, be open to their experiences, ask them questions, and express a willingness to learn from them. Making other people the center of your attention tells them that you feel they're important, it tells them that you regard their input as useful, and it tells them that you value their ideas." Barry Z. Posner and James M. Kouzes, *The Truth about Leadership: The No-fads, Heart-of-the-Matter Facts You Need to Know* (San Francisco, CA: Jossey-Bass, 2010), 140.

[6] "Mychal's Prayer" was composed by Fr. Mychal Judge, a fire department chaplain, and worn in the helmets of New York firefighters. Fr. Judge died responding to the 9/11 World Trade Center attack with New York firefighters. The day before his death, he said at a firehouse rededication: "Good days, bad days, but never a boring day on this job. You do what God has called you to do. You show up, you put one foot in front of the other, and you do your job, which is a mystery and a surprise. You have no idea, when you get in that rig, what God is calling you to. But he needs you … so keep going. Keep supporting each other. Be kind to each other. Love each other. Work together. You love the job. We all do. What a blessing that is." www.saintmychal.com

2.2 By Healing and Forgiving

[1] Among the early followers and apostles of Jesus, Matthew is mentioned in Matthew 9:9 and 10:3 as a former tax collector from Capernaum who was called into the circle of the Twelve by Jesus. Matthew is also named among the Twelve in Mark 3:18, Luke 6:15, and Acts 1:13. He is often identified with the figure of Levi, son of Alpheus, also a tax collector, who is mentioned in Mark 2:14–20 and Luke 5:27–35.

[2] Ken Blanchard and Phil Hodges, *Lead Like Jesus: Lessons from the Greatest Leadership Role Model of All Time* (Nashville: Thomas Nelson, 2005), 79.

2.3 By Shepherding

[1] Each of these directives is prefaced by the most important question:

"Do you love me?" Jesus is asking Peter, "Do you hear my voice?" We are not the Good Shepherd. Jesus is. And so our task is not just to lead others. Our task as pastors is helping Jesus to be present in the lives of others.

[2] Charles Spurgeon said:

> The lambs are the young of the flock. So, then, we ought to look specially and carefully after those who are young in grace. They may be old in years, and yet they may be, mere babes in grace as to the length of their spiritual life, and therefore they need to be under a good shepherd. As soon as a person is converted and added to the church, he should become the object of the care and kindness of his fellow-members. He has but newly come among us, and has no familiar friends among the saints, therefore let us all be friendly to him. Even should we leave our older comrades, we must be doubly kind towards those who are newly escaped from the world, and have come to find a refuge with the Almighty and His people. Watch with ceaseless care over those new-born babes who are strong in desires, but strong in nothing else. They have but just crept out of darkness, and their eyes can scarcely bear the light; let us be a shade to them until they grow accustomed to the blaze of gospel day.

[3] Phillip Keller, *A Shepherd Looks at Psalm 23* (Zondervan, 1997).

[4] 1 Peter 5:1–2 says, "Now as an elder myself and a witness of the sufferings of Christ, as well as one who shares in the glory to be revealed, I exhort the elders among you to tend the flock of God that is in your charge, exercising the oversight, not under compulsion but willingly, as God would have you do it—not for sordid gain but eagerly."

2.4 By Serving

[1] Rick Rusaw and Eric Swanson, *The Externally-Focused Church* (Loveland, CO: Group, 2004), 60-61.

[2] Ibid., 26.

[3] Henri J. M Nouwen, *In the Name of Jesus: Reflections on Christian Leadership* (New York: Crossroad, 1989), 61.

[4] Martin Luther described sin as *homo incurvatus in se* ("humanity 'curved in on itself'"). We sin by turning away from God and others and into ourselves. Desmond Tutu says, "we sin whenever we are less than we could be, when we miss the mark of our potential to be fully loving and caring human beings." *God Has a Dream: A Vision of Hope for Our Time* (New York: Doubleday, 2004), 81.

2.5 By Reconciling

[1] As Coretta [Scott King] remembered, "He just always talked about the fact that he didn't expect to have a long life. Somehow he always felt that he would die early and he saw no need always to be on guard against the inevitable." On the day John F. Kennedy was assassinated, Martin looked up from the television and said to [her]: "This is exactly what's going to happen to me. I just realized it. I don't expect to survive this revolution." Donald T. Phillips, *Martin Luther King, Jr., on Leadership: Inspiration & Wisdom for Challenging Times* (New York: Warner Business Books, 2000), 309–310.

[2] Compare Romans 12:14 and 17–21:

> Bless those who persecute you; bless and do not curse them. . . . Do not repay anyone evil for evil, but take thought for what is noble in the sight of all. If it is possible, so far as it depends on you, live peaceably with all. Beloved, never avenge yourselves, but leave room for the wrath of God; for it is written, "Vengeance is mine, I will repay, says the Lord." No, "if your enemies are hungry, feed them; if they are thirsty, give them something to drink; for by doing this you will heap burning coals on their heads." Do not be overcome by evil, but overcome evil with good.

[3] Dietrich Bonhoeffer wrote in *Discipleship* at page 144:

> Faced with the way of the cross of Jesus Christ . . . the disciples themselves recognize that they were among the enemies of Jesus who have been conquered by his love. This love makes the disciples able to see, so that they can recognize an enemy as a sister or brother and behave toward that person as they would toward a sister or brother. Why?

Because they live only from the love of him who behaved toward them as toward brothers and sisters, who accepted them when they were his enemies and brought them into communion with him as his neighbors. That is how love makes disciples able to see, so that they can see the enemies included in God's love, that they can see the enemies under the cross of Jesus Christ.

[4] Bonhoeffer, *Discipleship*, 108.

[5] Dietrich Bonhoeffer writes in *Discipleship* at page 144:

Our willingness to yield up everything when we are bidden to do so is our willingness to have enough in Jesus Christ alone, to desire to follow him alone. Our voluntary renunciation of counterviolence confirms and proclaims our unconditional allegiance to Jesus as his followers, our freedom, our detachment from our own egos. And it is only in the exclusivity of this adherence that evil can be overcome.

Bonhoeffer also speaks of the impossibility of doing this ourselves at page 185:

To give witness to and to confess the truth of Jesus, but to love the enemy of this truth, who is his enemy and our enemy, with the unconditional love of Jesus Christ—that is a narrow road. To believe in Jesus' promise that those who follow shall possess the earth, but to encounter the enemy unarmed, to prefer suffering injustice to doing ill—that is a narrow road. To perceive other people as being weak and wrong, but never to judge them; to proclaim the Good News to them, but never to throw pearls before swine—that is a narrow road. It is an unbearable road. The danger of falling off threatens every minute. As long as I recognize this road as the one I am commanded to walk, and try to walk it in fear of myself, it is truly impossible. But if I see Jesus Christ walking ahead of me, step by step, if I look only at him and follow him, step by step, then I will be protected on this path. If I look at the danger in what I am doing, if I look at the path instead of at him who is walking ahead of me, then my foot is already slipping. He himself is the way. He is the narrow road and the narrow gate. The only thing that matters is finding him. If we know that, then we will walk the narrow way to life through the narrow gate of the cross of Jesus Christ, then the narrowness of the way itself will reassure us.

6 An exception is that Jesus did act violently when he drove the money-lenders and merchants from the temple. This is disturbing for a man of peace and a person who loves all people. Certainly it leads us to consider when violence might be acceptable and what violence can achieve. There are some actions Jesus will not show patience for. There are situations where nonviolence will not achieve peace or resist evil, but where these ends still must be pursued. Dietrich Bonhoeffer faced one of these situations when he participated in an attempt to assassinate Adolph Hitler. We might imagine circumstances where the good shepherd would use violence to protect his flock, but we must also recognize that type of action as a very last resort to save others.

7 Walter Wink, *Jesus and Nonviolence: A Third Way* (Minneapolis: Augsburg Fortress, 2003), 39–40.

8 In his first example of loving use of nonviolent confrontation, Jesus tells his followers, "If any one strikes you on the right cheek, turn to him the other also." Walter Wink explains:

> To strike the right cheek with the fist would require using the left hand, but in that society the left hand was used only for unclean tasks [and using it this way was prohibited]. The only way one could strike the right cheek with the right hand would be with the back of the right hand ... unmistakably an insult, not a fistfight. The intention is not to injure but to humiliate. ... A backhand slap was the normal way of admonishing inferiors. Masters backhanded slaves; husbands, wives; parents, children; men, women; Romans, Jews. We have here a set of unequal relations, in each of which retaliation would be suicidal. The only normal response would be cowering submission. ... Why then does he counsel these already humiliated people to turn the other cheek? Because this action robs the oppressor of the power to humiliate. The person who turns the other cheek is saying, in effect, "Try again. Your first blow failed to achieve its intended effect. I deny you the power to humiliate me. I am a human being just like you. Your status does not alter that fact. You cannot demean me." Such a response would create enormous difficulties for the striker. Purely logistically, what can he do? He cannot use the backhand because his nose is in the way. He can't use his left hand regardless. If he hits with a fist, he makes himself an equal, ac-

knowledging the other as a peer. ... The oppressor has been forced, against his will, to regard this subordinate as an equal human being. The powerful person has been stripped of his power to dehumanize the other. This response, far from admonishing passivity and cowardice, is an act of defiance.

Walter Wink, *Jesus and Nonviolence: A Third Way* (Minneapolis: Augsburg Fortress, 2003), 14–16.

[9] In Jesus' second example of nonviolent confrontation ("and if anyone wants to sue you and take your coat, give your cloak as well"), Professor Wink points out that Jesus was dealing with the problem of debtor's rights—perhaps the "most serious social problem in first-century Palestine"—when poor debtors were frequently hauled into court by creditors trying to seize the last remnants of property:

Why then does Jesus counsel them to give over their inner garment as well? This would mean stripping off all their clothing and marching out of court stark naked! Put yourself in the debtor's place, and imagine the chuckles this saying must have evoked. There stands the creditor, beet-red with embarrassment, your outer garment in one hand, your underwear in the other. You have suddenly turned the tables on him. You had no hope of winning the trial; the law was entirely in his favor. But you have refused to be humiliated, and at the same time you have registered a stunning protest against a system that spawns such debt. You have said in effect, "You want my robe? Here, take everything! Now you've got all I have except my body. Is that what you'll take next?" Nakedness was taboo in Judaism, and shame fell not on the naked party, but on the person viewing or causing one's nakedness (Gen. 9:20–27). By stripping you have brought the creditor under the same prohibition that led to the curse of Canaan ... The entire system by which debtors are oppressed has been publicly unmasked. The creditor is revealed to be not a "respectable" moneylender but a party in the reduction of an entire social class to landlessness and destitution. This unmasking is not simply punitive, however; it offers the creditor a chance to see, perhaps for the first time in his life, what his practices cause, and to repent.

Wink, *Jesus and Nonviolence: A Third Way*, 18–20.

[10] Jesus' third example of nonviolent confrontation, about going the second mile, comes from the Roman law limiting the amount of forced labor soldiers could impress:

> A soldier could impress a civilian to carry his pack one mile only. ... In this way Rome attempted to limit the anger of the occupied people and still keep its armies on the move. Nevertheless, this levy was a bitter reminder to the Jews that they were a subject people even in the Promised Land. [Walking the second mile] is how the oppressed can recover the initiative, how they can assert their human dignity in a situation that cannot for the time being be changed. ... Imagine then the soldier's surprise when, at the next mile marker, he reluctantly reaches to assume his pack (sixty-five to eighty-five pounds in full gear), and you say, "Oh no, let me carry it another mile." ... From a situation of servile impressments, you have once more seized the initiative. ... Now you have forced him into making a decision for which nothing in his previous experience has prepared him. If he has enjoyed feeling superior to the vanquished, he will not enjoy it today. Imagine the hilarious situation of a Roman infantryman pleading with a Jew, "Aw, come on, please give me back my pack!" The humor of this scene may escape those who picture it through sanctimonious eyes, but it could scarcely have been lost on Jesus' hearers, who must have been regaled at the prospect of thus discomfiting their oppressors.

Wink, *Jesus and Nonviolence: A Third Way* (Fortress, 2003), 23–25.

[11] Martin Luther King, Jr., *Letter from Birmingham Jail*, April 16, 1963.

[12] Donald T. Phillips, *Martin Luther King, Jr. on Leadership: Inspiration & Wisdom for Challenging Times* (New York: Warner Business Books, 2000), 62–63 (quotes from Martin Luther King, Jr.).

[13] In his 1959 *Sermon on Gandhi*, Dr. King said, "The way of acquiescence leads to moral and spiritual suicide. The way of violence leads to bitterness in the survivors and brutality in the destroyers. But, the way of non-violence leads to redemption and the creation of the beloved community" (www.thekingcenter.org/king-philosophy#sub4). The King Center (established by Mrs. Coretta Scott King in 1968) describes Dr.

King's theology of the beloved community:

> Dr. King's Beloved Community is a global vision, in which all people
> can share in the wealth of the earth. In the Beloved Community, pov-
> erty, hunger and homelessness will not be tolerated because interna-
> tional standards of human decency will not allow it. Racism and all
> forms of discrimination, bigotry and prejudice will be replaced by
> an all-inclusive spirit of sisterhood and brotherhood. In the Beloved
> Community, international disputes will be resolved by peaceful
> conflict-resolution and reconciliation of adversaries, instead of mili-
> tary power. Love and trust will triumph over fear and hatred. Peace
> with justice will prevail over war and military conflict. Dr. King ...
> believed that conflicts could be resolved peacefully and adversaries
> could be reconciled through a mutual, determined commitment to
> nonviolence ... and all conflicts in The Beloved Community should
> end with reconciliation of adversaries cooperating together in a spir-
> it of friendship and goodwill."

[14] In *God Has a Dream: A Vision of Hope for Our Time* (New York: Doubleday, 2004), Desmond Tutu asks, "How could anyone really think that
true reconciliation could avoid a proper confrontation?" (52) and says:

> Forgiving and being reconciled to our enemies or our loved ones
> is not about pretending that things are other than they are. It is not
> about patting one another on the back and turning a blind eye to
> the wrong. True reconciliation exposes the awfulness, the abuse, the
> pain, the hurt, the truth. It could even sometimes make things worse.
> It is a risky undertaking, but in the end it is worthwhile, because in
> the end dealing with the real situation helps to bring real healing.
> Superficial reconciliation can bring only superficial healing. (55)

[15] In this kingdom of love, the king comes as a servant and persuades his
followers to love one another in the same Way, rather than forcing their
allegiance and obedience. Consider how false we are as Christians if we
attempt to coerce others to "follow" Jesus through threats or compulsion
or by creating fearfulness (as with threats of God's disfavor or the potential loss of eternal life). How we are missionaries is essential to others
experiencing God's love through Jesus.

[16] Donald T. Phillips, *Martin Luther King, Jr., on Leadership: Inspiration & Wisdom for Challenging Times* (New York: Warner Business Books, 2000), 67 (quoting May 1956 article by Martin Luther King, Jr.). King described the love of Jesus as the motivation for nonviolent actions and defined the Greek word "agape" as a "higher type of love" that is "understanding, creative good will for all men" and that "seeks nothing in return." This "love of God operating in the human heart" brings about love for "the person who does the evil deed, while hating the deed that the person does" (58). Only nonviolent action can bring about lasting change and show forth the reality of God's kingdom. Dr. King rejected violence as "immoral because it seeks to humiliate the opponent rather than win his understanding; it seeks to annihilate rather than to convert; it thrives on hatred rather than love; it destroys community and makes brotherhood impossible; it leaves society in a monologue rather than dialogue; [and] it creates bitterness in survivors and brutality in the destroyers" (268-269, quoting Martin Luther King, Jr., *Stride Toward Freedom*, 1959).

[17] Desmond Tutu, *God Has a Dream: A Vision of Hope for Our Time*, 56. He writes (at 54):

> Forgiveness gives us the capacity to make a new start. That is the power, the rationale, of confession and forgiveness. It is to say, "I have fallen but I am not going to remain there. Please forgive me." And forgiveness is the grace by which you enable the other person to get up, and get up with dignity, to begin anew. Not to forgive leads to bitterness and hatred, which, just like self-hatred and self-contempt, gnaw away at the vitals of one's being. Whether hatred is projected out or projected in, it is always corrosive of the human spirit.

[18] Phillips, *Martin Luther King, Jr. on Leadership*, 306–307.

[19] "The humiliating blow, the violent deed, and the act of exploitation all remain evil. Disciples are to know this and to give witness to it just as Jesus did, because otherwise the evil person will not be engaged and overcome. A disciple should not resist when challenged by evil that cannot be justified at all. Instead, by suffering, the disciple will bring evil to its end and thus will overcome the evil person. Suffering willingly endured is stronger than evil; it is the death of evil." Dietrich Bonhoeffer, *Disciple-*

ship, 136. And "Humiliation and debasement are revealed as sin when the disciple does not commit them, but bears them, without defense. Assault is condemned by not being met with violence. The unjust claim on my coat is answered by my giving up my cloak as well. The exploitation of my service becomes obvious as exploitation when I set no limit on it. Our willingness to yield up everything when we are bidden to do so is our willingness to have enough in Jesus Christ alone, to desire to follow him alone" (119).

[20] In *Jesus and Nonviolence: A Third Way*, on page 2, Walter Wink gives numerous examples of effective nonviolent confrontation, including the Philippines and Poland, and writes:

> In 1989–90 alone, fourteen nations underwent nonviolent revolutions, all of them successful except China, and all of them nonviolent except Romania. These revolutions total 1.7 billion people. If we total all the nonviolent movements of the twentieth century, the figure comes to 3.4 billion people, and again most were successful. And yet there are people who still insist that nonviolence doesn't work! Gene Sharp has itemized 198 different types of nonviolent actions that are part of the historical record, yet our history books seldom mention any of them, so preoccupied are they with power politics and wars [citing Gene Sharp, *The Politics of Nonviolent Action* (Boston: Sargent, 1973)].

[21] Tutu, *God Has a Dream: A Vision of Hope for Our Time*, 79–80. He adds (at 57), "Because we are not infallible, because we will hurt especially the ones we love by some wrong, we will always need a process of forgiveness and reconciliation to deal with those unfortunate yet all too human breaches in relationships. They are an inescapable characteristic of the human condition."

[22] Wink writes in *Jesus and Nonviolence: A Third Way*, 33–34:

> Sadly, Jesus' three examples have been turned into laws, with no reference to the utterly changed contexts in which they were being applied. His attempt to nerve the powerless to assert their humanity under inhuman conditions has been turned into a legalistic prohibi-

tion on schoolyard fistfights between peers. Pacifists and those who reject pacifism alike have tended to regard Jesus' infinitely malleable insights as iron rules, the one group urging that they be observed inflexibly, the other treating them as impossible demands intended to break us and catapult us into the arms of grace. The creative, ironic, playful quality of Jesus' teaching has thus been buried under an avalanche of humorless commentary. And as always, law kills.

[23] Ken Blanchard and Phil Hodges, *Lead Like Jesus: Lessons from the Greatest Leadership Role Model of All Time* (Nashville: Thomas Nelson, 2005), 30.

2.6 The Great Commandment

[1] In his response, Jesus is quoting from Deuteronomy and his answer unites his teaching with the great rabbis who summarized the most important teachings of the Torah. This "Great Commandment" is the part of the Hebrew Scriptures, the Law, and the prophets, that Jesus has come not to abolish but to fulfill (Matthew 5:17). Jesus says that the second greatest rule in the kingdom of God is to "love your neighbor as yourself" from Leviticus 19:18.

[2] Rick Warren, *40 Days of Purpose Small Group Study Guide* (Lake Forest, CA: Purpose Driven Publishing, 2005), 42.

[3] Henri J.M Nouwen, *In the Name of Jesus: Reflections on Christian Leadership* (New York: Crossroad, 1989), 28.

[4] Rob Bell, *Velvet Elvis: Repainting the Christian Faith* (Zondervan, 2005), 165–169.

[5] Desmond Tutu, *God Has a Dream: A Vision of Hope for Our Time* (New York: Doubleday, 2004), 61. In the postscript, he cites resources for ways to help others, including www.ActforChange.org; www.AmeriCorps. org; www.AntiRacismNet.org; www.GlobalVolunteers.com; www.Just-Give.org; www.NetAid.org; www.NetworkforGood.org; www.Senior-Corps.org; and www.VolunteerMatch.com.

3.1 Helping People Experience the Way of Jesus

[1] In a famous statement, William Temple, who served as the Archbishop of Canterbury from 1942 to 1944, said: "The Church is the only cooperative society in the world that exists for the benefit of those who are not its members." This statement is often quoted as a reminder that we cannot be church for ourselves, which is certainly true. The purpose of the church is sharing and showing forth God's love to all. At the same time, because love is mutual and reciprocal, the church is for members and nonmembers alike.

[2] In *The Church on the Other Side* (Grand Rapids: Zondervan, 2006), 190–191, Brian McLaren writes:

> The greatest apologetic for the gospel is and always has been a community that actually lives by the gospel. ... Our love for one another, our visible demonstration of living community, will prove both our legitimacy and his. This is truer than ever in a community-starved postmodern culture, where the pendulum has swung to extreme individualism, isolation, and loneliness. ... The church is to be a place in this world for "the poor, the crippled, the blind and the lame" (Luke 14:21), a place of real acceptance and love, where "the least of these" have importance, where you don't have to be a star to be valued, where your oddness (or sin) won't exclude you. Isn't the reality of a community of real people (odd people, people on the road, real world people)—people authentically loving one another—isn't that the one great apologetic without which all other apologetics taste flat and dry? And isn't this even more true in postmodern, community-poor times like today and tomorrow?

[3] In *The 5 Levels of Leadership: Proven Steps to Maximize Your Potential* (New York: Center Street, 2011) at 109, John C. Maxwell identifies a number of variations of the golden rule and the religions from which they come:

> Christianity: "Whatever you want men to do to you, do also to them." Islam: "No one of you is a believer until he loves for his neighbor what he loves for himself." Judaism: "What is hateful to you, do not do to your fellow man. This is the entire Law; all the rest is commentary."

Buddhism: "Hurt not others with that which pains yourself." Hinduism: "This is the sum of duty; do naught unto others what you would not have them do unto you." Zoroastrianism: "Whatever is disagreeable to yourself, do not do unto others." Confucianism: "What you do not want done to yourself, do not do to others." Baha'i: "And if thine eyes be turned towards justice, choose thou for thy neighbour that which thou choosest for thyself." Jainism: "A man should wander about treating all creatures as he himself would be treated." Yoruba Proverb (Nigeria): "One going to take a pointed stick to pinch a baby bird should first try it on himself to feel how it hurts."

[4] Dietrich Bonhoeffer wrote *Life Together* (*Dietrich Bonhoeffer Works* 5) (Fortress Press) as he brought students together in Christian community at underground seminaries in Nazi Germany. He wrote at 79:

> Where this discipline of the tongue is practiced right from the start, individuals will make an amazing discovery. They will be able to stop constantly keeping an eye on others, judging them, condemning them, and putting them in their places and thus doing violence to them. They can now allow other Christians to live freely, just as God has brought them face to face with each other. The view of such persons expands and, to their amazement, they recognize for the first time the richness of God's creative glory shining over their brothers and sisters. God did not make others as I would have made them. God did not give them to me so that I could dominate and control them, but so that I might find the Creator by means of them. Now other people, in the freedom with which they were created, become an occasion for me to rejoice, whereas before they were only a nuisance and trouble for me. God does not want me to mold others into the image that seems good to me, that is, into my own image. Instead, in their freedom from me God made other people in God's own image. I can never know in advance how God's image should appear in others. That image always takes on a completely new and unique form whose origin is found solely in God's free and sovereign act of creation. To me that form may seem strange, even ungodly. But God creates every person in the image of God's Son, the Crucified, and this image, likewise, certainly looked strange and ungodly to me before I grasped it.

We cherish one another's "freedom" by allowing God to create His image in each of us and taking joy in each person's "nature, individuality, and talent" as well as "weaknesses and peculiarities, that so sorely try our patience, and everything that produces the plethora of clashes, differences and arguments" between us.

[5] Dietrich Bonhoeffer wrote in *Life Together and Prayerbook of the Bible* (*Dietrich Bonhoeffer Works* 5) (Fortress Press), at 86–87:

> Not despising sinners, but being privileged to bear with them, means not having to give them up for lost, being able to accept them and able to preserve community with them through forgiveness. . . . As Christ bore with us and accepted us as sinners, so we in his community may bear with sinners and accept them into the community of Jesus Christ through the forgiveness of sins. We may suffer the sins of one another; we do not need to judge.

Saint Paul says, "My friends, if anyone is detected in a transgression, you who have received the Spirit should restore such a one in a spirit of gentleness" (Galatians 6:1). And James says, "There is one lawgiver and judge who is able to save and to destroy. So who, then, are you to judge your neighbor?" (James 4:12).

[6] Dietrich Bonhoeffer wrote in *Life Together and Prayerbook of the Bible* (Dietrich Bonhoeffer Works 5) (Fortress Press) at 89:

> The basis on which Christians can speak to one another is that each knows the other as a sinner who, even given all one's human renown, is forlorn and lost if not given help. This does not mean that the others are being disparaged or dishonored. Rather, we are paying them the only real honor a human being has, namely, that as sinners they share in God's grace and glory, that they are children of God. This realization gives our mutual speech the freedom and openness it needs. We talk to one another about the help we both need. We admonish one another to go the way Christ bids us to go. We warn one another against the disobedience that is our undoing. We are gentle and we are firm with one another, for we know both God's kindness and God's firmness. Why should we be afraid of one another since both of us have only God to fear? Why should we think that another Christian would not understand us when we understood very well

what was meant when somebody spoke God's comfort or God's admonition to us, even in words that were inept and awkward? Or do we really believe there is a single person in this world who does not need either comfort or admonition? If so, then why has God given us the gift of Christian community?

[7] Dietrich Bonhoeffer, *Life Together and Prayerbook of the Bible* (*Dietrich Bonhoeffer Works 5*) (Fortress Press), 96–97.

[8] See, e.g., "Agreeing and Disagreeing in Love: Commitments for Unity Congregations in Times of Disagreement," http://www.unityworldwideministries.org/sites/unityministries.oneeach.org/files/Agreeingand-DisagreeinginLove.pdf (adapted with permission Lombard Mennonite Peace Center) or http://stdavidspokane.org/about-us/community-covenants/.

[9] Religious orders often have rules that set boundaries and expectations for life together. Examples are The Rule of St. Augustine; The Rule of St. Benedict; The Rule of the Franciscan Order; and The Rule of the Society of St. John the Evangelist.

[10] Dietrich Bonhoeffer, *Life Together and Prayerbook of the Bible,* 20. He expands: "Christian community means community through and in Jesus Christ. Everything the Scriptures provide in the way of directions and rules for Christians' life together rests on this presupposition" (21). "The more genuine and the deeper our community becomes, the more everything else between us will recede, and the more clearly and purely will Jesus Christ and his work become the one and only thing that is alive between us" (22). "Christian community is not an ideal we have to realize, but rather a reality created by God in Christ in which we may participate. The more clearly we learn to recognize that the ground and strength and promise of all our community is in Jesus Christ alone, the more calmly we will learn to think about our community and pray and hope for it" (26). "For Jesus Christ alone is our unity. 'He is our peace.' We have access to one another, joy in one another, community with one another through Christ alone" (34).

[11] Christian A. Schwarz and Christoph Schalk, *Implementation Guide to Natural Church Development* (Carol Stream, IL: ChurchSmart Resources, 1998), 116.

3.2 Helping People Connect to Community

[1] These methods of church growth continued to be used because they were very effective! The history of the Christian movement after Jesus' resurrection and ascension is often expressed in the history of the Christian church. Within a generation of Jesus' crucifixion, Christianity had spread through the Roman Empire and become subject to persecution as a serious threat. Within three more centuries, the threat was realized, and the empire was absorbed into Christendom, which became the framework for medieval civilization and then for much of civilization well into the twentieth century. Between AD 250 and AD 350, the number of Christians grew from 1.7 million to 33.8 million. Rodney Stark, *The Rise of Christianity* (Princeton, NJ: Princeton University Press), 7.

Today, approximately one-third of the people in the world, or more than two billion people, consider themselves to be Christians. The 2001 edition of *The World Christian Encyclopedia* stated there were 2.1 billion Christians in the world, or 33% of the total population. Christianity, taken as a whole, is the largest religion in the world, although this figure undoubtedly comprises branches and denominations that various Christians would not consider to be Christians.

[2] We do a disservice to our churches when we suggest that we can simply make our worship or formation or outreach or whatever attractive and people will come, or that buzz is enough without personal faith sharing and invitation. Non-Christians are not looking for churches, and our world is just fine with that. In some ways, our times are not that much different from when Jesus sent his disciples out in Matthew 10.

[3] The 2020 Task Force Report in the Episcopal Church stated: "the largest proportion of any numerical expansion [65%–80%] is likely to take place in new congregations, which means that every effort should be made to make new church development a major priority of the church as a whole, and of dioceses in particular" and "we expect that dioceses and existing congregations will be the primary sponsors of new congregations" (www.episcopalchurch.org/congdev/2020full_rpt.html).

[4] This should not be surprising. People only follow leaders to make changes in their lives if they personally trust them. Trusting relationships come before and lead to action.

[5] Inviting friends to join small groups can happen either with the church community or in other places. Small groups are wonderful settings for relationships to develop and mature, for providing pastoral care, for promoting discipleship, and for reaching out in evangelism. In small groups, we grow together and support and encourage one another in walking in relationship with Jesus. There is more about this in the next chapter.

[6] Worship is more often a means of attracting people who are already in the church or denomination, but in contemporary society, it is generally not a means of reaching new members. Worship also is rarely the problem, so focusing on worship is not the solution. People come to join a community which they wish to be part of because of people they know (first) and a purpose they wish to participate in (second).

[7] George G. Hunter III, *The Celtic Way of Evangelism: How Christianity Can Reach the West ... Again* (Abingdon, 2000), 120.

[8] *The Interventionist* (Abingdon, 1997), 147–148, 184.

[9] Rick Warren, *The Purpose Driven Church: Growing Without Compromising Your Message & Mission* (Grand Rapids, MI: Zondervan, 1995), 234-235.

[10] Ibid., Chapters 13–16.

[11] Ibid., 222.

[12] Ibid., 220.

[13] Ibid., 222.

[14] Ibid., 209.

[15] Hunter, *The Celtic Way of Evangelism*, 52.

[16] Hunter points out that: "In significant contrast to contemporary Christianity's well-known evangelism approaches of 'Lone Ranger' one-to-one evangelism, or confrontational evangelism, or the public preaching crusade. ... Celtic Christians usually evangelized as a team—by relating to the people of a settlement; identifying with the people; engaging in friendship, conversation, ministry, and witness—with the goal of raising up a church in measurable time." *The Celtic Way of Evangelism*, 47.

[17] Hunter, *The Celtic Way of Evangelism*, 30. "The monastic community prepared people to live with depth, compassion, and power in mission" in solitude, with a soul friend, in a small group, in a corporate life, and in ministry with seekers (47–48).

[18] Hunter, *The Celtic Way of Evangelism*, 48.

[19] Hunter, *The Celtic Way of Evangelism*, 19–20. The goal is to "plant churches so indigenous to each people group 'that its expression will emerge from within their culture, in their language, style and flavours, yet still [embody] the counter-cultural values of the gospel'" (109). Connections made between Christianity and Irish understandings, beliefs, and values included: paradox, complex reality, rhetorical triads, heroism, stories, legends, nature, closeness of the divine, learning, openness to all (20, 80–94). "They affirmed and built on every indigenous feature that they could. They affirmed the Celtic people's religious aspirations, their sense of divinity's closeness, their belief in an afterlife, their love for creation and … their fascination with the number three." (92) Moreover, "they 'contextualized' Christianity's message. … The Biblical Revelation was primary, but understanding the people's cultural and historical context helped them to know what in Scripture to feature first and how to 'translate' it for the people … as David Bosch observes, 'The Christian faith never exists except as 'translated' into a culture.'" (77) In contrast to Celtic evangelism, the Roman church sought control, conservatism (vs. change), and cultural uniformity (vs. indigeneity). The "more Roman the monastic communities and churches became, the less they engaged in evangelization. … Not until the Renaissance and the Reformation would indigenous languages, cultures, and religious expressions resurface" (40–44). "As in the case of the ancient Roman wing of the Church, denominations are still substantially in the hands of the less apostolic wing of the Church, which works overtime to gain and retain institutional control; which assumes it knows best; and which works persistently to impose Roman, European, or other culturally alien forms upon the more indigenous and growing movements within the denomination. This pathology is observed today … in most of the denominations in the United States that were 'imported from Europe'" (95-96).

[20] Ibid., 31–32.

[21] Ibid., 21–22.

[22] Ibid., 53–54.

[23] The Celtic model follows an Aristotelian process of persuasion and recognizes that logic is only one basis for argument. Aristotle "taught that persuasion occurs from the interaction of the *ethos* of the speaker [the speaker can be trusted and believed—intelligence, character, good will, authenticity, credibility, integrity, dynamism, identification], the *logos* of the message [using both analytical and imaginative or artistic approaches effectively, including poetry, storytelling, music and visual arts], and the *pathos* of the audience [responding to the emotional appeal of the speaker and message]." Hunter, *The Celtic Way of Evangelism*, 56–75. "Their ethos, their identification with the people, their emotional appeal, and their imaginal appeal all helped communicate the gospel" (76).

[24] Ibid., 120.

[25] I agree with Ken Blanchard and Phil Hodges when they write in *Lead Like Jesus: Lessons from the Greatest Leadership Role Model of All Time* (Nashville: Thomas Nelson, 2005) at 206:

> We believe that the next great movement in Christianity will be demonstration. If we want people to be interested in our faith in the future, we as Christians must practice what we preach. In other words, people need to not only hear Christian leaders talking about the message of Christ, but they need to see us living out this message in the way we lead and serve others.

3.3 Building Community through Small Groups and Ministry Teams

[1] In *The Heart of Christianity: Rediscovering a Life of Faith* (HarperOne, 2004), Marcus Borg writes about a transformational "emerging paradigm" in Christianity, of loving God, and loving what God loves. This paradigm is replacing the centuries old paradigm of rigidly adhering to a specific set of beliefs. A church family today needs to support a personal

relationship with Jesus as a spiritual reality and way of life, not an ethic or law, and focus more on religious experiences than on principles or beliefs.

[2] This fundamental need is true for all people, not only those who are "suffering." We each have a deep need for relationships with God and other people (a "God-shaped hole" or an "ember" of God's love within us).

[3] Notice that the content of the group or team (theology, ministry) is always less important than the relational connections. We too often rely on (require) subject matter "experts" (such as clergy) to lead groups. Part of growing and replicating groups is always apprenticing other members to lead them.

[4] Christopher means "Christ bearer." This is a story of introducing an individual to closer relationship with God, welcoming him into a church family, and helping him prepare for Christian ministry. It integrates individual, small group, and collective spiritual experiences—because our contemporaries, while often desiring a spiritual life, are initially wary of encountering the collective church. It also integrates three different classical models of evangelism: the "missionary" model of going into the world and living with others who need God's healing love; the "monastery" model of the church as a spiritual home, refuge from the world, and place of pilgrimage that can set an example for life in the world; and the "cathedral" model of attraction to the center of community. This is an example of how we may reach more people through personal relationships that build trust and support faith sharing (i.e., *The Celtic Way of Evangelism: How Christianity Can Reach the West ... Again* by George Hunter [Abingdon, 2000]).

3.4 Helping People Act from Their Giftedness

[1] According to one study, the most important quality that healthy, growing Christian churches need and have in common is gift-oriented ministry. "When Christians serve in their area of giftedness, they generally function less in their own strength and more in the power of the Holy Spirit. ... No factor influences the contentedness of Christians more

than whether they are using their gifts or not." Christian A. Schwarz, *Natural Church Development: A Guide to Eight Essential Qualities of Healthy Churches* (Carol Stream, IL: ChurchSmart Resources, 1996), 24.

[2] In a recent church survey developed by Eric Swanson for the Leadership Network, 92 percent of the people responded that ministry to others enhanced their spiritual growth; not one person felt that it hindered their growth. 63 percent said ministering to others was at least as important to them as other spiritual disciplines such as prayer and Bible study, and 24 percent said serving others was more important in their spiritual development than other spiritual disciplines. 88 percent of the people who were ministering to others were satisfied with their spiritual growth, while 58 percent of the people who were not involved in ministry to others were less satisfied with their level of spiritual growth.

[3] Max DePree, *Leadership is an Art* (New York: Dell, 1989), 50.

[4] *Paradigm Shift in the Church: How Natural Church Development can Transform Theological Thinking* (Carol Stream, IL: ChurchSmart Resources, 1999), 178–179.

[5] Dennis Campbell, *Congregations as Learning Communities: Tools for Shaping Your Future* (The Alban Institute, 2000), 10.

[6] Ibid., 11.

[7] *Paradigm Shift in the Church*, 179.

[8] The issue of clergy centered churches is not new. Saint Augustine wrote, "What I am for you appalls me. What I am with you consoles me. For you I am a bishop, with you I am a Christian." St. Augustine, Sermon 340.

Shifting the paradigm to support a more involved laity is critical because more disciples can more effectively help Jesus make more disciples. Full involvement reaps significant rewards. In the body, church leadership is not limited to or centered in a single person, and ministry teams may take responsibility for entire areas of ministry. Church leaders do not have to manage all of the work of the church and may focus on visioning and discernment through prayer, study, and reflection.

[9] Good books about discernment include: Suzanne G. Farnham, Joseph P. Gill, R. Taylor McLean and Susan M. Ward, *Listening Hearts: Discerning Call in Community* (Harrisburg, PA: Morehouse, 1991); John Ackerman, *Listening to God: Spiritual Formation in the Congregation* (The Alban Institute, 2001). I also found Julia Cameron's *The Artist's Way: A Spiritual Path to Higher Creativity* to be a helpful tool for beginning discernment of personal gifts and vocations.

[10] A popular course is *Network Kit: The Right People, in the Right Places, for the Right Reasons, at the Right Time* by Bugbee, Bruce L., Don Cousins, and Wendy Seidman. (Grand Rapids, MI.: Zondervan, 2005).

[11] Rick Warren uses the acronym "SHAPE" in *The Purpose Driven Life* (Zondervan 2002), 227–256, as a way to describe your uniqueness as a human being. You can discover and use your SHAPE to serve others in ministry by identifying five key factors: Spiritual gifts, Heart (passions), Abilities, Personality and Experience. See also, Rick Warren, *The Purpose Driven Church: Growing Without Compromising Your Message & Mission* (Grand Rapids, Michigan: Zondervan, 1995), 369–375.

[12] Suzanne G. Farnham, Joseph P. Gill, R. Taylor McLean, and Susan M. Ward, *Listening Hearts: Discerning Call in Community* (Harrisburg, PA: Morehouse Publishing, 1991), 25–26.

3.5 Supporting Holistic Life in Community

[1] Definitions of "crucible" include (i) A vessel made of a refractory substance such as graphite or porcelain, used for melting and calcining materials at high temperatures; (ii) A severe test, as of patience or belief; a trial; and (iii) A place, time, or situation characterized by the confluence of powerful intellectual, social, economic, or political forces.

[2] Jack Jezreel, "Gospel-Driven Communities: Being a Church with the Biblical Vision of Justice," *Congregations* (Alban Institute), no. 2 (2012): 16.

[3] In the postmodern world, a primarily shepherding church is less equipped to reach nonchurch people and reaches growth limits because

the number of church people is declining. See, for example, Reggie Mc-Neal, *The Present Future* (Jossey-Bass, 2003); George G. Hunter III, *The Celtic Way of Evangelism* (Abingdon, 2000).

4 Jezreel, "Gospel-Driven Communities," 16.

5 Daniel P. Smith and Mary K. Sellon, *Pathways to Renewal: Practical Steps for Congregations* (Alban Institute, 2008), 9.

6 In *Traveling Together: A Guide for Disciple-Forming Congregations* (The Alban Institute, 2005), Jeffrey D. Jones also recognizes a threefold experience of God and points out that for a person to grow as a disciple, regular experiences of deepening, equipping, and ministering are essential. Deepening is a continuing process of growth in relationship with God as Creator, Christ, and Spirit—experiencing in ever-deepening ways the fullness of God. Equipping involves bringing together gifts/call and skills/knowledge. Call is based in the gifts God gives; skills we need may be particular to our call or something we all need to know, such as the Bible. Ministering is our participation in God's mission of redeeming all creation (within or outside the church).

7 Christian Schwarz introduced these concepts in *The Threefold Art of Experiencing God: The Liberating Power of a Trinitarian Faith* (ChurchSmart Resources, 1999) and further developed them in *Color Your World With Natural Church Development* (Churchsmart Resources, 2005). He identifies these areas with colors: green for head, red for hands, and blue for heart. We best respond to God's love with our whole being: through reflection, action, and emotion. Each person has a different balance and emphasis. We may deepen our relationships with God in each area. Exclusive focus on a single approach may take us out of close, balanced relationship with God: too much rationalism (head), activism (hands), or emotionalism (heart) can lead us away from experiencing God. Each individual (and denomination) has a different balance of these responses to God, so people may need to move in different directions to grow in relationship with God (more reflection, more action, more emotion).

8 Jim Collins writes about effective prioritizing in *Good to Great*,

> Most of us lead busy but undisciplined lives. We have ever-expanding "to do" lists, trying to build momentum by doing, doing, doing—and

doing more. And it rarely works. Those who build the good-to-great companies, however, made as much use of "stop doing" lists as "to do" lists. They displayed a remarkable discipline to unplug all sorts of extraneous junk.

Quoted in John C. Maxwell, *The 5 Levels of Leadership: Proven Steps to Maximize Your Potential* (New York: Center Street, 2011), 161.

[9] Jack Jezreel, "Gospel-Driven Communities: Being a Church with the Biblical Vision of Justice," *Congregations* (Alban Institute), no. 2 (2012): 17–18.

4.1 Leading from Relationship with Jesus

[1] Donald P. McNeill, Douglas A. Morrison, and Henri Nouwen, *Compassion: A Reflection on the Christian Life* (New York: Doubleday, 1983), 36–37.

[2] The most commonly acknowledged "servant" or "minister" in churches today may be the *diakonos* (or deacon) as used in Mark 10:43; Romans 13:4, 15:8; 1 Corinthians 3:5; 2 Corinthians 3:6, 6:4, 11:15, 15:8, 2:17; Ephesians 6:21; Colossians 1:7, 1:23–25, 4:7; 1 Thessalonians 3:2; and 1 Timothy 4:6. As might be expected in a hierarchical society, there were Greek designations for many different types and levels of servants, including *huperetes* (a rower or "any subordinate acting under another's direction") and *leitourgos* ("a steward" or "one who discharges a public office at his own expense"). Other nouns for servants include *misthios* or *misthotos* ("a hired servant"), *oiketes* ("a household servant"), *paidiske* ("a maidservant"), and *pais* ("a child household servant"). For citations of Biblical verses where each term is used, see *Vine's Greek New Testament Dictionary* online (http://www2.mf.no/bibel/vines.html). *Vine's* points out that each term is used to place people in relationship to their duties and their masters: "Speaking broadly, *diakonos* views a servant in relation to his work; *doulos*, in relation to his master; *huperetes*, in relation to his superior; *leitourgos*, in relation to public service." Another source for Greek translations is the Greek Interlinear Bible (http://www.scripture4all.org/OnlineInterlinear/Greek_Index.htm).

[3] C. Gene Wilkes, *Jesus on Leadership: Discovering the Secrets of Servant Leadership from the Life of Christ* (Wheaton, IL: Tyndale House Publishers, 1988), 113–114.

[4] Ken Blanchard and Phil Hodges remind leaders in *Lead Like Jesus: Lessons from the Greatest Leadership Role Model of All Time* (Nashville: Thomas Nelson, 2005) at 47:

> The term "leader" is mentioned only six times in the King James Version of the Bible, while the term servant is mentioned more than nine hundred times. That fact highlights [a key] distinction between a self-serving leader and a servant leader: who leads and who follows? Self-serving leaders think they should lead and others should follow. Servant leaders, on the other hand, seek to respect the wishes of those who have entrusted them with a season of influence and responsibility. Throughout His life and leadership, Jesus affirmed that God is not looking for leaders but for servants who will let Him be the Leader and who will focus first on the kingdom of God.

[5] Although any one of us may not be able to do what Jesus does, we can do the same things together as the body of Christ (1 Corinthians 12).

[6] Wilkes, *Jesus on Leadership*, 150–151.

[7] Metropolitan Anthony, *Courage to Pray*, trans. Dinah Livingstone (Crestwood, NY: St. Vladimir's Press, 1984), 30ff.

[8] One Family Story: A Primer on Bowen Theory (Washington DC, The Bowen Center). The classic text in the area of family systems is rabbi Edwin Friedman's *Generation to Generation: Family Systems in Church and Synagogue* (New York: Guilford Press, 1985).

[9] One Family Story: A Primer on Bowen Theory (Washington DC, The Bowen Center).

[10] Murray Bowen, Family Evaluation, Kerr and Bowen 1988, 342–43.

[11] A prime example of poorly differentiated leadership is Pontius Pilate's decision to crucify Jesus. Pilate clearly made an unjust decision to accommodate group anxiety and relationship pressures.

[12] Mike Bonem has pointed out that "rather than self-differentiation, which is as an act of personal willpower, we should be 'God-differentiated leaders.' … The God-differentiated person faces the same obstacles as every other leader but does so with a much greater sense of purpose and never does so alone." *In Pursuit of Great AND Godly Leadership: Tapping the Wisdom of the World for the Kingdom of God* (John Wiley and Sons, Kindle Edition 2011), 30.

[13] Desmond Tutu writes in *God Has a Dream: A Vision of Hope for Our Time* (New York: Doubleday, 2004), 84:

> We all need love and affection, but sometimes we become paralyzed by the fear that we will be disliked, or ridiculed, or ultimately that others will not love us. We might not go to a protest or get involved because we worry about what others will think. I have a horrible but human weakness in that I want very much to be loved. This desire to be loved, however, can become an obsession, and you can find that you are ready to do almost anything to gain the approval of others. We must remember that what God thinks is more important than what others think. Standing up for what we believe is right can ultimately help us to realize that even when we do not please our parents or our spouse or our friends or others, we may still be pleasing God. … God's love can sustain us even when others may hate us.

[14] Mike Bonem, *In Pursuit of Great AND Godly Leadership: Tapping the Wisdom of the World for the Kingdom of God* (John Wiley and Sons, Kindle Edition 2011), 29.

[15] Parker J. Palmer, *The Courage to Teach* (San Francisco: Jossey-Bass, 1998), 57.

[16] Bonem, *In Pursuit of Great AND Godly Leadership*, (John Wiley and Sons, Kindle Edition 2011), 23.

4.2 Sharing Leadership

[1] Christians identified references to the Trinity in the Hebrew Scriptures in Genesis 1:26, Psalm 110:1, Isaiah 48:16 and 63:10, and Hosea 1:7,

and in the New Testament in Matthew 3:16–17 and 28:19, 1 Corinthians 12:4–6, 2 Corinthians 13:14, Ephesians 4:4-6, 1 Peter 1:2, and Jude 20–21.

[2] We are like the body, and we need all of the parts of the body to function. We are not all the same. All of our gifts come from God, and we are each given something to do to glorify God, to show forth God's presence in our lives. The church can become the body of Christ in the world if we "grow up in every way into him who is the head, into Christ, from whom the whole body, joined and knit together by every ligament with which it is equipped, as each part is working properly, promotes the body's growth in building itself up in love" (Ephesians 4:15–16). When we ignore our gifts and calling, we diminish the body of Christ. When we share our gifts, we build up the body of Christ (Ephesians 4:11–13).

[3] Other Biblical support for the priesthood of all believers is 1 Peter 2:5 ("like living stones, let yourselves be built into a spiritual house, to be a holy priesthood, to offer spiritual sacrifices acceptable to God through Jesus Christ"); Revelation 1:6 ("[Jesus] made us to be a kingdom, priests serving his God and Father"); Revelation 5:10 ("you have made them to be a kingdom and priests serving our God, and they will reign on earth"); and Exodus 19:6 ("you shall be for me a priestly kingdom and a holy nation").

[4] Contemporary leadership research agrees:

> Conventional wisdom portrays leadership as something found mostly at the top. Myth and legend treat leadership as if it were the private reserve of a very few charismatic men and women. Nothing is further from the truth. Leadership is much more broadly distributed in the population, and it's accessible to anyone who has passion and purpose to change the way things are.

Barry Z. Posner and James M. Kouzes, *The Truth about Leadership: The No-fads, Heart-of-the-Matter Facts You Need to Know* (San Francisco: Jossey-Bass, 2010), 5.

[5] Notice also that this third effort of reconciliation is not necessarily final: "Then Peter came and said to him, 'Lord, if another member of the church sins against me, how often should I forgive? As many as seven

times?' Jesus said to him, 'Not seven times, but, I tell you, seventy-seven times'" (Matthew 18:21–22).

[6] Malcolm Gladwell, *The Tipping Point: How Little Things Can Make a Big Difference* (Back Bay Books, 2002).

[7] See, e.g., Arlin J. Rothage, *Sizing Up a Congregation for New Member Ministry* (New York: The Episcopal Church Center); Alice Mann, *Raising the Roof: The Pastoral-To-Program Size Transition* (Bethesda, MD: The Alban Institute, 2001).

[8] In *The Interventionist* (Abingdon, 1997), 185–186, Lyle Schaller writes:

> One part of the explanation for the recent emergence of scores of very large independent churches is that many of them have found it easy to create a congregational culture that is based on unreserved trust of the lay leadership and encouraged lay initiative. One part of the explanation for the recent numerical decline of several mainline Protestant denominations is that culture is built on a distrust of local leadership and a response to the perceived need for the denomination to function as a regulatory body.

He adds:

> The younger the current generation of influential leaders and/or the larger the size of the congregation and/or the faster the rate of numerical growth and/or the higher the level of formal educational attainment of the new members and/or the larger the proportion of individual entrepreneurs among the new members and/or the higher the income level of the members and/or the greater the degree of diversity within the membership and/or the larger the proportion of the total workload carried by volunteers and the smaller the proportion carried by paid staff, the greater the need for the congregation to function on a high level of trust and to encourage lay initiative.

[9] Different structures work for different sized congregations. See, e.g., Alice Mann, *The In-Between Church: Navigating Size Transitions in Congregations* (Washington, D.C.: Alban Institute, 1998); Alice Mann, *Raising the Roof: The Pastoral-To-Program Size Transition* (Alban Institute, 2001); Arlin Rothauge, *Sizing Up a Congregation for New Member Min-*

istry (The Episcopal Church Center, 1986); Kevin Martin, *The Myth of the 200 Barrier: How to Lead through Transitional Growth,* (Abingdon Press, 2005).

[10] Loren B. Mead, *The Once and Future Church: Reinventing the Congregation for a New Mission Frontier* (Washington D.C.: The Alban Institute, 1991), 10.

[11] Ken Blanchard, Susan Fowler, and Laurence Hawkins, *Self Leadership and the One Minute Manager: Increasing Effectiveness Through Situational Self Leadership* (William Morrow, 2005).

[12] Susan Scott, *Fierce Conversations: Achieving Success at Work & in Life, One Conversation at a Time* (New York: Berkley, 2004), 118–121.

[13] Ibid., 120.

[14] Ibid., 122.

[15] Contrast this controlling style to Rick Warren's success with Saddleback Church (*The Purpose Driven Church: Growing Without Compromising Your Message & Mission* [Grand Rapids, MI: Zondervan, 1995], 378):

> I haven't known about everything that happens at Saddleback for years. I don't need to know about it all! You might ask, "Then how do you control it?" My answer is: "I don't. It's not my job to control the church. It's my job to *lead* it." There is a very big difference between leading and controlling. Our pastors and staff are responsible to keep the church doctrinally sound and headed in the right direction, but the day-to-day decisions are made by the people actually doing the ministries of the church.

4.3 Guiding and Serving

[1] Donald T. Phillips, *Martin Luther King, Jr., on Leadership: Inspiration & Wisdom for Challenging Times* (New York: Warner Business Books, 2000), 61.

[2] Barry Z. Posner and James M. Kouzes state in *The Truth about Lead-*

ership: The No-fads, Heart-of-the-Matter Facts You Need to Know (San Francisco, CA: Jossey-Bass, 2010), 78:

> There's a positive relationship between risk and trust. The more people trust, the more they'll risk. When people feel secure, because they trust that you and the organization will protect their welfare, they can focus their energies on meeting higher-order needs, such as forming strong and cohesive relationships, mastering tasks, achieving organizational objectives, gaining a greater sense of self-efficacy, learning new skills and knowledge necessary to prepare for future assignments, and pursuing activities that promote growth and develop innate potential.

[3] Posner and Kouzes, *The Truth about Leadership*, 19. They add, "Even in a traditional command-and-control environment, trust comes first and following comes second, not the other way around. Trust motivates people to go beyond mere compliance with authority. It motivates them to reach for the best in themselves, their team, and their organization" (77). And, "Your ability to take strong stands, to challenge the status quo, and to point people in new directions depends on just how credible you are" (23).

[4] Posner and Kouzes, *The Truth about Leadership*, 32.

[5] Posner and Kouzes, *The Truth about Leadership*, 16. They add, "when people say their immediate manager exhibits high credibility, they're significantly more likely to: be proud to tell others they're part of the organization, feel a strong sense of team spirit, see their own personal values as consistent with those of the organization, feel attached and committed to the organization, and have a sense of ownership of the organization" (25).

[6] Ken Blanchard and Phil Hodges, *Lead Like Jesus: Lessons from the Greatest Leadership Role Model of All Time* (Nashville: Thomas Nelson, 2005), 31.

[7] Ken Blanchard and Phil Hodges write in *Lead Like Jesus*, 182: "We're all vulnerable. We all fall short. Don't be afraid to share your vulnerability. Being vulnerable is one of the most powerful things you can do to build a team and to build relationships with people you're leading. They know

you're not perfect, so don't act as if you are. More times than not, they know your imperfections long before you reveal them."

[8] Posner and Kouzes, *The Truth about Leadership*, 19.

[9] Posner and Kouzes, *The Truth about Leadership*, 66. They add, "The very best leaders understand that it's about inspiring a shared vision" (68).

[10] Posner and Kouzes, *The Truth about Leadership*, 41. They add, "What people really want to hear is not the leader's vision. They want to hear about how their own aspirations will be met. They want to hear how their dreams will come true and their hopes will be realized" (68).

[11] John C. Maxwell, *The 5 Levels of Leadership: Proven Steps to Maximize Your Potential* (New York: Center Street, 2011), 153.

[12] Diana Butler Bass, *The Practicing Congregation: Imagining a New Old Church* (Herndon, VA: The Alban Institute, 2004).

[13] Gil Rendle, "Telling the Better Story," *Congregations* (The Alban Institute) 31, no. 1 (Winter 2005), 23–25.

[14] Posner and Kouzes, *The Truth about Leadership*, 90. They add, "Research indicates that the highest performing managers and leaders are the most open and caring. The best leaders demonstrate more affection toward others and want others to be more open with them. They are more positive and passionate, more loving and compassionate, and more grateful and encouraging than their lower performing counterparts" (136).

[15] Ron Ricci and Carl Wiese, *The Collaboration Imperative: Executive Strategies for Unlocking Your Organization's True Potential* (San Jose, CA: Cisco Systems, 2011), 49 – 50.

4.4 Developing followers and leaders

[1] John C. Maxwell, *The 5 Levels of Leadership: Proven Steps to Maximize Your Potential* (New York: Center Street, 2011), 265.

[2] Marcus Buckingham and Curt Coffman, *First, Break All the Rules: What the World's Great Managers Do Differently* (New York: Simon & Schuster, 1999), 28.

[3] Ibid., 45.

[4] Ibid., 67.

[5] Barry Z. Posner and James M. Kouzes write in *The Truth about Leadership: The No-fads, Heart-of-the-Matter Facts You Need to Know* (San Francisco, CA: Jossey-Bass, 2010) at 63: "Leadership is not about the leader per se. It is not about you alone. It's about the relationship between leaders and their constituents. It's about the connection you and your teammates have with each other. It's about how you behave and feel toward each other. It's about the emotional bond that exists between you and them. Exemplary leaders know that they must attend to the needs, and focus on the capabilities, of their constituents if they are going to get extraordinary things done."

[6] Posner and Kouzes, *The Truth about Leadership*, 7.

[7] Traditional churches seem thrilled with Bill Hybels' "shocking confessions" following Willow Creek's multi-year study on the effectiveness of their programs and philosophy of ministry in *Reveal: Where Are You?* (Willow Creek Association, 2007) by Cally Parkinson and Greg Hawkins. Hybels called the findings "groundbreaking," "earthshaking" and "mindblowing," saying "some of the stuff that we have put millions of dollars into thinking it would really help our people grow and develop spiritually, when the data actually came back it wasn't helping people that much. Other things that we didn't put that much money into and didn't put much staff against is stuff our people are crying out for." Since the study, Willow Creek has shifted from a central effort to be "seeker friendly" to a greater focus on more committed "mature believers" who want "someone to hold me accountable," and "speak the truth to me." Bill Hybels said, "We made a mistake. What we should have done when people crossed the line of faith and became Christians, we should have started telling people and teaching people that they have to take responsibility to become 'self feeders.' We should have gotten people, taught people, how to read their Bible between services, how to do the spiri-

tual practices much more aggressively on their own." Willow Creek has raised expectations.

[8] Lyle Schaller says, "Most Christian congregations write a self-fulfilling prophecy. At one end of the spectrum are the churches that create a high commitment congregation by projecting high expectations of people in general and members in particular. At the other end of that spectrum are the congregations that project low expectations of people." *The Interventionist* (Abingdon, 1997), 179.

[9] Rick Warren's *The Purpose Driven Life* (Zondervan 2002) is a good example of identifying Christian expectations.

Most denominations or nondenominational churches have statements of expectations for members. An example is the Baptismal Covenant from the Book of Common Prayer (304):

- Continue in the apostle's teaching and fellowship, in the breaking of the bread, and in the prayers;

- Persevere in resisting evil, and, whenever falling into sin, repent and return to the Lord.

- Proclaim by word and example the Good News of God in Christ.

- Seek and serve Christ in all persons, loving your neighbor as yourself.

- Strive for justice and peace among all people, and respect the dignity of every human being.

[10] Christian A. Schwarz, *Natural Church Development* (Carol Stream, IL: ChurchSmart Resources, 1996), 22.

[11] Posner and Kouzes, *The Truth about Leadership*, 69.

[12] Ibid., 69.

[13] Ibid., introduction.

[14] John C. Maxwell, *The 5 Levels of Leadership: Proven Steps to Maximize Your Potential* (New York: Center Street, 2011), 201.

[15] Max DePree, *Leadership is an Art* (Dell Publishing, 1990), 38.

[16] Posner and Kouzes, *The Truth about Leadership*, 73.

4.5 Discerning God's Call to the Community

[1] Stephen Bryant, "Discernment as Worshipful Work," *Alban Weekly*, January 21, 2013, www.alban.org/conversation.aspx?id=10173, based on Danny E. Morris and Charles M. Olson, *Discerning God's Will Together: A Spiritual Practice for the Church*, (Upper Room, 1997).

[2] Lists on the Internet of serious world problems run into hundreds of issues. In *High Noon 20 Global Problems, 20 Years to Solve Them* (Basic Books, 2003), J. F. Rischard breaks twenty critical issues into three groups. Group one (sharing our planet) includes global warming, biodiversity and ecosystem losses, fisheries depletion, deforestation, water deficits, and maritime safety and pollution. Group two (sharing our humanity) includes poverty; peacekeeping, conflict prevention, and combatting terrorism; education for all; global infectious diseases; the digital divide; and natural disaster prevention and mitigation. Group three (sharing our rule book) includes reinventing taxation for the twenty-first century, biotechnology rules, global financial architecture, illegal drugs, trade-investment-competition rules, intellectual property rights, e-commerce rules, and international labor and migration rules.

[3] Many churches do not have any real plans. They operate more by the seat of their pants, dealing with issues as they come up, either based on "where we happen to be at the moment" or "the way we've always done it." Excuses for this are that "we want to be open to the Holy Spirit" and "we don't want to run the church like a business." In fact, people often resist planning because they don't like to be accountable for results. But God holds us accountable (e.g., Matthew 25:14–46), and the absence of a plan frequently contributes to fragmentation and chaos in our spiritual communities.

[4] Excellent "Practical Ideas for Measurement" for various church goals are included in Appendix C of Mike Bonem, *In Pursuit of Great AND Godly Leadership: Tapping the Wisdom of the World for the Kingdom of*

God (John Wiley and Sons, Kindle Edition 2011), 235–239.

4.6 Working for Transformation

[1] Donald T. Phillips, *Martin Luther King, Jr., on Leadership: Inspiration & Wisdom for Challenging Times* (New York: Warner Business Books, 2000), 263.

[2] Barry Z. Posner and James M. Kouzes, *The Truth about Leadership: The No-fads, Heart-of-the-Matter Facts You Need to Know* (San Francisco, CA: Jossey-Bass, 2010), 93.

[3] In *The Church on the Other Side* (Grand Rapids: Zondervan, 2006), 28, Brian McLaren describes this evolutionary process of church communities in a way that would be shocking to Pharisees and most church people:

> The new church never expects to "get it right." It doesn't expect to finally find the magic pattern or resurrect the lost, last detail that will suddenly spell supernatural success for the body of Christ. It assumes that as long as the church grows, it will have to adapt and change and learn. As long as there are people, there will be problems; as long as there is history, there will be struggle; as long as the church exists in this troubled world, it will compete neck and neck against the gates of hell to see who will prevail against whom. As long as we keep having children, those offspring will eventually rise up and call us outdated.

[4] These lessons about flexibility and adaptation are explored in the best-selling fable by Spencer Johnson, *Who Moved My Cheese: An A-Mazing Way to Deal With Change in Your Work and Life* (New York: G.P. Putnam's Sons, 1998).

[5] Phillips, *Martin Luther King, Jr. on Leadership*, 261, 263.

[6] Everett Rogers, *Diffusion of Innovations* (New York: Free Press, 1962), 150. Rogers popularized a theory about how, why, and at what rate new ideas and technology spread through cultures and become widely adopted and self-sustaining. Rogers identified four main elements that

influence the spread and acceptance of a new idea: innovation, communication channels, time, and a social system. Diffusion of innovations manifests itself in different ways in various cultures and fields and is highly subjective to the type of adopters and innovation–decision process, but at some point, a successful innovation reaches a point of adoption by a critical mass.

[7] For outstanding books about an eight step process of leading change, see John P. Kotter, *Leading Change* (Cambridge: Harvard Business School Press, 1996) and John P. Kotter and Holger Rathgeber, *Our Iceberg Is Melting: Changing and Succeeding Under Any Conditions* (St. Martin's Press, 2006).

[8] Phillips, *Martin Luther King, Jr. on Leadership*, 263–264.

[9] Ibid., 263–264.

[10] John C. Maxwell, *The 5 Levels of Leadership: Proven Steps to Maximize Your Potential* (New York: Center Street, 2011), 164.

[11] Thomas Merton shared this prayer for our journey:

My Lord God, I have no idea where I am going.

I do not see the road ahead. I cannot know for certain where it will end.

Nor do I really know myself, and the fact that I think that I am following your will does not mean that I am actually doing so.

But I believe that the desire to please you does in fact please you.

And I hope I have that desire in all that I am doing.

I hope that I will never do anything apart from that desire.

And I know that if I do this you will lead me by the right road though I may know nothing about it.

Therefore will I trust you always though I may seem to be lost and in the shadow of death.

I will not fear for you are ever with me, and you will never leave me to face my perils alone.

Thomas Merton, *Thoughts in Solitude* (New York: Farrar, Straus & Cudahy, 1958).

[12] Maxwell, *The 5 Levels of Leadership*, 168.

[13] Ronald A. Heifetz, *Leadership Without Easy Answers* (Cambridge, MA.: Belknap Press of Harvard University Press, 1994), 106.

[14] These challenges are natural and not unique or new. They are all subjects of Saint Paul's letters. How we deal with them determines our health as the body of Christ.

[15] This is inherently part of the "shepherd" leadership of Jesus, who truly cares for his followers *and* challenges them to transformational change. Jesus doesn't coddle but instead challenges and prepares his followers to lead, to care for other followers, and to make followers into leaders. Accordingly, I would disagree with a position in "The Work of Leadership" by Ronald A. Heifetz and Donald L. Laurie (*Harvard Business Review*, December 2001), that "shepherd" leaders give people false assurance that their best is good enough, smooth over conflicts, and protect their flock from harsh surroundings—instead of exposing them to the painful reality of their condition, demanding that they fashion a response and insisting that people surpass themselves. In the case of Jesus, doing the latter is part of loving, protecting, and giving peace.

[16] Heifetz, *Leadership Without Easy Answers*, 128.

[17] Ronald A. Heifetz and Marty Linsky, "Managing Yourself: A Survival Guide for Leaders" (*Harvard Business Review*, June 2002), Reprint R0206C, 6.

[18] Presentation by Matthew Sallman to Christ Episcopal Church in Dearborn, Michigan, during worship on Sunday, February 10, 2013. References to the vestry of the congregation have been changed to read "board".

Conclusion: Follow Where Jesus Leads

[1] Barry Z. Posner and James M. Kouzes write in *The Truth about Leadership: The No-fads, Heart-of-the-Matter Facts You Need to Know* (San Francisco, CA: Jossey-Bass, 2010) at 1: "Before you can lead others, you have to lead yourself and believe that you can have a positive impact on others. You have to believe that your words can inspire and your actions can move others. You have to believe that what you do counts for something. If you don't, you won't even try. Leadership begins with you."

[2] Desmond Tutu writes in *God Has a Dream: A Vision of Hope for Our Time* (New York: Doubleday, 2004), at 127–128:

> Our God hears. Our God cares. Our God knows and our God will come down to deliver his people. Our God will come to deliver his people everywhere. When will this deliverance from oppression, from hunger, from war happen? Today? Maybe not today. Tomorrow? Maybe not tomorrow. But God will come "in the fullness of time" because God has a dream and God will make his dream come true through us. For we are His partners. We are the ones He has sent to free the oppressed, to feed the hungry, and to shelter the homeless. We will turn our sadness into resolve, our despair into determination. ... All over this magnificent world God calls us to extend His kingdom of shalom—peace and wholeness—of justice, of goodness, of compassion, of caring, of sharing, of laughter, of joy, and of reconciliation. God is transfiguring the world right this very moment through us because God believes in us and because God loves us. What can separate us from the love of God? Nothing. Absolutely nothing. And as we share God's love with our brothers and sisters, God's other children, there is no tyrant who can resist us, no oppression that cannot be ended, no hunger that cannot be fed, no wound that cannot be healed, no hatred that cannot be turned to love, no dream that cannot be fulfilled.

Leading Change in Church Communities:
10 Important Questions

[1] Everett Rogers, *Diffusion of Innovations* (New York: Free Press, 1962), 150.

[2] See Ronald A. Heifitz, *Leadership Without Easy Answers* (Cambridge, Mass.: Belknap Press of Harvard University Press, 1994). Steps to successful adaptive confrontations are (1) identify the adaptive challenge; (2) keep the distress within a tolerable range; (3) focus attention on ripening issues and not on stress-reducing distractions, (4) give the work back to people, but at a rate they can stand, and (5) protect voices of leadership without authority.

[3] We need to encourage confrontation to have the community question its attitudes, actions, behavior, or beliefs. At the same time, we need to manage people's passionate differences in a way that diminishes their destructive potential and constructively harnesses their energy. First, create a secure place where the conflicts can freely bubble up. Second, control the temperature to ensure that the conflict doesn't boil over—and burn you in the process. Third, make sure that the leader does not come up with an answer or solution on the leader's own, but encourages the confrontation. Beware that identifying or raising issues that everyone else is avoiding puts the leader in the position of having anger and resentment surrounding the issue directed toward him or her.